Charles I

Charles I provides a detailed overview of Charles Stuart, placing his reign firmly within the wider context of this turbulent period and examining the nature of one of the most complex monarchs in British history.

The book is organised chronologically, beginning in 1600 and covering Charles' early life, his first difficulties with his parliaments, the Personal Rule, the outbreak of Civil War, and his trial and eventual execution in 1649. Interwoven with historiography, the book emphasises the impact of Charles' challenging inheritance on his early years as king and explores the transition from his original championing of international Protestantism to his later vision of a strong and centralised monarchy influenced by continental models, which eventually provoked rebellion and civil war across his three kingdoms. This study brings to light the mass of contradictions within Charles' nature and his unusual approach to monarchy, resulting in his unrivaled status as the only English king to have been tried and executed by his own subjects.

Offering a fresh approach to this significant reign and the fascinating character that held it, *Charles I* is the perfect book for students of early modern Britain and the English Civil War.

Mark Parry read History at Cambridge and completed a doctorate on the political role of the episcopate under the early Stuarts. He teaches History at Westminster School. He is the author of several academic articles on the political and religious history of the early Stuart period and of an A-level textbook *Stuart Britain and the Crisis of Monarchy, 1603–1702* (2015).

ROUTLEDGE HISTORICAL BIOGRAPHIES
Series Editor: Robert Pearce

Routledge Historical Biographies provide engaging, readable and academically credible biographies written from an explicitly historical perspective. These concise and accessible accounts will bring important historical figures to life for students and general readers alike.

In the same series:
Louis XIV by Richard Wilkinson (second edition 2017)
Martin Luther by Michael A. Mullet (second edition 2014)
Martin Luther King Jr. by Peter J. Ling (second edition 2015)
Mao by Michael Lynch (second edition 2017)
Marx by Vincent Barnett
Mary Queen of Scots by Retha M. Warnicke
Mary Tudor by Judith M. Richards
Mussolini by Peter Neville (second edition 2014)
Nehru by Benjamin Zachariah
Neville Chamberlain by Nick Smart
Oliver Cromwell by Martyn Bennett
Queen Victoria by Paula Bartley
Richard III by David Hipshon
Thatcher by Graham Goodlad
Trotsky by Ian Thatcher
Stalin by Christopher Read
Thomas Cranmer by Susan Wabuda
Ho Chi Minh by Peter Neville
Isabella d'Este by Christine Shaw
Charles I by Mark Parry

Forthcoming:
Churchill by Robert Pearce
Gandhi by Benjamin Zachariah
Khrushchev by Alexander Titov
Wolsey by Glenn Richardson

Charles I

Mark Parry

Taylor & Francis Group

LONDON AND NEW YORK

First published 2020
by Routledge
2 Park Square, Milton Park, Abingdon, Oxon OX14 4RN

and by Routledge
52 Vanderbilt Avenue, New York, NY 10017

Routledge is an imprint of the Taylor & Francis Group, an informa business

© 2020 Mark Parry

The right of Mark Parry to be identified as author of this work has been asserted by him in accordance with sections 77 and 78 of the Copyright, Designs and Patents Act 1988.

All rights reserved. No part of this book may be reprinted or reproduced or utilised in any form or by any electronic, mechanical, or other means, now known or hereafter invented, including photocopying and recording, or in any information storage or retrieval system, without permission in writing from the publishers.

Trademark notice: Product or corporate names may be trademarks or registered trademarks, and are used only for identification and explanation without intent to infringe.

British Library Cataloguing-in-Publication Data
A catalogue record for this book is available from the British Library

Library of Congress Cataloging-in-Publication Data
Names: Parry, Mark, author.
Title: Charles I / Mark Parry.
Description: Abingdon, Oxon ; New York : Routledge, 2020. | Series: Routledge historical biographies | Includes bibliographical references and index. | Summary: "Charles I provides a detailed overview of Charles Stuart, placing his reign firmly within the wider context of this turbulent period and examining the nature of one of the most complex monarchs in British history."— Provided by publisher.
Identifiers: LCCN 2019032618 (print) | LCCN 2019032619 (ebook) | ISBN 9781138637733 (hardback) | ISBN 9781138712225 (paperback) | ISBN 9781315200309 (ebook)
Subjects: LCSH: Charles I, King of England, 1600-1649. | Great Britain—History—Stuarts, 1603-1714—Biography. | Great Britain—Kings and rulers—Biography.
Classification: LCC DA396.A2 P37 2020 (print) | LCC DA396.A2 (ebook) | DDC 940.06/2092 [B]—dc23
LC record available at https://lccn.loc.gov/2019032618
LC ebook record available at https://lccn.loc.gov/2019032619

ISBN: 978-1-138-63773-3 (hbk)
ISBN: 978-1-138-71222-5 (pbk)
ISBN: 978-1-315-20030-9 (ebk)

Typeset in Sabon
by Swales & Willis Ltd, Exeter, Devon, UK

For my parents

Contents

	Acknowledgements	viii
	Stuart family tree	x
	Introduction	1
1	Early life and Prince of Wales (1600–25)	13
2	Patriot king (1625–29)	43
3	Imperial monarch (1629–40)	74
4	Royalist-in-chief (1640–42)	119
5	Warlord (1642–46)	156
6	Conscientious objector (1646–49)	196
	Epilogue: the legacy of a royal martyr	246
	Guide to further reading	258
	Index	262

Acknowledgements

An author incurs many debts. My interest in the early Stuart period began at university and I was fortunate in the thriving post-graduate community there and above all, the stimulating environment provided by the Early Modern British and Irish History Seminar and the Tudor and Stuart History Seminar at the Institute of Historical Research. The experience of giving papers there on the early Caroline regime was hugely valuable in helping to evolve my thinking about the period. Having completed a PhD on the political role of the episcopate in the 1620s, I benefited from having as examiners Professors John Morrill and Kenneth Fincham, whose searching questions forced me to re-think several of my interpretations. The idea for writing this book came from a former colleague, Dr Max von Habsburg, and his encouragement and friendship during the early stages of writing it were immensely appreciated. I owe particular gratitude to my former PhD supervisor, Dr David L. Smith, who read most of the manuscript and saved me from numerous infelicities. Needless to say responsibility for any remaining errors is entirely my own. I have also profited over the last few years from useful conversations with, among others, Simon Healy, John Adamson, Anthony Milton, Kenneth Fincham, Peter Gaunt and Miranda Malins. Discussion and debate with former colleagues and fellow-enthusiasts for the seventeenth century, particularly Philip Pedley, Colin Pendrill and Richard Mather, often in the congenial surroundings of a country pub, have also been hugely valuable. Perhaps above all, the experience of teaching the reign of Charles I to successive cohorts of sixth form historians, first at Oundle and then at Westminster,

Acknowledgements ix

has been not only enormous fun but also formative: while instinctively less than impressed by Charles as a king ('Oh Charles!') was one commonly characteristic reaction to the latest part of the story in lessons, their perceptive questions, refusal to be satisfied with simplistic explanations and their keenness to question and challenge received wisdom has frequently challenged me in my own thinking and led me to modify my own views about the reign. In so far as there is an intended audience for this book, I hope it might not prove unuseful for sixth-formers studying the period in the future.

Stuart family tree

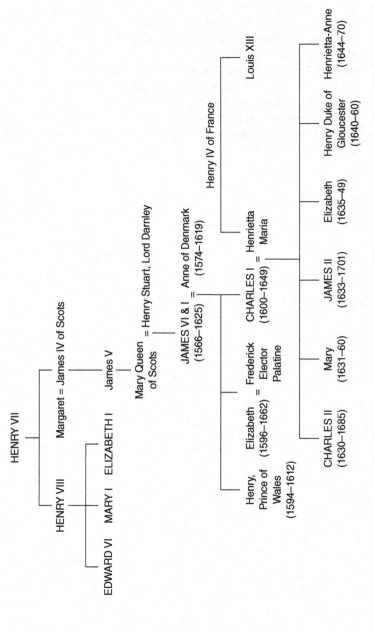

Introduction

The historical reputation of Charles I

King Charles I looms large in the British historical imagination. His equestrian statue (by Hubert Le Sueur) stands proudly, albeit on a traffic island, just in front of Trafalgar Square, while his bust stares out from the porch of St Margaret's Church opposite the Houses of Parliament. The Banqueting House at Whitehall, the only surviving part of the Whitehall Palace complex, and which contains the grand Rubens ceiling that he commissioned, and in front of which the king was beheaded in 1649, is among London's most visited tourist attractions while a recent exhibition at the Royal Academy entitled 'Charles I: King and Collector', an examination of Charles's artistic tastes and patronage, was hailed as one of the cultural highlights of the year. Charles is one of the few English monarchs to have a society dedicated to him (Richard III being another) in the shape of the Society of St Charles King & Martyr, as well as an attendant feast day in the Church of England calendar. In the nineteenth century the romantic obsession with the defeated royalist cause had a habit of intruding into the pages of popular fiction, including Charles Dicken's *David Copperfield* (in Mr Dick's inability to stop Charles I taking over his memoirs) as well as Conan Doyle's 'The Musgrave Ritual', where Charles's crown is discovered buried in an aristocrat's garden, while his escape from Hampton Court is the backdrop to the events in Captain Maryatt's *Children of the New Forest* (occasionally adapted for television). He appears in cinema too, perhaps most memorably portrayed by Alec Guinness in an entertaining (if not

2 Introduction

always terribly historically accurate) 1970 film, *Cromwell* and by Rupert Everett in *To Kill a King*. His status, as the only British monarch ever to be publicly executed, ensures that he is a perennial point of reference for political failure and guarantees that, in an age sometimes considered 'post-historical', he continues to be the subject of popular and media attention.

His historical reputation is much contested. Victorian historians, among whom the great Samuel Rawson Gardiner had the most lasting impact, tended to see Charles as an aspiring but ineffective tyrant, not entirely devoid of good qualities but failing to grasp the fundamental principles of a constitutional system upheld and defended by Parliament. His reign was from the start hindered by his defects as king, chiefly his stubborn refusal to appreciate the views of others and concomitant tendency to divide 'mankind into two simple classes – into those who agreed with him, and those who did not'.[1] In this account, the early Stuarts generally were seen as misguided architects of 'divine-right' kingship, an error only finally corrected by the Glorious Revolution of 1688. Nevertheless, Gardiner's work, identified several key themes which remain central to modern work on the period, chiefly an awareness of the importance of the British context to the Civil Wars, the centrality of religion, and a belief that the royalists were as worthy of study as the parliamentarians.[2] The 'Revisionist' history of the 1970s onwards, while picking up these themes, modified his narrative substantially, emphasising, instead of long-term political and constitutional clashes, the more short-term crisis caused by the divisiveness of Charles's religious policies within the wider context of the challenges of ruling three distinct 'British' kingdoms and the 'functional breakdown' of the financial system.[3] Both of these preoccupations led to a re-appraisal of the first early Stuart monarch, James I, seeing him, despite some occasionally tactless pronouncements upon the basis of his royal power, as a moderate and competent manager of religious tensions with a shrewd understanding of the political and religious differences within his three kingdoms. By extension, for the kingdoms to dissolve into bitter civil war by 1642, the mistakes must be those of James's son and successor, Charles. The best tribute paid to him, in this analysis, is that he was not incompetent enough to be deposed in the way that his royal predecessors, Edward II, Richard II and

Introduction 3

Henry VI were: rather, he was an adept enough 'party leader' to rally a body of supporters and fight a civil war.[4]

Some subsequent scholarship, sometimes labelled 'post-revisionist', has sought to step back from this by suggesting that longer-term political and ideological tensions did exist within the early Stuart polity, and have also focused on politics beyond Whitehall and Westminster to demonstrate the vibrancy of early seventeenth-century political discourse, particularly print culture. Within this framework, Charles's failure has tended to be seen as one of public relations, as a distant monarch suspicious of 'popularity', who refused 'to resort to print to woo public opinion as his opponents were doing', and in the process, lost battle for hearts and minds.[5] Attempting to reconcile these positions, and synthesise the revisionist as well as the post-revisionist legacy, other historians such as Tim Harris have emphasised the room for differing interpretations of the extent of both royal and parliamentary power within the early Stuart polity, which allowed ideological conflict to emerge when practical disagreements ensued. As such, the minimalisation of ideological conflict on the grounds that all political agents were operating within the same world-view and using the same language, is misconceived.[6] This is not to resurrect the old Whig narrative of righteous common lawyers in the House of Commons 'winning the initiative' from overweening monarchs but rather to appreciate that there were competing world-views and competing conspiracy theories in which Puritans in Parliament could view the existence of a 'Popish Plot' as a genuine reality and Charles, his court, and key advisers as aspiring architects of tyrannical government; but Charles and his political and episcopal lieutenants could also see his opponents as deliberately seeking to undermine the efficacy of executive government and the royal prerogative, while cloaking their radical and rebellious political designs in insincere religious rhetoric. Viewing the early Stuart period in this way also prompts some qualification of the formerly positive appraisal of James I, highlighting his failure to address some of the Crown's structural problems (notably its financial weakness) as well as the continuities between his policies and those of his son, notably, as shown by the work of Laura Stewart, in

4 Introduction

relation to the 'confessionalisation' they pursued in Scotland, contributing to the difficulties faced by Charles and so highlighting the invidious nature of the Jacobean inheritance.[7]

Charles's character in context

Many existing biographies students are arguably out of date or fail to give coverage to the entirety of the reign. Charles Carlton's *Charles I: The Personal Monarch* employed a psychoanalytical approach which has now been largely discredited. It is also rather simplistic in its conclusions. In the preface to the second edition Carlton states bluntly: 'I maintain that the king – more than anyone else – was to blame for the bloodiest war known to English history. In sum, Charles failed because of his own personal defects'. He is also guilty of anachronism, suggesting that 'Charles was less a Burkean, even Thatcherite Conservative, than he was a reactionary, whose insecurity made him an authoritarian'.[8] Kevin Sharpe's revisionist account of the Personal Rule, *The Personal Rule of Charles I* highlighted some more positive features of the 1630s, notably artistic patronage, court culture, and the systematic nature of Charles's attempts to reform government and society. Even if he overstated the case for the establishment of 'conciliar government', and underplayed the role of Laud in the formation of Caroline religious policy, this grand work did show that there was an integrity and consistency to Charles's project for governing his three kingdoms and encouraged historians of the period to begin viewing events according to Charles's world-view in which hierarchy, dignity, honour, and their political expression, the royal prerogative, mattered.[9] Biography has rarely produced positive views of the king. Michael B. Young's analysis was ultimately quite conventional, seeing Charles as an anachronistic reactionary who, 'In his view of the relationship between a king and his subjects. . .had a medieval mentality while increasing numbers of his subjects had early modern mentalities'.[10] While there is certainly mileage in considering Charles's medievalism, in areas ranging from his fiscal policy to his relations with his nobility, Young's overriding conclusion was somewhat simplistic, concluding that ultimately the king's untrustworthiness was the 'fundamental, unforgiveable defect in Charles's character that in

Introduction 5

the end made his execution necessary. It was truly his fatal flaw'.[11] While the charge of untrustworthiness is not without foundation, to label it 'unforgiveable' rather overlooks the complexities of the problems he faced and it is important to uncover why Charles behaved in this way (notably in his negotiations with Army and Parliament between 1646 and 1648) and to see it as part of a wider breakdown of trust between the king and his parliamentary critics, a breakdown that had many of its roots in the crucial failures of the parliaments of 1625–29.

The best recent biography of the king is that by Richard Cust, *Charles I: A Political Life*, which is balanced and and reflects many years of study of the period. Cust's analysis of Charles's personality, with its emphasis on the twin dimensions of prudence and conscience (made popular among contemporaries by the renewal of interest in the works of the Roman historian, Tacitus), and on Charles's own obsession with honour and loyalty, is much more persuasive than Carlton's psychoanalysis or Young's simplistic conclusion that Charles was, essentially, a 'reactionary'. Cust presents a sympathetic but nevertheless critical account of Charles's reign, highlighting his understanding of the need for political manipulation and tactical manoeuvre, even if he did not always make the right judgements. In addition, he shows that his performance as a war-leader during the Civil Wars was more impressive than often thought (this picks up Conrad Russell's verdict that Charles was a much better 'party leader' than he was a king), and that he was a competent military commander. He shows awareness of changes in the king's views and approaches over the course of his reign but at the same time stresses certain continuities, particularly his deep hostility to puritanism and his fear of 'popularity'.[12] As will be seen, when combined with others of his character-traits (notably his sensitivity to slights upon his honour and challenges to his authority), this prevented both his working effectively with his parliaments in the 1620s and reaching agreement with his enemies in the later 1640s.

There is, however, more recent work on Charles's reign that needs to be taken account of in any new biography. Cust's own book on *Charles I and the Aristocracy* (2011) has shown the depth of Charles's attachment to chivalry and aristocratic culture at the Caroline court.[13] This links in to John Adamson's work on the role

6 Introduction

of the nobility in the reign as a whole but particularly in bringing about the crisis in England in 1640–42.[14] Charles's relationship with his nobility is an important theme in his reign and helps explain much about the course of it. Work on the political culture of the 1630s also requires us to consider the king's presentation of himself as an 'imperial' ruler and consider the way in which he and his councillors tried to solve the problems of ruling three distinct kingdoms in the shape of England, Scotland, and Ireland. It is worth reflecting on the extent to which Charles had a 'vision' for ruling his three kingdoms, one that was more than an attempt to repress dissent and stifle opposition, and actually contained an intentional project which promoted unity and conformity as positive features.[15] Resonances have been detected with the wider seventeenth-century European context, and approaches such as that of Geoffrey Parker have highlighted the extent to which Charles faced some of the same sorts of political and religious problems, and attempted some of the same sorts of solutions, as his contemporary monarchs in France and Spain. It is also important to appreciate how post-Reformation politics in Europe generally produced significant diplomatic as well as religious difficulties for British monarchs, and, as Michael Questier has recently argued, it is possible to consider that, given the circumstances of the times, the move towards peace and the dispensing with parliament in 1629 was an instance of how 'the Stuart monarchy had, at the end of the 1620s, read the political tea-leaves correctly'.[16] This strengthens the case for treating the Personal Rule and Charles's approach to government on their own terms, embodying an alternative, if ultimately unsuccessful, vision of how the country should be governed as a partnership between Charles and his elite subjects within a turbulent European context of which he and his contemporaries were fully aware.

Perhaps the most important recent writing on Charles, however, is that by the late Mark Kishlansky. In a provocative article, 'Charles I: A Case of Mistaken Identity', *Past and Present* (2005) and a short biography in the new Penguin series, *Charles I: An Abbreviated Life* (2014), Kishlansky sought to demolish some of the shibboleths surrounding Charles's reign, notably the charges that he was inflexible and untrustworthy. Though Kishlansky's argument becomes less convincing for the mid-late 1640s (Charles's duplicity in his

Introduction 7

negotiations with Parliament, the Army, and the Scots seems indisputable, even if Kishlansky is able to cite one or two factors in mitigation), his carefully articulated case that Charles has been unfairly blamed for underhandedness in his response to the Petition of Right in 1628 as well as blunt intransigence in his dealings with the Scots Covenanters in 1638–40 and with the Long Parliament in 1640–1, is more cogent. Indeed several of his courtiers and advisers, notably his wife, Henrietta Maria, were infuriated by his tendency to make concessions after having appeared to wish to stand firm. This should lead us to re-evaluate Charles's performance in the crisis of 1637–42, his overriding mistakes being borne of indecisiveness and failure of nerve in defending and upholding the vision of monarchy pursued during the Personal Rule rather than a total unwillingness to engage with his opponents. The evidence from his private correspondence highlights his negative view of the Scottish rebels, his concessions being a means to buy time, but paradoxically this was a strategy he would baulk at in his dealings with both the Scots and his parliamentary opponents in the years 1646–48.

Another recent pre-occupation in the literature on the period has been the role of popular politics. Alistair Bellany and Tom Cogswell have explored the richly dramatic means by which rumours that James I was murdered by the duke of Buckingham and that Charles had knowledge of, or was in some way complicit in, the plot, helped to stoke parliamentary opposition to the duke and to undermine confidence in Charles's rule early on his reign.[17] The theme of popular opposition and criticism has been related specifically to Charles I and his style of ruling by David Cressy. Cressy's view differs substantially from that of Kishlansky, who had suggested that Charles was an open and accessible monarch. Instead, Cressy suggests that Charles was the author of his own downfall, citing evidence of dissent and criticism from all social strata to argue that Charles's worst mistake was, above all, his failure to appreciate and live up to popular expectations of his rule.[18] As Kevin Sharpe argued in his *Image Wars*, in some ways Charles's approach to public relations transitioned from a willingness to justify and defend his policies in the written word in the 1620s to a narrower, more elite-oriented, and aesthetically based image-projection in the 1630s, through portraiture and court culture.[19] He then, however, returned to a

8 Introduction

more active cultivation of public opinion through proclamations and printed defences of his actions following the outbreak of the Scottish rebellion in 1638, continuing during the Short and Long Parliaments and the contest for the raising of support in 1641–42, and both during and after the Civil Wars, culminating in his very successful attempt to keep the royalist cause alive even in death through his posthumously published memoir, *Eikon Basilike*, the 'Image of the King'. While some of this could be seen as a desperate response to political crisis in having to argue a case to his subjects, it is important to appreciate that print was not the only medium through which an image could be crafted and loyalty engendered, and that Charles did not shirk the public-relations battle when it mattered most.

Other important work has considered the character and nature of royalism during the 1640s, as Charles performed the role of 'party leader' (in Russell's phrase). Several recent works re-assess various aspects of the royalist cause and the war effort.[20] The contribution by David Scott, and his essay in Adamson (ed.) *The English Civil War: Conflicts and Contexts* (2009), stresses the factional rivalries which beset the royalist court at Oxford and the council of war.[21] The divisions between 'swordsmen' and more moderate royalist politicians were often bitter and affected decision-making; their exposure further highlights the difficulties with which Charles was confronted as a war-leader and also begs further criticism of his failure to manage those around him and discern which was the best 'counsel' to follow. His virtues as a leader in war, namely his single-mindedness and ability to inspire loyalty to a cause, need to be set against his undeniable failings.

There has also been a lot of writing on the period between the end of the First Civil War and the king's execution, as historians attempt to explain the failure to reach a settlement. A particular source of controversy, as reflected in the ongoing debate between Sean Kelsey and Clive Holmes, is the question of when regicide came to be intended by the king's enemies, and what the trial was actually for. Cust, for instance, regards Kelsey as being ultimately convincing in his assertion that the trial was part of an extended negotiation-strategy rather than the implementation of the Army's resolution to put Charles to death; Holmes refutes Kelsey's case strongly in an article and, for the most part,

Introduction   9

convincingly.[22] The debate does affect how we view Charles as a negotiator and political strategist: if Kelsey is right then Charles is an astute politician who nevertheless 'overplays his hand', and the episode might be seen as a final failure in his approach to political negotiations, whereas, if Holmes is right, Charles, while still very much to blame for his own fate on account of his duplicity in starting the Second Civil War in 1648, nevertheless becomes, in 1649, more the victim of forces beyond his control (chiefly the Army). By emphasising the political context in which the key events took place, it is therefore possible to reach a more nuanced appraisal of Charles's reign up to and including his trial and execution, without seeking to absolve him of his failings or to overlook his mistakes.

David Hume gave this verdict upon Charles's character in his *History of England*, first published in 1754:

> He deserves the epithet of a good, rather than a great man; and was more fitted to rule in a regular established government, than either to give way to the encroachments of a popular assembly, or finally to subdue their pretensions. . .Had he been born an absolute prince, his humanity and good sense had rendered his reign happy, and his memory precious: had the limitations on prerogative been in his time quite fixed and certain, his integrity had made him regard as sacred the boundaries of the constitution. . .And if his political prudence was not sufficient to extricate him from so perilous a situation, he may be excused; since even after the event, when it is commonly easy to correct all errors, one is at a loss to determine what conduct, in his circumstances, could have maintained the authority of the Crown, and preserved the peace of the nation.[23]

While Hume's analysis of Charles is not without serious shortcomings, notably a tendency, unsurprising on the part of an Enlightenment atheist, to regard the king's religious conviction as 'superstition', his verdict nevertheless highlights the extent to which Charles's weaknesses were exposed by the challenges he was forced to confront during his reign. While resisting too extended a counter-factual excursus, Hume also implies that it is possible to imagine that if Charles had possessed the power

10   *Introduction*

wielded by his contemporaries in France and Spain, who might claim to be 'absolute' princes in the sense that they were not directly dependent (in a financial or legislative sense) upon national representative assemblies, his failings of temperament would have been less evident and his qualities more apparent. It also reinforces the sense in which the ill-defined political and constitutional parameters he inherited were susceptible of different interpretations and, at times, provoked heated ideological conflicts. The sincerity he brought to religious matters might have been manifest in political and constitutional ones had the parameters (and his inheritance) been clearer.

Moreover, the suggestion that negative judgements of Charles rely too heavily on an alternative universe in which a better king (including, as much revisionist scholarship might imply, his father James) resolved all of the political and religious tensions and avoided Civil War also reminds us of the need to appreciate the difficult nature of his inheritance and of the crises that emerged across his three kingdoms. Charles was a human being: a product of his time, of his inheritance, and of his political apprenticeship as Prince of Wales, while his first five years on the throne as a young and energetic king anxious to live up to his subjects' expectations were formative in his evolving conception of monarchy. He was sincere in his religious convictions and took his role as Supreme Governor of an episcopal Church of England extremely seriously, was loyal to those whose support he valued, a devoted husband and father, and a cultivated connoisseur of the arts; he was also genuine in his pursuit of a partnership between Crown and nobility, and a recovery of royal prerogative power which chimed with the spirit of his age on the continent. He also had a sense of the importance of public relations and of political manoeuvre and negotiation. At the same time, he could also be insecure, stubborn, indecisive at crucial moments, and unwilling to see things from his opponents' point of view. His success as a motivator of his royalist supporters is at the same time an indictment of his performance as a unifier of the realm, while he failed to manage disagreements among his advisers during the Civil War, chose commanders based on narrow social conservatism and, in his negotiations with parliamentarian and military leaders after the First Civil War, failed to pursue a consistent and sustainable policy. Yet context

Introduction 11

remains crucial: an invidious inheritance, intransigent parliamentary opponents, a radical puritanism which threatened the foundations of his Church and by extension the State, created a perfect storm of political and religious tensions across three kingdoms which few rulers would have been equipped to manage.

Notes

1 S.R. Gardiner, *History of England from the Accession of James I to the Outbreak of the Civil War, 1603–1642* (10 vols, London, 1883–4), V, p. 318.

2 John Adamson, 'Introduction: High Roads and Blind Alleys – The English Civil War and its Historiography', in John Adamson (ed.), *The English Civil War: Conflicts and Contexts* (Basingstoke, 2009), pp. 1–35, at pp. 5–7.

3 Nicholas Tyacke, *Anti-Calvinists: The Rise of English Arminianism, c.1590–1640* (Oxford, 1987); Conrad Russell, *The Fall of the British Monarchies, 1637–1642* (Oxford, 1991).

4 Conrad Russell, *The Causes of the English Civil War* (Oxford, 1990), pp. 185–211, at pp. 209–10.

5 Michael Braddick, *God's Fury, England's Fire: A New History of the English Civil Wars* (London, 2008), p. 26; Richard Cust, 'Charles I and Popularity', in Tom Cogswell, Richard Cust and Peter Lake (eds.), *Politics, Religion and Popularity* (Cambridge, 2002), pp. 235–58.

6 A view found in particular in the work of Glenn Burgess, *Absolute Monarchy and the Stuart Constitution* (New Haven, 1996); Peter Lake, 'From Revisionist to Royalist History; or Was Charles I the First Whig Historian?', *Huntington Library Quarterly*, 78 (2015), pp. 657–81.

7 Tim Harris, 'Revisiting the Causes of the English Civil War', *Huntington Library Quarterly*, 78 (2015), pp. 615–35; idem, *Rebellion: Britain's First Stuart Kings, 1567–1642* (Oxford, 2014); Laura A.M. Stewart, *Rethinking the Scottish Revolution: Covenanted Scotland, 1637–1651* (Oxford, 2016).

8 Charles Carlton, *Charles I: The Personal Monarch* (2nd edn, London and New York, 1995), pp. xiv, xviii.

9 Kevin Sharpe, *The Personal Rule of Charles I* (New Haven and London, 1992), pp. 443–8; cf. Richard Cust, *Charles I: A Political Life*, pp. 138–41.

10 Michael B. Young, *Charles I* (Basingstoke, 1997), p. 178.

11 Young, *Charles I*, p. 180.

12 Cust, *Charles I*, pp. 17–24, 414–19.

12 *Introduction*

13 Richard Cust, *Charles I and the Aristocracy* (Cambridge, 2011).

14 John Adamson, *The Noble Revolt* (London, 2007).

15 For example, Malcolm Smuts, 'Force, Love and Authority in Caroline Political Culture', in Ian Atherton and Julie Sanders (eds.), *The 1630s: Interdisciplinary Essays on Culture and Politics in the Caroline Era* (Manchester, 2006), pp. 28–49; idem, 'The Court and the Emergence of a Royalist Party', in Jason McElligott and David L. Smith (eds.), *Royalists and Royalism during the English Civil Wars* (Cambridge, 2007), pp. 43–64; John Peacock, 'The Image of Charles I as a Roman Emperor', in Atherton and Sanders (eds.), *The 1630s*, pp. 50–73.

16 Michael Questier, *Dynastic Politics & the British Reformations, 1558–1630* (Oxford, 2019), pp. 457–8.

17 Alistair Bellany and Thomas Cogswell, *The Murder of King James I* (New Haven, 2015).

18 David Cressy, *Charles I and the People of England* (Oxford, 2015).

19 Kevin Sharpe, *Image Wars: Promoting Kings and Commonwealths in England, 1603–1660* (New Haven and London, 2010), p. 143; Lake, 'From Revisionist to Royalist History', p. 670.

20 David Scott, 'Counsel and Cabal in the King's Party, 1642–1646', in Jason McElligott and David L. Smith (eds.), *Royalists and Royalism during the English Civil Wars* (Cambridge, 2007), pp. 112–35.

21 David Scott, 'Rethinking Royalist Politics, 1642–1649', in John Adamson (ed.), *The English Civil War: Conflicts and Contexts* (Basingstoke, 2009), pp. 36–60.

22 Sean Kelsey, 'The Death of Charles I', *The Historical Journal*, 45 (2002), pp. 727–754; Kelsey, 'The Trial of Charles I', *The English Historical Review*, 118 (2003), pp. 583–616; cf. Clive Holmes, 'The Trial and Execution of Charles I', *The Historical Journal*, 53 (2010), pp. 289–316.

23 David Hume, *History of England from the Invasion of Julius Caesar to the Glorious Revolution of 1688* (9 vols, London, 1810), VIII, pp. 140–1.

1 Early life and Prince of Wales (1600–25)

Duke of York

There is an obvious point of comparison between Charles I and Henry VIII. Both were second sons born into dynasties newly established on the English throne; both saw their elder brothers being groomed for the succession while they were restricted to a more minor role as dukes of York; both suddenly found themselves propelled into the limelight and the succession by the untimely deaths of their elder siblings. Yet, aside from the fact that they turned out to be very different monarchs in wildly differing circumstances, there is a further difference: while Henry found himself king at the age of only 17, scarcely an adult by contemporary reckoning, and without having been in any sense schooled in the art of government by his predecessor, Charles was 24 at his accession and had spent the preceding decade being gradually introduced to political life, meeting with foreign ambassadors, attending two parliaments as Prince of Wales, (the second of which was summoned at his urging), and mounting a daring expedition to Madrid in pursuit of his intended bride on his own initiative. As such, Charles in many ways had the ideal preparation for kingship within the context of his age and that needs to be remembered when examining his subsequent reign.

Charles was born at Dunfermline Castle on 19 November 1600. His birth was not greeted with any great fan-fare: his father, James, was away in Edinburgh at the time, and was at that stage merely James VI of Scotland. In England, one leading newsletter writer only found room in his latest missive to

14   Early life and Prince of Wales

say that 'The Scottish king hath another sonne'.[1] Though James was already being lined up by Elizabeth's wily councillor, Robert Cecil, as her successor on the throne of England, by now he had a son and heir in the shape of Prince Henry, born in 1594. As such Charles's dynastic importance at the time of his birth was limited. He was christened at Holyrood Palace in Edinburgh on 23 December and placed in the care of Lady Margaret Stewart as his governess. As well as being, until 1612, a younger son not destined to inherit the throne, and as a consequence very much in the shadow of his elder brother, the other significant feature of his early life was that he suffered fragile health as a child, and these infirmities prompted sustained concerns about his physical wellbeing and informed much contemporary comment about him. This has also been widely used to explain his subsequent conduct as king. As with other rulers who suffered from physical frailty in infancy, such as Kaiser Wilhelm II, it is sometimes seen as having produced a negative psychological reaction which in turn created an inflexible and autocratic temperament.[2] Some have gone so far as to employ crude Freudian analyses to suggest that weak limbs and a stammer, together with a distant mother and a homosexual father, determined his personality not only as a child but for long afterwards.[3] Even historians who affect to disavow such approaches appear unable to resist the suggestion that his childhood 'explains a great deal about Charles's later behaviour'.[4] They are not wholly mistaken but closer examination of Charles's early life would suggest that these claims have been overstated.

Undoubtedly Charles was a sickly child. When James VI of Scotland made his triumphant progress south to take up his English Crown in 1603, Charles was left behind in Scotland as being too weak to accompany him. A few weeks after his father's departure, Charles's governor, Lord Fyvie, wrote to James from Edinburgh to report on his health, celebrating the fact that he was 'for the present at better health far then he was' and relating that he now 'eats, drinks, and uses all natural functions as we would wish in any child of his graces age, except that his nights rest is not as yet as sound as we hope in God it shall be shortly'. These encouraging signs, however, were to be seen in the context of 'The great weakness of his body, after so long and heavy sickness', and his physical frailties were outweighed by 'the might and strength of his

Early life and Prince of Wales 15

spirit and mind', which ensured that he 'looks as stately, and bears as great an majesty in his countenance, as could be required of any prince, albeit four times above his age'.[5] Aside from the clear effort to accentuate the positive, and assure James of Fyvie's own care and competence, the report suggests that despite acknowledged poor health as a young child, Charles already displayed a natural dignity and bearing which would become much more apparent as he grew to adulthood. A month later, Fyvie assured James that 'although yet weak in body', Charles 'continues, praise be God, in good health, good courage, and lofty mind', and reported that he had even begun to 'speak some words', so that he was 'far better as yet of his mind and tongue nor of his body and feet'.[6]

Such was Charles's progress that James decided to bring his younger son south to join him in England, and sent Dr Henry Atkins to verify that Charles was fit enough to travel. Atkins reported to Cecil on 17 June 1604 that 'The happy health wherein the Almighty at this time does bless his grace is a happy concurrent with his Majesty's designs', while a fortnight later he could assure Charles's mother, Anne of Denmark, that 'our noble young Prince' was 'daily growing from one perfection of health to another', including walking up and down the chamber of Dunfermline Castle 'like a gallant soldier all alone', and expressing a keen desire 'of going to London' to see his mother.[7] Charles duly began his journey, reaching Berwick 'in very good health' on 21 July and enjoying a lengthy stay at Worksop in Nottinghamshire, a residence of the earl of Shrewsbury, where he enjoyed music and acquired his life-long love of the chase, having 'been intiate in the sports of hunting', after watching 'the quarries of deer killed', before finally reaching his parents at Windsor.[8]

Once in England, other observers noted Charles's continued physical frailty: when Charles was created Duke of York in January 1605, Sir Dudley Carleton commented that 'we have a Duke of York in title, but not in Substance', and suggested that courtiers were much more interested in the Twelfth Night celebrations that began later that day.[9] The following month, he was placed in the care of Lady Elizabeth Carey as his governess. She was the wife of Sir Robert Carey, and her appointment was reward for her husband's enthusiasm (and opportunism) in riding post-haste from Elizabeth I's deathbed in London in March 1603 to Edinburgh to

16 Early life and Prince of Wales

deliver the news of James's accession to the English throne. The Careys took their governorship very seriously: Lady Carey complained stridently in October 1607 that the young prince's household was insufficiently provisioned and needed more money to provide a suitably regal diet.[10] It may well, however, have been in their interests to exaggerate Prince Charles's physical infirmities. Sir Robert later wrote that when the prince came into their charge he was 'past four years old' but 'was not able to go, nor scant able to stand alone' and 'was so weak in his joints and especially his ankles, insomuch, as many feared they were out of joint'. He also noted, however, that his enemies were thrilled when his wife was appointed to look after the prince, in case 'the Duke should die in our charge' and then Carey get the blame.[11] It therefore perhaps made sense for him to talk-up Charles's ill-health lest he die prematurely, which also allowed him to emphasise the scale of Charles's physical and medical improvement over the following years and therefore his own and his wife's diligence and loyalty, useful when lobbying the king for jobs and pensions at the end of their governorship.[12] Thus of the seven years for which the Careys had charge of the young Duke of York, Carey later wrote that 'he daily grew more and more in health and strength, both in body and mind, to the amazement of many that knew his weakness, when she [Lady Carey] first took charge of him'. During that time, Lady Carey seems to have saved Charles from the rather terrifying treatments that James prescribed both for his stammer, namely that 'the string under his tongue should be cut', and for his difficulties walking, that he be made to wear 'iron boots, to strengthen his sinews and joints'. The king is said to have given way before Lady Carey's protests, and Charles spared these rather brutal remedies.[13]

During this time, and based in the Careys' household, Charles was rather distant from political events. The Gunpowder Plotters had planned to abduct him but he was not their primary target and interrogation of Guy Fawkes revealed that they thought to kidnap Princess Elizabeth instead when they realised they 'knew not how to seize Prince Charles'.[14] His father's court was notably bibulous, even allowing for the bitter exaggeration of the disappointed courtier, Sir Anthony Weldon, upon which so many judgements about it have been based. In 1606 Charles's uncle, King Christian IV of Denmark, visited, and there were reports of

Early life and Prince of Wales 17

vomiting in the aisles and general drunkenness. Charles is often said to have found this all very distasteful, as reflected in the much more staid and decorous tone of his own court when he became king, but there is nothing to suggest that the young Charles was actively disapproving of his father's more relaxed court and household. As will be seen, Charles's court was indeed very different, but Charles himself expresses nothing but gratitude and admiration towards his father, suggesting that talk of a priggishly negative reaction is somewhat exaggerated.[15]

Instead Charles's main focus was his education. Tutored by Thomas Murray, who later became Provost of Eton, Charles appears to have been a hard-working pupil, who 'followed his Booke seriously', and was a 'good Mathematician, not unskilful in Musicke, wel read in Divinity, excellently in History, and no lesse in the Lawes and Statutes of this Nation'.[16] He impressed his father by his diligence and application, and James used Charles's scholarly habits as a stick with which to beat his elder brother. This reportedly led Henry to scoff at Charles's bookishness, and to suggest that when he was king he would make him his archbishop of Canterbury.[17] It may be misleading to draw too sharp a contrast between the two princes, however. Though Henry was celebrated for his athleticism and was certainly more physically imposing, Charles was regarded as an 'excellent Horseman' who could 'shoot well at a marke', and whose introduction to hunting at Worksop in 1604 clearly gave him a love of the chase.[18] If he was the butt of his brother's jokes, it did not diminish his affection for him. When Henry caught typhus after swimming in the Thames following an energetic game of tennis, Charles visited him on his deathbed and tried to comfort him by presenting his favourite toy, a small bronze horse.[19] Henry's death in November 1612 produced an outpouring of public sorrow, and, Charles, chief mourner at the funeral and who reportedly displayed a 'grief beyond his years', was deeply affected. Above all it also brought a radical change in Charles's role in the world.

Prince Charles

At the time of Prince Henry's death, concerns about his younger brother's health remained. Sir Simonds D'Ewes wrote later that

18   *Early life and Prince of Wales*

Charles 'was then so young and sickly, as the thought of their enjoying him did nothing at all alleviate or mollify the people's mourning' at the loss of Henry.[20] Charles's sister, Princess Elizabeth, was on the point of marrying a German prince, Elector Frederick of the Palatinate (part of James's policy of pursuing a middle way in international relations between the increasingly hostile Catholic and Protestant alliance systems), but it was suggested that she remain in England for a couple of years 'until Prince Charles has grown stronger'. In the event, however, the marriage took place as planned in February 1613, a welcome release from the recent period of mourning, and Charles went to see his sister off as she departed for Germany.[21]

While he would not be created Prince of Wales for another three years, itself partly a reflection of concerns about his health, Charles's household now became a more important theatre for political aspiration. He was given an independent establishment at Richmond Palace, moving there on 1 July 1613, and contemporaries discussed the competition for places within it.[22] Charles's enhanced position as heir to the throne also prompted a much higher level of interest in him among the courts and chancelleries of Europe. The Venetian ambassador commented in April 1613 that

> in the few months since the death of Prince Henry he has developed greatly in body, far more than in many preceding months. His health is becoming sound, he advances in his studies . . . He is quite aware of his rise in importance, as he is now the only son but all this only makes him more humane.[23]

This increased attention was also reflected in discussions about Charles's possible marriage, even though he had not yet reached marriageable age (fourteen). Barely was Prince Henry in his grave than it was being suggested that he replace his brother as candidate for the hand of a French princess, Christine, though, in a foreshadowing of the problems encountered with the later proposed Spanish match, likely French religious demands were seen as an obstacle.[24] (In the end the proposals came to nothing and Christine married the Duke of Savoy). Charles also began to take an interest in foreign affairs, being reported as having detailed

Early life and Prince of Wales   19

discussions with foreign ambassadors about the diplomatic situation in Italy and political developments in France.[25]

The politics of the Jacobean court

Charles was also gradually introduced to the world of domestic politics. He accompanied the king to the opening of Parliament in 1614.[26] The Parliament was not a happy one: indeed, it is known to history as 'The Addled Parliament' because it passed no legislation. Its unhappy outcome reflects in many ways the extent to which James's court had become a hotbed of factionalism. Following the death of Robert Cecil, Earl of Salisbury, in 1612, the man who had orchestrated James's accession in Elizabeth's final months and who had dominated the new government as Lord Treasurer and the king's chief councillor, James had come under the influence of the Howard family. Its leading members were the earls of Northampton and Suffolk, who favoured a policy of friendship towards Spain and opposed the summoning of Parliament. The Howard faction increased its dominance at court by winning over the royal favourite, Robert Carr, a young Scot upon whom James's very susceptible eye had lighted several years previously, and who became Viscount Rochester in 1611 and Earl of Somerset in 1613. They even engineered Carr's marriage to Suffolk's daughter, Lady Frances Howard, but only after, to the scandal of many, her previous marriage to the earl of Essex (a childhood companion and playmate of the late Prince Henry) had been annulled on the grounds of his alleged impotence. When James summoned Parliament in 1614, it was largely in order to resolve the Crown's financial difficulties (despite Salisbury's efforts at retrenchment, the total debt had reached over £500,000 by 1613) but Carr and Suffolk conspired to sabotage the session by encouraging attacks upon the Crown's practice of levying 'impositions' (additional taxes on trade levied through the royal prerogative and a long-standing grievance of parliaments).[27] The failure of the Parliament (James would not summon another for seven years) cemented the dominance of the Howard faction at court, at least for a time, and led to the more aggressive pursuit of the policy of a proposed marriage alliance with Spain, a policy that directly concerned the young Charles and which will be dealt with in greater detail on pp.XXX.

20 *Early life and Prince of Wales*

The rise of George Villiers

The Howard dominance was gradually weakened in the wake of the scandal that erupted when it was revealed that Carr and his Howard bride had conspired to murder another courtier, Sir Thomas Overbury, who had been threatening to sabotage their proposed marriage. Carr and his wife were disgraced and while Suffolk, by now Lord Treasurer, survived for a time (indeed in March 1617 he and Charles rode as far as Huntingdon to see James off on his visit to Scotland), he too would fall in 1618 amidst accusations of corruption.[28] As the Howard star waned, their rivals at court, the so-called 'Protestant' faction, led by the Archbishop of Canterbury, George Abbot, and the earl of Pembroke, and associated both with a more anti-Spanish foreign policy and a positive attitude to parliaments, were in the ascendant. The improbable instrument of their new-found favour was a young man from minor Leicestershire gentry stock, one George Villiers, who was introduced to James by Abbot in 1615 and who supplanted the disgraced Somerset in the king's affections. Charles's relations with Villiers have been the subject of debate. Those who favour psychological explanations of Charles's later misfortunes as king are inclined to suggest that he resented the presence of a rival for his father's affections and that, as such, relations between prince and favourite were strained. There certainly appears to have been some friction at first, as reflected in the famous story of Charles's having turned a water fountain onto Villiers in the gardens at Greenwich Palace in 1616 and in an episode reported in June 1618 when there 'fell out some words betwixt the Prince and the Marquiss of Buckinghame playing at the balloun'; but they soon began to get on better, as reflected in the Venetian ambassador's observation in January 1620 that Buckingham was apparently 'as great a favourite with the prince as with his father' after he watched them perform in a court masque together.[29] The explanation for this improved relationship might at least partly lie in the fact that Charles's mother, Queen Anne, had died in March 1619, removing one obstacle to Buckingham's domination of the king's affections, and that shortly afterwards, James himself, who had not attended his wife's funeral (once again deputing Charles to be chief mourner), became seriously ill and nearly died. If only

Early life and Prince of Wales 21

for pragmatic reasons, a more positive relationship with the royal favourite now seemed advisable for Charles, while Buckingham had seen how close he might have come to losing everything that he had so rapidly acquired should his royal patron have died.[30] As such it suited both parties to start to work together more effectively as the two most important figures in the ageing king's life.

Prince of Wales (1616)

Villiers's rise coincided with the time when Charles was beginning to be given more independence and responsibility. Charles was present at the new favourite's creation as Viscount Villiers in September 1616, just two months after he himself began attending the Privy Council (he did not formally become a member of the Council Board until March 1622),[31] and two months before he was finally invested with the title of Prince of Wales. It was noted of the latter event that the ceremonies and celebrations did not to match those which had been afforded his late brother at the same stage.[32] Charles came from Richmond to Whitehall for the ceremony but Queen Anne refused to attend, reportedly due to the uncomfortable reminder of Prince Henry, who, it was said, 'runs still so much in some men's minds'.[33] There is a sense, perhaps, in which Charles remained in his elder brother's shadow even after the latter's death. Charles's household was reconfigured as a mark of his new-found status, and in which his former guardians received their rewards: Sir Robert Carey, previously a gentleman of the bedchamber was, after much lobbying, and thanks to Queen Anne's intervention, made Lord Chamberlain, while Charles's former tutor, Thomas Murray, was made the prince's secretary.[34]

The Spanish match

The question of Charles's marriage also now became one of huge diplomatic significance. Having married his daughter Elizabeth to one of the leading German Protestant princes, James sought to pair his son with a Catholic princess in order to achieve a balance in England's foreign alliances and avoid becoming drawn into the increasingly confessionalised politics of contemporary Europe.

22 Early life and Prince of Wales

For some time, and encouraged by the Howards, James had been inclining towards a potential marriage alliance with the most powerful Catholic state of the age: Habsburg Spain. Amidst years of tentative diplomatic wrangling, Charles does not seem personally to have been overly keen on the idea of a Spanish marriage. In August 1619 it was reported that Spanish commissioners returned from England having 'found the prince very averse from an alliance with a Spaniard'. However, while this lack of 'inclination' to a Spanish match is repeatedly remarked throughout 1620, so is Charles's desire to please his father and to carry out his wishes.[35] By now the question was bound up with an urgent diplomatic crisis: Princess Elizabeth's husband, Elector Frederick of the Palatine, had foolishly (and against James's advice) accepted the offer of the Bohemian Crown from the country's rebel Protestant aristocracy, in defiance of the Habsburg emperor, whose virtual hereditary possession the Crown was. Having incurred Habsburg wrath, Frederick was in a vulnerable position and Charles, for one, showed sympathy with his brother-in-law and rebutted Spanish attempts to convince him that Frederick was in the wrong. Charles and Buckingham, in a further sign of their increasing political closeness, jointly lobbied James to offer help to his benighted son-in-law.[36] Frederick's catastrophic defeat at the battle of White Mountain in November 1620, followed by his eviction from his short-lived Bohemian kingdom (hence his soubriquet, 'The Winter King') and the occupation of his electorate by Habsburg forces, changed the game significantly, however. Now, amidst an increasingly belligerent public mood, reflected in pamphlet's such as Thomas Scott's *Vox Populi* (1620), which was demanding military action to aid Frederick, James sought, in accord with his firm attachment to peace, to use the marriage negotiations with Spain as leverage in a deal to return Frederick's territory without resort to force. This project, and apparent defiance of the public mood, would last for nearly three years, and it was one which would have a profound effect upon Charles's formation as heir to the throne.

'A Prince Bred up in Parliaments'

In pursuit of his policy of negotiating a return of his son-in-law's territory, James summoned the Parliament of 1621. In the words

Early life and Prince of Wales 23

of Conrad Russell, the most distinguished historian of the parliamentary politics of these years, James had called it 'in the hope that the threat of war would fortify the efforts he was making to negotiate a successful peace', or, in the words of his one of his secretaries of state, 'When so many swords are drawn, it is very inconvenient his Majesty's should be sheathed'.[37] Parliaments were a symbol of national unity as well as the means by which kings could raise the sorts of sums required to wage war. James had no intention of going to war, but hoped that the appearance of his willingness to do so would focus Spanish minds. He also hoped that this Parliament would serve to complete his son's political apprenticeship. It will be remembered that when a Parliament had last met, in 1614, it had sat for only a few weeks and then been abandoned. Now nearly 21 years old, Charles would need to know how parliaments worked in order to manage and understand them when he should accede to the throne. As Prince of Wales, Duke of Cornwall and of York and Earl of Chester, Charles was entitled to sit in the House of Lords, eligibility for which depended merely upon the issue of a writ of summons by the king. The vicissitudes of dynastic succession, royal childlessness and female rule meant that this was nevertheless a rare occurrence: the last Prince of Wales to sit in Parliament had been the future Henry V in 1410–13.[38] While healthy adult male heirs had been in short supply in recent English history, Charles's participation in two parliaments prior to his becoming king, along with his central role in the formation of foreign policy (which was tied up with the negotiations for his marriage), arguably made him the most politically experienced heir to the English throne for two centuries.

Having ridden in state in the ceremonial procession at the parliament's beginning, Charles sat to the left and just below the throne as James made his opening speech setting out his aims for the session. He was reported going to Parliament 'with a faire retinue and his guard' on foot on subsequent days and was regular in his attendance in the House of Lords (sitting, when the king was not present, at the head of the earls' bench).[39] In response to James's request for subsidies to enable him to look as if he might be prepared to use military force against Spain, a request that was then fleshed out by the Lord Treasurer's statement of the Crown's financial position, Charles made a speech in support

24 *Early life and Prince of Wales*

of the Crown's case, one which demonstrates his capacity to act as a royal messenger. He was responding to apparent expression of 'doubts', made in his presence, as to the king's intentions. He therefore affirmed the Crown's sincerity, insisting that the king's determination to go to war was genuine, and that parliament was summoned as he 'was not able of himself and of his own strength to engage himself in a war without your assistance'. He then answered what he (or more likely, his father) saw to be the chief fear of the assembled MPs:

> Another doubt there was in mine own mind that some amongst you might fear that when those businesses were settled, the King would be slow in calling you together again. I will put you in mind of the last part of the King's speech, that he hoped to be in love with Parliament; but having occasions to send to the King upon other occasions I find him willing and very willing to call you often; but this I speak of mine own head.

Perhaps Charles's claim to speak 'of mine own head' was disingenuous: he was in constant consultation with privy councillors and his father about affairs in Parliament. Nevertheless, he does appear able to gauge the parliamentary mood and show himself conscious of the some of the unease and suspicion within the houses. As he reached his peroration, he also demonstrated an acute sense of the importance of the royal honour, a characteristic he would display frequently as king. Urging the Commons to make haste with a grant of funds, he encouraged them to

> prepare yourselves so as that you may not only show your teeth but bite also if there be occasion', and reminded that 'how much the King's honour and mine much more are engaged; if you should fail in this it would be dishonourable to yourselves as well as to me.

Charles's reference to 'honour' here is significant for the way it reflects what was clearly an increasing preoccupation, and one that was to be central to his kingship, while the concept of 'engagement' would be one he would have bitter cause to use in relation to his first Parliament as king, that of 1625, when

Early life and Prince of Wales 25

it failed to honour the 'engagements' of its predecessor to fund a war against Spain with adequate subsidies. The slight hint of admonition also anticipates the tone he would adopt towards some of his early parliaments, while his last, more personal flourish, acknowledged his own relative inexperience:

> You shall oblige me who am now entering into the world; and when time shall serve hereafter you shall not think the labour ill bestowed.[40]

As James received a prompt grant of two subsidies, hardly enough to fight a war but an apparent endorsement of his policy, Charles's first significant speech to Parliament can be considered to have done the trick.

As the Commons turned in April to attack the leading patentees, Sir Giles Mompesson and Sir Francis Michell, and in doing so revived the long-dormant practice of parliamentary impeachment, Charles was active, sitting on the committee charged with investigating Mompesson and taking part in the interrogation of Matthias Fowles, the patentee for gold and silver thread.[41] Much of this involved treading carefully, as Mompesson was Buckingham's cousin and the latter's brother was also implicated.[42] When the Lord Chancellor, Sir Francis Bacon, was also impeached for allegedly taking bribes to issue some of the offending patents, Charles supported the action, and showed himself mindful of precedent when discussion of Bacon's punishment ensued. Perhaps most notably, he was trenchant in his defence of his father's honour against the slight offered by the Attorney General, Sir Henry Yelverton, who had dared to compare Buckingham to Hugh Despenser, and thereby implicitly James to Edward II.[43] Charles was observed to have 'asked leave of the Lords to interrupt him as not able to indure his fathers government to be so paralleled and scandalised', an indication of his acute sense of the royal honour and dignity.[44] The episode also foreshadowed a similar incident that was to occur in the Parliament of 1626 when Charles reacted furiously to the comparison made by one MP between the royal favourite, Buckingham, and the Roman soldier Sejanus, which, as Charles realised, implied that he was being likened to the Emperor Tiberius.

26 Early life and Prince of Wales

Charles also acted as a conduit for messages between Parliament and the king.[45] Politically speaking, Charles's presence as an effective representative of the king may also have deterred certain peers, notably the earl of Southampton, from launching a widely anticipated attack on Buckingham himself, whose family's neck-high involvement in patents was an acute embarrassment.[46] Indeed contemporaries witnessed to his impressive performance in the first session of the Parliament: John Chamberlain commented that his 'affabilitie and curtesie in the parlement hath won him great reputation and love, and yt seems he is much improved by his diligent frequenting the parlement house'.[47] The Venetian ambassador, meanwhile, reported that 'The prince constantly increases his popularity therein [in Parliament] by his modesty and other great qualities'. His assessment at the end of the session was that 'in some sense the prince has served as a tie to unite his Majesty and his people'.[48]

Charles's role in the second session of the Parliament was considerably greater. This was largely because James was away in Newmarket throughout, and so the prince became the key figure in the management of the Parliament and the principal point of contact for royal councillors, meeting with them regularly in the evenings in order to discuss the day's proceedings and plan for the next day's sitting as well as compiling reports to be sent to the king. At last foreign policy came to be debated, though against the wishes of the king, who had sought more funds but who had banned discussion of affairs of state of this kind. Charles showed himself intolerant of opposition, recommending to the king that 'seditius fellus' be made an example of.[49] His main contribution was to notify the king of his outrage at the Commons 'for busying themselves about his marriage'.[50] Indeed several MPs had spoken out against the match and Sir Edward Coke went so far as to demand that the Commons 'peticion the king to match the prince with a wife of his owne Religion', though James's response was an emphatic ban upon further discussion of the topic.[51] Personal affront was coupled with political confrontation as the Commons and the king clashed over the Lower House's claims to freedom of speech. Charles, after a meeting with the privy councillors on 7 December, advised the king to take a conciliatory line, to accept the Commons' Declaration on freedom of speech

Early life and Prince of Wales 27

and take time to read it on condition that the Lower House got on with granting further subsidies (i.e. behaved themselves), or, if they proved obdurate, to have Charles activate a pre-prepared ('Dormant') commission for adjourning the Parliament to a later date. James followed his son's advice, telling MPs to 'goe on with bills', but, as the Commons dug their heels in, the outcome was an adjournment, which turned into an outright dissolution after Buckingham lobbied strongly for an end to the recalcitrant assembly.[52] The scene in which James summoned the Commons to him at Whitehall and, in front of them, ripped the text of their Protestation regarding freedom of speech from the official journal of the House, illustrated the king's sensitivity to perceived attacks upon his prerogative. It was a trait which his son was to more than inherit.

Charles's role in the Parliament of 1621 has been the subject of debate. Historians such as Conrad Russell and Chris Kyle suggest that Charles enjoyed a positive and constructive relationship with the institution, while Richard Cust has recently shown the picture to be more complicated: while true for the first session, in the second session he began to show some of the frustrations and anxieties, shared with his father, about threats posed by elements within the House of Commons to the royal prerogative.[53] The difference in tone between the two sessions is partly explained by the issues under discussion: though it had been anticipated that preparations for a possible war with Spain would predominate, the first session had swiftly became side-tracked by economic issues arising from the ongoing depression, a development that suited James's reluctance to actually undertake to fight a war, and which was assisted by the hiatus in diplomatic negotiations produced by the king of Spain's death at the end of March. As such, while the House of Commons quickly granted the king two subsidies towards the potential war, it had soon began to focus upon the grants of patents and monopolies to courtiers and royal servants.[54] What ought we to make of Charles's parliamentary debut? While he had shown himself willing to learn the rudiments of parliamentary procedure and had been a diligent participant in the revival of judicature in the first session, representing his father's interests and seeking to steer Parliament towards achievement of the Crown's objectives, he had also seen how

28   Early life and Prince of Wales

parliaments could go awry by challenging the royal prerogative and standing jealously on their privileges.

The journey to Madrid

One of the most mysterious and puzzling episodes in Charles's life was his impromptu journey to Madrid in February 1623.[55] It seems that the motivation behind it was straightforwardly to expedite the negotiations for Charles's marriage to the Spanish Infanta (what James's father, rather indelicately, called the 'cod-piece point'). The traditional view was that the venture was Buckingham's initiative. Clarendon, whose history of these years, written much later, was keen to refute criticisms of his former royal master, claimed that it was 'contrived wholly by the duke'.[56] Others subsequently saw it as part of Buckingham's by now near total political dominance over an ageing and ailing king. That, however, underestimates Charles's political autonomy: James told the Privy Council that it was 'the Princes owne desire' rather than the initiative of Buckingham, and while Buckingham (soon to be made a duke to increase his status abroad and give him parity with the Spanish chief minister, Olivares) seems to have encouraged the enterprise, it would be overly simplistic to regard Charles as his 'tool'.[57] Other, well-informed contemporaries, such as Godfrey Goodman (later Bishop of Gloucester) and Henry Wootton (diplomat and later Provost of Eton) felt sure that the plan was Charles's idea. Indeed Goodman argued that it was evidence of his youthful and energetic disposition, being 'active, an excellent horseman, and never perfectly well but when he was in action', attributing some of this to his tutor, Murray, who 'put this spirit in him' and to the knowledge that his own father, James, had once risked life and limb by sailing to Denmark to win his bride. Further, and while Goodman conceded that Gondomar might have encouraged him in these thoughts, Charles felt that personal diplomacy, face-to-face with Philip IV, would not only be better able to settle the treaty but also that it 'might greatly improve his experience, and the world might thereby take notice of his abilities'.[58] As such, confident both in his physical and intellectual attributes, for Charles the journey to Madrid was as much about his self-fashioning and growth to maturity as a king-in-waiting as it was

Early life and Prince of Wales 29

about the marriage treaty itself. In any case it made little political sense for Buckingham to absent himself from the court and allow his enemies scope to plot against him, while at the same time he had to maintain his relationship with Charles as the reversionary interest and so had good reason to go along with the plan once Charles had put it forward.[59]

Very few people knew beforehand of the secret mission. Only Buckingham, Francis Cottington (Hispanophile diplomat and later one of Charles's most long-standing councillors), Endymion Porter, and James, were 'acquainted with the Prince's resolution'.[60] Disguised as 'Jack and Tom Smith', they travelled to Dover, where they were recognised, and then on through France, reaching Madrid by the 7 March, completing a 750-mile journey in only thirteen days, and news of their safe arrival prompting widespread relief in London.[61] The intrepid pair were 'royally received' by the Spanish, though both they and the English ambassador, the earl of Bristol, were astonished to see them. After only a few days Charles asked to see his future bride and Buckingham engineered a surreptitious trip by coach to watch the Infanta walking with the king and queen in the Prado Park.[62] He subsequently astonished Spanish courtiers by attempting to speak to his intended bride after leaping over the wall of a garden in which she was walking, prompting her to shriek and flee in fear of her virtue.[63] Quite quickly, however, it became apparent that the Spanish were more interested in converting Prince Charles to Catholicism or at least in extracting concessions for their co-religionists in England. Charles displayed a degree of naivety in this regard, writing to his father to enquire how much of the pope's spiritual supremacy within Christendom he might legitimately acknowledge, a move that would of course have caused horror back home. Desultory talks persisted throughout May, with Charles making tentative promises to seek toleration for English Catholics, and, in England, preparations were made for the Infanta's reception, including Inigo Jones's design of a splendid chapel at St James's for her to worship in.[64] Relations between the English and Spanish in Madrid began to become strained, however, not helped by Buckingham's very public quarrel with the Spanish chief minister, Olivares. Charles felt himself by now to be little better than a hostage at the Spanish court, a

30 Early life and Prince of Wales

fact that his returning emissary, Francis Cottington, reported to James in London in June.[65]

The sluggish pace of the negotiations at least allowed Charles to explore Madrid and to indulge his developing artistic tastes, exploring Philip IV's considerable collection, purchasing pictures to take back to England with him, and even sitting for a (sadly now lost) drawing by the young Velázquez. His patience with the prolonged diplomatic wrangling wearing thin, Charles showed now showed a willingness to engage in the double-dealing for which his enemies would later castigate him: at the start of July he told James that he would promise all that the Spanish demanded regarding freedom of worship for English Catholics and allowing any children of the marriage to remain with their mother (and therefore be raised as Catholics) until the age of twelve, but that he would not honour the agreement unless he was able to take the Infanta Maria home with him there and then. Knowing as he did the Spanish reluctance to allow her to leave the country until the concessions to English Catholics were actually enacted, this was a game of bluff. His courtiers, and the Spanish, however, were amazed at his willingness to make these promises. Back home, James duly had his Privy Council swear to uphold the articles of the marriage treaty. In any event, the almost simultaneous death of Pope Gregory XV, whose dispensation was required for the marriage to go ahead, produced a further delay, and an excuse for Charles and Buckingham to break things off.[66] In late August Charles requested James order his return in order to justify a hasty departure.[67] He left his proxy with Bristol as ambassador (but instructed him not to exercise it), and set off back for England at the beginning of September, though not before he had received the famous Titian portrait of the Habsburg Emperor Charles V as a gift from Philip IV, perhaps a sign that the Spanish king had indeed been taken in by the English prince's game-playing, but also in many ways an inducement to join the Habsburg family by marriage.[68] Indeed Philip erected a stone pillar on the spot outside Madrid upon which they had finally parted.[69] Charles arrived back in England to bonfires of popular rejoicing and wine-fuelled street parties the following month, an illustration of the relief felt in England that the prince's religion had not been suborned at the Spanish court. James too was relieved at the return of his heir and

Early life and Prince of Wales 31

his favourite, greeting them, in his eagerness, on the stairs of his hunting lodge at Royston whereupon he 'fell on their necks, and they all wept'.[70]

Charles was also noted to have grown a beard, a sign perhaps that he himself regarded his recent experience as a seminal moment in his passage to manhood.[71] His Spanish sojourn had demonstrated youthful bravura and determination to secure his bride in the original venture, naivety in some of his initial dealings with the Spanish negotiators, and finally ruthlessness and deceit in his last, equivocal statements and ultimately false promises. He had imbibed a wide-eyed admiration for the dignified aura of the Habsburg court, embodied in Philip IV's statuesque public appearances and the sobriety of his sable garb, as well as a deepening love of Renaissance art, both of which he was to seek to replicate at his own court when he became king. As such the visit to Madrid captures two sides of Charles's developing public persona that were to become deeply familiar to his future English subjects.

The prince's parliament

Upon their return, Charles and Buckingham sought to maximise their new status as Protestant heroes. The 'strong alliance' between them was noted by contemporaries, while Charles was observed to be much more politically self-confident, and open in his anti-Spanish utterances.[72] They began agitating for the summoning of a Parliament with the aim of using it to pressure the king into war against Spain for the restitution of the Palatinate. This is sometimes seen as jarring with Charles's later reputation for a peaceful foreign policy; indeed Charles was later heavily criticised in the 1630s for his failure to intervene in the continental war in defence of fellow Protestants. It is important to emphasise, however, as Tom Cogswell has done, that the young Charles was distinctly warlike in his instincts. Unlike his father, who adopted the *Rex Pacificus* mantle from an early stage in his reign, Charles was every inch the patriot prince and indeed patriot king in his first five years on the throne, until his troubled relationship with Parliament changed his view and his policy by 1629. It is important also to realise that the pique felt by Charles and Buckingham upon their return from Spain in 1623 was less

32 *Early life and Prince of Wales*

to do with a perceived personal humiliation in pursuit of marital ardour at the Spanish court, and much more to do with the realisation of the Spanish refusal to link any Anglo-Spanish marriage to a restitution of the Palatinate to Charles's sister and brother-in-law, the original intention behind the policy of the Spanish match.[73] This also usefully highlights a key aspect of Charles's character: his sensitivity to perceived slights upon his or his family's honour (a point to which we shall return). As a report of his conversation with the Spanish ambassador a few years before had revealed, Charles cared deeply about his sister Elizabeth's fortunes. In January 1620 he told a Spanish agent that 'I have nothing else to do at present than to think of the affairs of the Bohemians and of my brother-in-law and nothing occupies my mind more', and it was said that 'at every opportunity he displays his friendly feeling towards his sister and the new King [of Bohemia]'.[74] As the work of Richard Cust has shown, and as the language he used in Parliament in 1621 would suggest, Charles's sense of regal and noble honour was acute, expressed not only in his personal and political utterances as Prince of Wales but also in his keen promotion of chivalric culture as king.[75] It helps to understand the swiftness of his apparent *volte face* regarding Spain and the vigour with which he championed the case for war in the ensuing Parliament of 1624.

Though reluctant, by the end of the year James had been persuaded to summon a Parliament to meet the following February, a decision Gardiner argued effectively ushered in the 'reign of Buckingham'.[76] This, however, underestimates not only the continued exercise of James's political will but also the significant role played by Charles in the forthcoming events. He appeared single-mindedly focused on pursuing war with Spain, and the famous remark he made to William Laud around this time, that he could never have been a lawyer as he could not 'defend a bad, nor yield in a good cause', suggested an unshakeable conviction of the rightness of his stance.[77] Building on the knowledge and experience he had acquired during the previous Parliament, the prince played an even bigger role. Prior to the meeting of Parliament, Charles took the lead in reconciling Buckingham with some of his many enemies among the peerage, especially the earl of Pembroke.[78] It was he who moved for a joint conference between Lords and

Early life and Prince of Wales 33

Commons to hear Buckingham's narrative of their recent expedition to Spain and then exerted consistent early pressure for the House to focus its attention on the recovery of the Palatinate.[79] In many ways Charles's handling of the Parliament was impressive, helping Buckingham to construct a 'patriot coalition' including his former opponents the earls of Southampton, Pembroke, and Oxford, which enabled them to generate a striking level of war-fever in the House of Lords, even among the bishops.[80] Early on in the session, to curry favour with the Commons, and reflecting a sense of grievance at his treatment in Madrid, the prince strongly supported the enforcement of laws against recusants (this was not yet the Charles who would later be criticised for being 'soft' on the Catholic threat).[81]

He and Buckingham constructed a narrative of their time in Madrid calculated to push all of the right anti-Spanish buttons of the assembled MPs, accusing their hosts of 'cunning and fraud' and telling of the 'various slights and offences received in Spain'.[82] They were also critical of the English ambassador in Madrid, the earl of Bristol, the beginnings of a quarrel that was to escalate and sour relations between Crown and Parliament in the next reign. As this Parliament unfolded, however, Charles's role was central and multifaceted, his parliamentary management in many ways astute: not only in his regular attendance in Parliament and playing on his status as heir to the throne, but also commanding respect by his apparent devotion to Parliament as an institution and his crucial function of mediating between the Commons and his father.[83] When James appeared to be trying to exploit circumstances to get money from them to pay off his debts, Charles, who was privately hugely agitated by his father's actions (indeed the king's speech invoking his debts was said to have turned him pale with anxiety) assured the Lower House that he meant only after the foreign-policy situation had been addressed.[84] The suspicion that James was trying to sabotage the push towards war was fed by refusal to declare war before subsidies were voted, while the Commons feared if it voted the money (an unprecedented demand for five subsidies) then the king would merely use it to pay off his debts. In the end a scheme of 'appropriation', by which three subsidies and three fifteenths were voted for the sole and express purpose of funding the forthcoming war, ended the impasse.[85]

34 Early life and Prince of Wales

Charles and Buckingham also had to withstand a Spanish counter-attack towards the end of April, when the agents Inijosa and Coloma accused them to James of being involved in a conspiracy to side-line the king and rule in his place. James appeared to believe it, at least initially, but Charles managed to salvage the situation by protecting Buckingham and exploiting anti-Spanish sentiment in the Commons.[86] He also, in conjunction with Buckingham, made use of parliamentary impeachment to attack, on charges of corruption, Lord Treasurer Middlesex, whose real crime was opposition to the war on financial grounds (and alleged involvement in the Spanish plot against them), which had made him an enemy of Buckingham and Charles.[87] While Charles did speak up for Middlesex before sentence in order to reduce his fine, he helped to defeat the former Treasurer's attempts to recover favour at court by excluding him from the royal bedchamber and had James remove him from the list of subsidy commissioners in his home county.[88] In a typically prescient foreshadowing of things to come in the next reign, however, James, who let the impeachment proceed, a clever tactic to ensure tension was defused and criticism channelled away from the Crown, warned Charles that the use of this weapon would later come back to haunt him.[89]

When Parliament was prorogued on 29 May until November (though in the event it would not meet again), Charles emerged with his political reputation immeasurably enhanced. We might not quite go as far as Gardiner, whose Whiggish tendencies were never more evident than when he claimed that 'Headed by the Prince of Wales, the House of Commons appeared suddenly to have become the first power in the State', but his sense that Charles had captured the mood of the political nation, and placed himself at its head, certainly has merit.[90] Charles was described by the Venetian ambassador as having 'drawn all the popularity to himself and as against the royal authority. . .he can in this case adduce the cause and the argument of his own succession'.[91] In the ambassador's remark was recognition that not only was Charles basking in the glow of near-universal popularity and acclaim, but also of the discovery that his status as heir to the throne gave him significant political leverage over his father and with members of the political nation anxious to preserve their position into the next reign. This courting of popularity by the prince did not meet

Early life and Prince of Wales   35

with approval in all quarters, however. The earl of Kellie suggested that 'their is not that harmonye betwixt the Kings Majestie and the Prince as I culd wishe' and that in his eagerness to win supply Charles was 'a lytill more populare then was fitting for him', something for which James had upbraided him and which, it was presciently suggested, 'will sume tyme meete him' if and when he should become king himself.[92]

The main historical debate about the importance of the Parliament is that between Conrad Russell and Tom Cogswell. Russell argued that it was a 'meeting of ships that pass in the night', in which Buckingham and Charles on the one hand and the Commons on the other 'had little interest in each other's business', a dissonance that was ultimately reflected in the refusal of the Commons in 1625 to vote sufficient funds for the war.[93] Cogswell, by contrast, shows that the parliamentary enthusiasm for war was genuine, as reflected in the generosity of the subsidy voted, and indeed extended beyond Westminster (a context Russell did not adequately consider), as shown by the flood of virulently anti-Catholic and anti-Spanish literature throughout London in the summer of 1624. The problem was rather that their success in encouraging and exploiting pro-war sentiment in 1624 led Charles and Buckingham to the mistaken conclusion that managing parliaments was easy and that future parliaments would be similarly enthusiastic for their policy agenda, while in addition the predominantly naval war that Parliament had thought it had been promised gave way to a continental expedition that was ineffective as well as expensive.[94]

The Parliament of 1624 is often regarded as an illustration of what could be achieved when court and Parliament were singing from the same hymn sheet: events would soon show that such harmony was rare indeed. The difficulties Charles experienced in his dealings with his parliaments in his first few years as king have their roots in the Parliament of 1624.

The French marriage

The proposal that Charles marry the French princess, Henrietta Maria, sister of King Louis XIII, was under consideration very soon after the negotiations for a Spanish match began to collapse.

36 *Early life and Prince of Wales*

Lord Kensington, future Earl of Holland, was dispatched to Paris soon after Parliament opened in February 1624 to sound out the French court. As negotiations proceeded more seriously after the proroguing of Parliament, Charles himself, despite reportedly being unimpressed by her portrait, was keen on the idea of the marriage.[95] Aside, as his Spanish venture had shown, from being anxious to acquire a wife, his enthusiasm also likely reflected diplomatic considerations: the French were seen as possible participants, along with the Dutch, in a military alliance for the recovery of the Palatinate. Though Kensington reported initially that the French were seeking only the freedom for Henrietta Maria and her attendants to worship as Catholics, rather than a more general toleration, the vicissitudes of French court politics soon brought demands from the French, as from the Spanish before them, for significant concessions to English Catholics as part of any marriage treaty, something to which Charles, the French ambassador in London noted, was particularly averse.[96] As talks between the English and French continued, and it became clear that granting liberty of worship to English Catholics was to be the French price for a meaningful military alliance, by September Charles and James were eventually won over to the suspension of the laws against the recusants, despite their undertakings to Parliament to the contrary, making its promised recall in the autumn politically impossible and forcing a further prorogation until late February of the following year.[97]

As the realities of European diplomacy began to risk undermining Charles's anti-Catholic public persona, amidst all of this he suffered a painful fall from his horse while out hunting in September, a reminder, if any were needed, of the fragility of the succession and therefore of the dynastic importance of the marriage.[98] That Charles should have appeared to backtrack in this way is easily explained: at this stage, his and Buckingham's absolute priority, in continued pursuit of their patriot agenda, was securing French military help to recover the Palatinate, and the ground given on religion was a means to that end. The rejoicing in November among the people of London, thus far still ignorant of the religious concessions, at news of an impending marriage treaty, reflected the wider optimism that the alliance strengthened the English military position against Spain. In addition, as D'Ewes noted, 'The English generally so detested the Spansh match, as

Early life and Prince of Wales 37

they were glad of any other which freed them from the fear of that'.[99] As Charles put his signature to the treaty at Cambridge in December 1624 in the presence of the king, Buckingham, and the French delegation, he could not have yet realised what a significant impact it would have upon not only on him personally but upon English politics more generally.

The war and the death of James I

Meanwhile Charles was exercised about the preparations for military intervention on the continent, which continued but were strikingly ineffectual. The mercenary general, Count Mansfeld, was stuck at Dover in December and January short of funds while his troops were noted to be poor in quality and even poorer in behaviour, his expedition delayed while resources were found. In desperation, Charles even borrowed money on his own personal security to tide Mansfeld over.[100] He was reportedly becoming impatient at Mansfeld's lack of action, urging him to get to Calais as soon as possible in the hope that this would prompt the French to action on behalf of the English cause, though in fact the French refused to permit an English landing on French soil. When the expedition finally did depart, it went to Holland instead, though by early February the troops were starving and disease-ridden. Hamstrung by James's desire to avoid all-out war with the Spanish, the troops were forbidden from acting to relieve the siege of Breda, a meaningful military action that might actually have contributed to the war effort.

This was still the situation when James entered his final illness in March 1625. His declining health had been evident at Christmas, when he had remained in his chamber and avoided court festivities, but he had then recovered. Now he took to his bed at his favourite palace of Theobalds in Hertfordshire with a tertian ague, subsequently exacerbated by a stroke and then dysentery. The duke of Buckingham delayed his planned visit to Paris, where he was to finalise arrangements for Charles's marriage, in order to tend James on his deathbed. This would later give rise to rumours that he had poisoned the king with medicines he personally recommended, some even suggested in collaboration with Charles, an accusation that was to spawn a rich and lurid literature and which would

38   Early life and Prince of Wales

not only contribute to the campaign to impeach the favourite in 1626 but would also re-surface against Charles in the 1640s.[101] If the potions did worsen James's condition then this was almost certainly inadvertent: the subsequent charges against Buckingham say more about his extreme unpopularity and the general mystery surrounding most medical matters in the seventeenth century than about any likely plot to kill the king.

As he lay dying, James reportedly offered his son various pieces of advice as to how he should govern his kingdom. Aside from commending several courtiers to him as good servants and urging him to protect the Church, a responsibility which, as will be seen, Charles was to take extremely seriously, James also implored Charles to seek to restore the Palatinate to the Elector and his wife, Charles's sister Elizabeth.[102] While in James's mind this was entirely consistent with the avoidance of war, the likely effect of issuing this injunction to the prince, who was already at the forefront of the campaign to reclaim the Palatinate by force, was only to stiffen his resolve to prosecute the war with Spain. The first few years of his own reign were to be dominated by exactly this mission.

Notes

1 *Letters of John Chamberlain*, ed. Norman Egbert McLure, (2 vols, Philadelphia, 1939), I, p. 113.
2 See for example, John C.G. Röhl, 'Kaiser Wilhlem II: a suitable case for treatment?', in Röhl, *The Kaiser and his Court: Wilhelm II and the Government of Germany* (Cambridge, 1994), pp. 9–27 at pp. 25–7. Cf. Christopher Clark, *Kaiser Wilhelm II: A Life in Power* (London, 2009), pp. 29–34.
3 Charles Carlton, *Charles I: The Personal Monarch* (London, 1983), pp. 7–9.
4 Michael B. Young, *Charles I* (1997), p. 15.
5 George Seton, *Memoirs of Alexander Seton, Earl of Dunfermline, President of the Court of Session, and Chancellor of Scotland* (Edinburgh and London, 1882), p. 53.
6 Ibid., p. 56.
7 *HMC Salisbury MSS.*, XVI, pp. 137–8, 163.
8 Ibid., p. 227.
9 Ralph Winwood, *Memorials of Affairs of State*, ed. E. Sawyer (2 vols, London, 1725), II, p. 43.
10 *HMC Salisbury*, XIX, pp. 412–3.

Early life and Prince of Wales 39

11 *Memoirs of Robert Carey, Earl of Monmouth, Written by Himself* (Edinburgh, 1808), pp. 138–9, 140–1.
12 Carlton, *Charles I*, p. 5.
13 *Memoirs of Robert Carey*, p. 141.
14 *Calendar of State Papers Domestic, 1603–1610*, p. 246.
15 See for example Carlton, *Charles I*, pp. 6, 9.
16 William Lilly, *Monarchy or No Monarchy in England* (London, 1651), p. 75.
17 Mark Kishlansky and John Morrill, 'Charles I', *Oxford Dictionary of National Biography* [*ODNB*].
18 William Lilly, *Monarchy or No Monarchy in England*, p. 75.
19 Catherine Macleod, Malcolm Smuts and Timothy Wilks, *The Lost Prince: the Life and Death of Henry Stuart* (London, 2012), pp. 131, 160.
20 *The Autobiography and Correspondence of Sir Simonds D'Ewes, Bart., during the reigns of James I and Charles I*, ed. J.O. Halliwell (2 vols, London, 1845), I, p. 46.
21 *Calendar of State Papers Venetian, 1610–1613*, pp. 493, 531–2.
22 *The Court and Times of James I*, ed. Thomas Birch (London, 1848), I, 246–7, 252.
23 *CSPV, 1610–1613*, p. 524.
24 BL Stowe MS 173, ff. 205, 252.
25 *CSPV, 1613–1615*, p. 98; *CSPV, 1615–1617*, p. 502.
26 *CSPV, 1613–1615*, p. 115; Chamberlain, *Letters*, I, 522.
27 Tim Harris, *Rebellion: Britain's First Stuart Kings* (Oxford, 2014), pp. 134–5.
28 Harris, *Rebellion*, pp. 137, 139.
29 Carlton, *Charles I*, p. 24; *HMC MSS Earl of Mar and Kellie* (HMSO, 1930), p. 85; *CSPV, 1619–1621*, p. 138.
30 Carlton, *Charles I*, pp. 25–26.
31 Quoted in Cust, 'Prince Charles', p. 431; *CSPD, 1619–1623*, p. 362.
32 Chamberlain, *Letters*, II, p. 22; *CSPV, 1615–1617*, pp. 269, 350.
33 Birch, *Court and Times of James I*, I, p. 435.
34 Chamberlain, *Letters*, II, p. 58.
35 *CSPV, 1619–1621*, pp. 151, 238.
36 *CSPV, 1619–1621*, pp. 151, 275.
37 Conrad Russell, *Parliaments and English Politics, 1621–1629* (Oxford, 1979), p. 87.
38 Chris R. Kyle, 'Prince Charles in the Parliaments of 1621 and 1624', *Historical Journal*, 41 (1998), pp. 603–24, at p. 604.
39 Ibid., p. 605; Chamberlain, *Letters*, II, 343–44; *CSPD, 1619–1623*, p. 225.
40 *HMC Salisbury MSS, XXII* (1971), p. 145.
41 Chamberlain, *Letters*, II, p. 351; *Notes of the Debates in the House of Lords, officially taken by Henry Elsing, Clerk of the Parliaments,*

40 *Early life and Prince of Wales*

A.D. 1621, ed. Samuel Rawson Gardiner, Camden Society (London, 1870–71), pp. 27, 35.

42 Russell, *Parliaments and English Politics*, p. 105.

43 *Notes of Debates. . .1621*, pp. 62–3, 71, 73

44 Chamberlain, *Letters*, II, p. 369.

45 *Notes of Debates. . .1621*, p. 58.

46 Russell, *Parliaments and English Politics*, p. 107; Cust, 'Prince Charles', p. 428.

47 Chamberlain, *Letters*, II, p. 359.

48 *CSPV, 1621–1623*, pp. 36–7, 67.

49 Cust, 'Prince Charles', pp. 428–30, 431.

50 *CSPD, 1619–1623*, p. 321.

51 *Commons Debates 1621*, eds. Wallace Notestein, Frances Helen Relf and Hartley Simpson (7 vols, New Haven and London, 1935), VI, pp. 220–4.

52 Ibid., 233; Cust, 'Prince Charles', pp. 435–7.

53 Kyle, 'Prince Charles in the Parliaments of 1621 and 1624', pp. 603, 619–21; Richard Cust, 'Prince Charles and the Second Session of the 1621 Parliament', *English Historical Review*, 122 (2007), pp. 427–441.

54 Russell, *Parliaments and English Politics*, pp. 87–8, 91.

55 The best account is Glyn Redworth, *The Prince and The Infanta: The Cultural Politics of the Spanish Match* (New Haven and London, 2003).

56 Edward Hyde, Earl of Clarendon, *The History of the Rebellion and Civil Wars in England*, ed. W. D. Macray, (6 vols, Oxford, 1888), I, p. 20.

57 See for example, Samuel R. Gardiner, *History of England from the Accession of James I to the Outbreak of the Civil War, 1603–1642* (10 vols, London, 1883–4), V, pp. 1–2.

58 Godfrey Goodman, *The Court of King James the First. . .To which are added letters illustrative of the personal history of the most distinguished characters in the court of that monarch and his predecessors. Now first published from the original manuscripts by J. S. Brewer* (London, 1839), I, pp. 363–4.

59 Redworth, *The Prince and The Infanta*, p. 77.

60 Simonds D'Ewes, *Autobiography*, I, pp. 224–5.

61 *Court and Times of James I*, II, pp. 368–9, 374–5, 377–8, 381.

62 *HMC Report on the MSS of the Duke of Buccleuch and Queensberry* (HMSO, 1899), I, p. 256; *HMC Salisbury MSS*, pp. 173–4

63 Gardiner, *History of England*, V, p. 52.

64 Ibid., p. 55. 'The Queen's Chapel', of course, still stands across from what remains of St James's palace.

65 Redworth, *The Prince and The Infanta*, pp. 105–06, 110–11; Gardiner, *History of England*, V, p. 57.

66 Redworth, *The Prince and The Infanta*, pp. 112–13, 123–9.

Early life and Prince of Wales 41

67 Gardiner, *History of England*, V, p. 100.
68 Redworth, *The Prince and The Infanta*, pp. 133, 135–6; Jerry Brotton, *The Sale of the Late King's Goods: Charles I and his Art Collection* (London, 2006), pp. 97–8. The painting was sold off by the Commonwealth regime after Charles's execution, for which see Brotton, *Sale of the Late King's Goods*, pp. 244, 246.
69 *Court and Times of James I*, II, p. 440.
70 Chamberlain, *Letters*, II, p. 515; *Court and Times of James I*, II, pp. 422–3.
71 *Court and Times of James I*, II, p. 420.
72 *CSPV, 1623–1625*, pp. 142–3, 169.
73 Tom Cogswell, *The Blessed Revolution: English Politics and the Coming of War, 1621–1624* (Cambridge, 1989), pp. 61–4.
74 *CSPV, 1619–1621*, p. 151.
75 Richard Cust, *Charles I and the Aristocracy, 1625–1642* (Cambridge, 2013).
76 Gardiner, *History of England*, V, p. 160.
77 *The works of the Most Reverend Father in God, William Laud, D.D. sometime lord archbishop of Canterbury*, ed. W. Scott and J. Bliss (7 vols, Oxford, 1847–60), III, pp. 146–7.
78 *CSPV, 1623–1625*, p. 169.
79 *Notes of the Debates in the House of Lords, Officially Taken by Henry Elsing, Clerk of the Parliaments, A.D. 1624 and 1626*, ed. Samuel Rawson Gardiner, Camden Society (London, 1879), pp. 1, 6, 9.
80 On the creation of the 'patriot coalition', see Cogswell, *Blessed Revolution*, pp. 77–105, 137–8, 146.
81 *Notes of Debates 1624*, pp. 56–7. 64.
82 *CSPV 1623–1625*, p. 232.
83 Cogswell, *Blessed Revolution*, p. 148.
84 *CSPV 1623–1625*, p. 255; Gardiner, *History of England*, V, p. 196.
85 For the text of the bill, see J.R. Tanner (ed.), *Constitutional Documents of the Reign of James I, A.D. 1603–1625 with an historical commentary* (Cambridge, 1960), pp. 374–9.
86 Cogswell, *Blessed Revolution*, pp. 251–2.
87 *Notes of Debates 1624*, pp. 75–6, 88; *CSPV, 1623–1625*, p. 279.
88 *CSPV, 1623–1625*, p. 279; Cogswell, *Blessed Revolution*, pp. 268–9; *Court and Times of James I*, II, pp. 459–60.
89 Gardiner, *History of England*, V, p. 231.
90 Ibid., pp. 231, 235.
91 Alvise Valaresso, Venetian Ambassador in England, to the DOGE and SENATE, 17 May 1626, https://www.british-history.ac.uk/cal-state-papers/venice/vol18/pp305-315.
92 *HMC Kellie and Mar MSS*, pp. 201–03.
93 Russell, *Parliaments and English Politics*, p. 202.
94 Cogswell, *Blessed Revolution*, pp. 309–19.
95 *CSPV, 1623–1625*, p. 355.

42 *Early life and Prince of Wales*

96 *Court and Times of James I*, II, p. 464; Gardiner, *History of England*, V, pp. 251, 253.
97 Gardiner, *History of England*, V, pp. 261–3.
98 *HMC Kellie and Mar MSS*, pp. 211–12; *Court and Times of James I*, II, p. 476.
99 Sir Simonds D'Ewes, *Autobiography*, I, p. 257.
100 *Court and Times of James I*, II, pp. 490, 493; Gardiner, *History of England*, V, p. 283; Lockyer, *The Early Stuarts*, p. 163.
101 For a thorough account of all of this, see Alastair Bellany and Thomas Cogswell, *The Murder of King James I* (New Haven and London, 2015).
102 Ibid., p. 28.

2 Patriot king (1625–29)

Accession

Charles's accession was greeted with 'universal applause and rejoicing', a reflection of the optimism and zeal which had attached to him after his return from Spain and his championing of an aggressive Protestant foreign policy.[1] As will be seen, however, within five years this positive atmosphere had dissipated and been replaced by one of scepticism and dismay in many quarters at the new king's conduct of politics, of foreign war, and his treatment of his parliaments in particular. Some of this was undoubtedly due to Charles's character and attitudes, but much was also due to the circumstances and wider context within which he was having to operate in the later 1620s.

Having attended his father's deathbed at Theobalds in Hertfordshire, Charles made his way to London to take up temporary residence in St James's Palace and from there appointed his Privy Council, confirming most of his father's councillors in post, at least until he had had time to consider matters further. Contemporaries noticed both change and continuity from the previous reign. The most obvious change was in the tone of the royal court, which the avid newsletter-writer, John Chamberlain, noted was 'kept more strait and private than in the former time' and which others saw as a reflection of the new monarch's character, 'being temperate, moderate and of exchanging all the prodigality of the past for order and profit'.[2] The most obvious continuity, meanwhile, was in the role of Buckingham. Contemporaries naturally wondered if the death of the old king would presage the end

44 Patriot king (1625–29)

of Buckingham's period as royal favourite, as was often the case in personal monarchies. The Venetian ambassador observed that

> Every one was watching to see what would happen to the Duke of Buckingham, to observe whether the new King's affection for him was sincere or if it was policy and to note if things change or go on as before.

As it turned out, Charles quickly made several 'demonstrations of esteem' including letting him ride in the same coach 'as an equal' at the royal entry into London and assigning him apartments in St James's Palace close to his own, the result being that 'this gentleman retains his former influence and estimation'.[3] This might suggest that James had recommended Buckingham's counsels to his son or that their shared experience of the journey to Madrid and the campaign for war in the Parliament of 1624 had genuinely brought them into a relationship of both personal and political dependency. It had been remarked in 1624 that Buckingham's influence was 'wonderfull great, and more with the Prince then with the King, at the leaste no less', and as will be seen, arguably Buckingham's power grew to its greatest height in the period 1625–28.

James's funeral took place on 7 May, with Charles as chief mourner.[4] After the obsequies, Charles set himself to the immediate priorities of his reign: namely arranging the coronation, finalising the French marriage, and the summoning of a Parliament to grant funds for the war that was now underway. These events were largely interdependent. He could not meet Parliament until the details of the marriage were settled, as the French were demanding more concessions for English Catholics, a condition certain to inflame the anti-Catholic prejudices of the House of Commons. As such, Parliament was repeatedly prorogued from 17 May until 18 June, two days after the arrival of his bride in London.[5] Further disruption would be caused by a severe outbreak of plague in London, which lasted for the entire summer.

Marriage

The marriage of Charles to Henrietta Maria took place by proxy on 1 May outside of the west door of Notre Dame (on account of the Protestantism of the absent groom). As part of the treaty, Charles ordered the suspension of the recusancy laws in England, but he and Buckingham doubted whether the French would offer the hoped-for military assistance against Spain. As such, Buckingham tried to cajole the French government into action by journeying to Paris himself on 14 May and, while he failed in his enterprise, he was still in France when Charles's bride sailed to meet her new husband.[6] The delay in Henrietta Maria's arrival in England caused widespread surprise, Chamberlain commenting that he and others 'expect the queen's coming and marvel it is so long deferred'. Charles went to Dover to meet her, but her voyage was delayed by the illness of her mother, Marie de Medici, and by bad weather. She finally landed on 12 June and the couple moved on to Canterbury for dinner and there the marriage was consummated. They journeyed along Watling Street as far as Gravesend and then made the rest of the journey into London along the Thames by barge. It was a rainy day but the entry was made quite a spectacle, with many barges of honour and 'thousands of boats' as well as cheering crowds.[7] Contemporaries noted of the royal bride that she was 'a most absolute delicate lady. . .[whose] deportment amongst her women was so sweet and humble, and her speech and looks to her other servants so mild and gracious'.[8] While Charles's relationship with his wife, and with her French entourage, would be strained for the first few years of marriage, of more interest to the politically interested in the capital were the implications his marriage to a Catholic queen, complete with her own chapel (designed by Inigo Jones) at St James's, was likely to have for the future of Protestantism in England.

The Parliament of 1625

Despite his experience of attending parliaments early in the decade, Charles was clearly unacquainted with some of the constitutional proprieties surrounding the process of summoning one. Eager as he was to receive a grant of supply to press on with the war, Charles assumed that he could merely re-summon the Parliament of 1624, the one that had seemingly been so enthusiastic in support of his foreign policy. He was therefore disappointed

46 Patriot king (1625–29)

to be informed by the Lord Keeper, John Williams, that the previous Parliament had died with 'his death that call'd it', and that constitutionally Charles was obliged to issue writs for fresh elections. Ordering Williams to do this immediately, the new king was then told that it was usual for the Privy Council to make preparations in the constituencies first.[9] As such, Charles was already becoming frustrated in his efforts to get his war off the ground. He was clearly in a hurry: Viscount Mandeville noted that 'The King hath already professed it is not to sit long, and if his errand were dispatched, which is for money, all other business should expect a new session'. While some thought the outbreak of plague should lead the Parliament to be moved out of London, Charles instead believed it merely added to the urgency for 'doing something instantly' in a short session.[10] When Parliament did finally meet, on 18 June, two days after the arrival of his queen, Charles impressed upon the MPs that 'they had drawn him into a war, and they must find means to maintain it', the first articulation of what was to become his central and persistent argument for generous supply. Rumours in London seemed to suggest, however, that while 'there is much urging and spurring the parliament for supply and expedition, in both which they will prove somewhat rusty', at least partly on account of concerns about religion, concerns Charles seemed anxious to rebut by adding in his speech that 'they need not doubt nor suspect his religion, seeing he was brought up at the feet of Gamiliel', a reference to the learning as well as the impeccable Protestant orthodoxy of his late father.[11] The invocation of his father's memory might also have drawn attention, however, to qualities that Charles appeared to lack. For instance, while James was accustomed to address his parliaments at some length, relishing imparting regal wisdom (perhaps too often and at too great a length for some MPs), Charles made only a short speech and announced he was reviving the practice of having his Lord Keeper speak for him 'in most things' a reflection perhaps of nerves about his stammer ('Now, because I am unfit for much speaking') but hardly designed to impress his audience. In addition, Charles showed some signs of complacency. First he suggested that the matter of the war was 'no new business (being already happily begun by my father. . .), therefore it needs no narrative', appearing to take their assent to what had gone before

Patriot king (1625–29) 47

entirely for granted, but he also implied an obligation on them 'to maintain [i.e. pay for] it as freely as you were willing to advise my father to it' as royal policy had been formed based on what he described repeatedly as 'your entreaties, your engagements'. He acknowledged his own role in whipping up war-fever, something he had done 'like a young man, and consequently rashly' but insisted that it was 'begun by your advice and entreaty' and, the sting in the tail, 'what a great dishonour it were both to you and me if this action, so begun, should fail for that assistance you are able to give me'.[12]

Charles's hopes for a generous grant of taxation were to be disappointed. The Venetian ambassador reported that MPs 'are not very pleased with these speeches, as they do not want to contribute without making sure of their laws'.[13] The Commons voted a mere two subsidies (equating to around £140,000) when the cost alone of the navy being prepared was estimated at £300,000. They also denied him the customary grant of tonnage and poundage for life (afforded to all of his predecessors since 1485), granting it for one year only, and hoping thereby to incentivise financial reform of the customs and the hated impositions inherited from the previous reign.[14] The explanation for this reluctance may have been the fact that MPs had been home to the shires since the previous Parliament and realised that their constituents were reluctant to pay the taxes required to fund the war; alternatively, MPs were merely objecting to the type of war being waged, angry that Buckingham had appeared to disregard their preference for a blue-water strategy based around the navy rather than land campaigns.[15] They also criticised the way that the monies granted in the previous Parliament were spent, complaining 'that the three subsidies granted to the late King were expended fruitlessly and ask to see the accounts', a reference to the disastrous expedition by Count Mansfeld in January 1625. Having been bitten before, they were now more cautious, as 'they perceive that the granting of subsidies in advance has not served them for obtaining subsequently the satisfaction which they claim', and therefore it is likely 'that matters will take a long time, or the contributions will be scanty'.[16] What is certain is that hostility to Catholicism had certainly not abated, and this was manifested in the way in which MPs diverted their attention to religious matters, demanding the enforcement of the laws against Catholics

48   Patriot king (1625–29)

and also taking up the case of Richard Montagu, whose printed works were alleged to minimise the differences between the Church of England and Rome and who was seen as being linked to a growing 'Arminian' movement within the English Church which sought to institutionalise such a position. Fusing with concerns at what might have been agreed with the French as part of the marriage treaty by way of concessions towards English Catholics and the presence now on English soil of a Catholic queen with a Catholic entourage, this served as a powerful set of grievances within the Parliament.[17] For Charles, however, this was an unwelcome distraction from the real priority of funding his war and his frustration began to become apparent.

It was decided to try again to secure the necessary funding by adjourning the Parliament to Oxford for a second session, ostensibly due to the plague rife in London, and with the hope that in surroundings less influenced by the febrile anti-Catholic atmosphere of the capital MPs would prove more pliant. MPs were not enthusiastic, however, and the meeting 'aroused dissatisfaction, being considered unreasonable owing to the plague and the harvest and the excessive inconvenience to the members', and, as a consequence, 'men spoke very freely against the government'.[18] Charles, residing at the royal manor at Woodstock just outside the city, travelled in on 4 August and addressed both Lords and Commons in Christ Church Hall. He once again sought to convince them of their obligation to fund a war whose origin lay in their advice to his father, expressing gratitude for the subsidies already granted but stressing their inadequacy for the purpose.[19] He also once again invoked the extent to which 'his honour was engaged' and went so far as to suggest that he 'would rather half the fleet perished at sea than abandon the preparations already made without doing anything'.[20]

Instead, they refused to vote further supply until the details of military action were clarified and continued to demand full execution of the laws against Catholics; in addition, they complained of corruption in the distribution of offices and honours and began to link these grievances to the royal favourite, the duke of Buckingham. They objected that 'the government should not be in the hands of one man alone', a reflection of the untrammelled influence over the king that Buckingham was perceived to wield. In an apparent slight against the king's inexperience and

Patriot king (1625–29) 49

the quality of those from whom he took advice (Buckingham in particular), they also complained about 'the government being in the hands of young men', a comment upon the character of the regime which, as will be seen, in many ways accurately reflects the demographics of the Caroline court in the 1630s.[21] As a result, Charles dissolved the Parliament on 12 August rather than tolerate what he saw as an attempt to remove Buckingham from his counsels.[22] Again, it was suggested that Charles's actions were determined by his sense of honour: 'It is said that the king was influenced by his intention to maintain his honour and authority supreme', as well as the fact that Buckingham 'promised to furnish the cost of the fleet' by other means.[23] Others lamented the failure of a Parliament which 'should have been an happy occasion and means to have united and settled the affections of Prince and people'.[24] The king's intransigence in the face of what he perceived to be an attempt to dictate to him his choice of advisers or direction of policy would be a running theme over the next few years.

It did not help Buckingham's cause, nor Charles's, that when the duke, as Lord Admiral, decided to launch a naval campaign against Cadiz the following month, funded by Henrietta Maria's dowry of £120,000 and money borrowed from the Dutch against the value of his own jewels, it proved a disastrous failure characterised by disease and drunkenness among the poorly supplied and badly equipped troops. The return of the remains of the fleet in November from its ignominious expedition would only lead to an increase in Buckingham's unpopularity on account of his alleged mismanagement and a hardening of Charles's belief that the failure was Parliament's for having failed to provide sufficient funds to equip the force properly.[25]

Charles also reconfigured his Council, exacting a degree of revenge for what he and Buckingham believed was disloyal conduct in the recent parliamentary session. Williams was replaced as Lord Keeper (by Sir Thomas Coventry), accused of aiding the duke's critics at Oxford, and perhaps Charles also remembered his refusal to infringe constitutional precedent by re-summoning the 1624 Parliament. Williams had the seals of office taken from him at Salisbury, where the court was in the autumn. Charles would also display his vindictiveness by forbidding him to officiate as dean of Westminster at his coronation the following February (he would be

50   Patriot king (1625–29)

replaced by Laud as sub-dean) and denying him his writ of summons to the subsequent parliamentary session.[26]

Coronation and Parliament of 1626

Charles's coronation had been delayed by the plague. When it finally did take place, on 2 February 1626, the feast of Candlemas (a perhaps not accidental choice of the church's festival of light) it was a slightly less grand affair than usual. The king travelled to Westminster from Whitehall by barge rather than in procession, partly because of the plague and an aversion to riding through the filthy streets amidst crowds of onlookers, partly due to economy when funds were so desperately short for the ongoing military preparations. Though it has been suggested that this was an early indication of the more distant and inaccessible form of kingship which Charles practised compared with many of his recent predecessors.[27] A further departure was that the queen was not crowned, apparently due to the influence of her priests against her participating in a Protestant ceremony. One contemporary, Joseph Mead, who referred to her standing 'at a window in the mean time, looking on, and her ladies frisking and dancing in the room', was clearly not impressed.[28] Charles was crowned by Archbishop George Abbot and Laud presided in place of Williams as dean, another sign of the former's growing favour. After the ceremony, the new king received, as was customary by way of emphasising the continuing feudal relationship between the Crown and his leading subjects, the homage of the nobility. The favour in which Charles held Buckingham was demonstrated by his being appointed Lord High Constable for the day of the coronation, effectively giving him primacy among the nobility with the temporary revival of this quasi-medieval office.[29] In addition, when, during the ceremony Buckingham offered his arm to help Charles ascend the specially erected stage, Charles instead offered his arm to Buckingham, reportedly saying 'I have more need to help you, than you have to help me'.[30] One interesting source of later controversy was the coronation oath. Devised by a committee in which Laud was the leading participant, it differed from those of Charles's predecessors in some ways, notably when promising to uphold the laws of the kingdom 'agreeable to

Patriot king (1625–29) 51

the prerogatives of the kings thereof', which was raised at Laud's trial as evidence of an attempt to enhance the royal prerogative, while the omission of the phrase *quae populus elegerit*, 'which the people have chosen, or shall choose', albeit following the precedent of James I's coronation, was seen in a similar light.[31] Even while making allowance for the much altered political climate in which the oath came to be raked over, there is much in Charles's subsequent conduct as king to suggest that the reference to the prerogative was by no means insignificant.

The coronation was followed only four days later by the opening of Parliament. The Parliament of 1626 was, in many ways, the most formative experience of Charles's early years as king, colouring as it did his view of the institution and entrenching him in his association of opposition with disloyalty and affronts to his honour and dignity as king. Indeed Mark Kishlansky goes as far as to say that: 'In 1626, Charles lost whatever innocence he may once have had regarding assemblies of his subjects'.[32] He tried to head off possible opposition by having some of the Crown's leading critics from 1625 'pricked' as sheriffs prior to the session, rendering them ineligible to sit. He then had William Laud, Bishop of St David's, preach the sermon at the opening of Parliament on 6 February, in which he delivered a scarcely veiled admonition to the 'disjointed factions' that had ruptured the previous assembly and made a plea for 'unity' as 'the strongest wall of a State'.[33] Charles's own appearance at the opening was noteworthy for the queen's absence. In a further sign of uneasy marital relations, she was reported to have quarrelled with the king over her refusal to watch the ceremonial opening from the countess of Buckingham's rooms, ostensibly because it would involve walking across a muddy courtyard, and she only consented to go eventually at the prompting of the French ambassador, infuriating Charles 'at not being obeyed at first'.[34] Charles's own address made his most explicit admission of his lack of confidence in his public-speaking. In marked contrast to his famously verbose predecessor, he said that 'Of my own nature I do not love long speeches and I know I am not very good to speak much', declaring himself to be 'a an rather of action than words' and announcing that henceforth he would revive the old custom of having his Lord Keeper (now Sir Thomas Coventry) speak for him at the opening of Parliament. The longer speech that

52 Patriot king (1625–29)

followed, which can be taken to reflect the king's own intentions, was calculated to reassure MPs uneasily anticipating a demand for hefty subsidies. Referring to his recent coronation as having 'lately solemnised the scared rites of that blessed marriage between him and his people', it gave the king's undertaking to use Parliament 'to consult and advise of provident and good laws'. Beyond a reference to 'his Majesty's pressing occasions and urgent affairs of state, both at home and abroad' the speech 'touched not upon any matters of money'.[35]

If, however, Charles hoped that this more subtle approach would yield financial fruit, he was to be sadly mistaken. In a bold move, the House of Commons requested redress of their grievances before they would vote supply. While the king complained of this delay, anxious as he was to press on with the war, it quickly became clear that their grievances could all be traced to the duke of Buckingham, the '*causa causarum* of all the mischief'.[36] The House of Lords, which had its own axe to grind regarding the perceived infringement of its privileges (through the denial of writs of summons to Bishop Williams and the earl of Bristol), also contained vocal opponents of the duke, and the king was faced with a parliament-wide assault upon his favourite. Buckingham was accused of, among other things, mismanaging the war, corrupting the administration and even of poisoning the late king, an accusation which Charles interpreted as particularly offensive given the implication of his own complicity. The key to Charles's attitude to the parliamentary attack upon his favourite is that he perceived it to equate to an attack upon himself. In a speech that 'was considered threatening', Charles told MPs on 29 March that 'this was not a parliamentary way or the way to deal with a king', and warned them that 'Parliaments are altogether in my power for the calling, sitting and continuance of them, therefore as I find the fruits of them either good or evil, they are to continue or not to be'.[37] He insisted that 'they should not meddle any more with the duke's person, which he defended' and made quite clear that 'their supply was far too mean and insufficient for the king's necessities'.[38]

This is further indicated by the tone of his address to the Lords on 11 May, which reinforced the sense of his sensitivity to perceived slights upon his honour:

Patriot king (1625–29)   53

My Lords, The Cause and only cause of my coming unto you this day is to express the sense I have of all your honours, for he that touches any of you touches me in a very great measure. . .I have been too remiss heretofore in punishing those insolent speeches that concerned myself. . .For, as touching the occasions against him [Buckingham], I myself can be a witness to clear him in every one of them. . .and now I hope you will be as tender of my honour when time shall serve as I have been sensible of yours.[39]

In a conversation overheard between the king and Buckingham at around this time, Charles was supposed to have said: 'What can I do more? I have engaged mine honour to mine uncle of Denmark, and other princes. I have, in a manner, lost the love of my subjects. What wouldst thou have me do?'[40] This sense of obligation to family honour, not only his sister, Elizabeth of Bohemia, for whom the whole war against Spain was ostensibly being fought, but also to his uncle, Christian IV of Denmark, who had entered the war the year previously against the Habsburg emperor in Germany, was one that Charles seems to have felt acutely and genuinely. As will be seen, it continued to be a key part of his psychological and political make-up throughout his reign.

By investing so much of himself, and his own sense of slighted honour, in his defence of Buckingham, he was unable to take advantage of impeachment as a safety valve for parliamentary grievances in the way that his father had done in the cases of the monopolists or of Francis Bacon in 1621. That said, though he excoriated them for doing so, Charles did in fact allow the attack against Buckingham to proceed. The only way to squash the impeachment proceedings entirely was to dissolve the Parliament, and though Charles had considered this at the end of March, Buckingham himself had persuaded him to keep it in being rather than suffer the ignominy of being unable to fight the war. As the clearly intrigued Venetian ambassador reported, 'The king on one hand allows the torrent to run against the duke, on the other he seems to do everything that can satisfy him', while telling the Commons 'to hasten supplies and to rest satisfied with the proceedings against the duke without looking for fresh grievances'.[41] It would be a mistake, therefore, to think that Charles was entirely

54 *Patriot king (1625–29)*

devoid of political pragmatism. As Kishlansky has pointed out, it is an error to suggest Charles dissolved the Parliament to prevent Buckingham's impeachment. Rather, when the Commons, unable to convict Buckingham of the various crimes of which he had been accused (perhaps unsurprisingly given the rather peculiar mixture of paranoia and bile they reflected), tried to have him removed from the king's counsels regardless of guilt or innocence, as well as denying the king the collection of tonnage and poundage, Charles decided enough was enough.[42] He would just have to fight his war using alternative means.

The effect of this bitter ending to the Parliament upon Charles's political world-view was, however, considerable. When Charles dissolved the Parliament, he was at pains to lay the blame upon the House of Commons and to absolve the Lords. Lord Keeper Coventry delivered to them a message of the king's 'resolution to dissolve the parliament not for anything he found fault with us, but some of the Lower House were carried with such malice as they all neglected him and counted him for nobody'.[43] It is striking that Charles interpreted their attack on Buckingham and criticism of the conduct of the war as 'malice'. His tendency to personalise the politics of parliament was exacerbated by the tone of some of the criticism in the Commons, notably, for example, the likening by Sir John Eliot of Buckingham to Sejanus. This led Charles to conclude that 'implicitly he must intend himself Tiberius' and then to send both Eliot and another MP, Sir Dudley Digges, to the Tower.[44] Charles's subsequent treatment of others who had spoken against Buckingham (Bristol was also imprisoned in the Tower), and his increasingly Manichean view of the political universe, bred a sense of the adversarial and would colour his view of parliaments in the future.

Arminianism and religious controversy

A few days into the Parliament of 1626, a significant religious conference had taken place at Buckingham's London residence, York House. A grand mansion on the Strand close to Whitehall and backing on to the river, the water-gate, added by Buckingham, is the only part of the house that survives (albeit set some way back from the river since the embankment of the Thames in the

Patriot king (1625–29) 55

nineteenth century). The conference was held to examine the ideas of Richard Montagu, who, it will be recalled, had been the subject of complaint in the previous Parliament for writing works appearing to downplay the theological differences between the Churches of England and Rome. While the outcome of the conference was in many ways indecisive, it being said by the earl of Pembroke that 'none returned Arminians thence, save such who repaired thither with the same opinions', its timing, against the backdrop of a highly charged parliamentary session, was significant for the way in which it helped to infuse the political climate with the fear of religious innovation.[45] Those who instigated the conference, namely the earl of Warwick and viscount Saye and Sele, by asking the king and Buckingham to help to settle the burgeoning religious controversy, aimed to prove that Montagu's works, *A New Gagg for an Old Goose* (1624) and *Appello Caesarem* (1625), were heretical in their content, chiefly by denying core tenets of Calvinist theology surrounding predestination. In this they failed.

Buckingham chaired the conference, and with some skill, in such a way as to demonstrate his (and by extension, his royal master's) support for Montagu against these charges. The clerical participants, including John Preston, a former protégé of Buckingham's, were made to prove their case meticulously with reference to the text of Montagu's works and to scripture, the sort of approach one could imagine Charles commending. Meanwhile the linkage between innovations in religion and government, which was to re-appear in the parliamentary sessions of 1628–29 and prompt Charles to a robust defence, and which would lead to challenges to the royal supremacy over the Church of England in the way that Charles exercised it, arguably had an origin in the agreement at York House as to the orthodoxy of Montagu's beliefs. Charles himself was not present, but by having Buckingham, previously a patron to Puritan preachers such as Preston but increasingly associated with the Arminian clergy such as Laud (his chaplain since 1622), oversee the conference as he did, the king was signalling the trajectory of his own religious policy quite clearly, and with significant consequences for the rest of the reign.[46] Meanwhile the Arminian clergy repaid Buckingham's support of them handsomely, notably by helping to get him elected as chancellor of the University of Cambridge in June 1626.

56 *Patriot king (1625–29)*

New counsels

One of Charles's privy councillors, Sir Dudley Carleton, had threatened that the king might have no alternative but to resort to 'new counsels' if Parliament proved unwilling to provide him with what he needed. He was as good as his word. Peace with Spain was not an option in Charles's mind. It was reported that he would not consider negotiating for peace until he had 'first performed some feat'. Clearly, he still conceived of himself as a patriot king who needed and desired a military success in order to bolster his image and add lustre to the opening years of his reign. In addition, however, he still felt deeply his familial obligation to aid his sister, and that withdrawing from the conflict now would amount to a 'desertion' of her.[47] Anxious also to assist his embattled uncle, Christian IV (this was a family affair), and having forfeited the three subsidies offered by the Commons after his dissolution of Parliament, Charles resorted to non-parliamentary methods of raising revenue. In many ways, as Richard Cust has argued, he behaved as if he would not have to face a Parliament again in the near future: for instance, he issued orders through the Privy Council authorising the collection of tonnage and poundage by letters patent under the Great Seal, and the imprisonment of anyone refusing to pay. He also attempted to raise a voluntary 'benevolence' (or 'free gift') from his wealthier subjects under the privy seal, a loan that he assured them 'in the word of a King, shall be wholly employed in the common defence of the kingdom, and not to any other use whatsoever. We doubt not but you will be tender of the safety of your Prince and Country'.[48] When this failed he changed the name of what they were requesting to a 'Loan', a policy supported by Buckingham (who dreaded the prospect of another parliament) and his partisans.[49] This would require (rather than request) subsidy-payers to assist the Crown with funds comparable to those raised by parliamentary taxes.

Privy Seal loans were by no means unheard of. Indeed, Charles's father had levied more than one when short of cash and anxious to avoid summoning a Parliament. A royal proclamation of 7 October 1626 strongly implied that any future meeting of Parliament was contingent upon compliance, 'by our people's

Patriot king (1625–29)   57

affection nowe shewed unto us in this waie of necessitie'.[50] The Loan was justified by 'the accidents in Germany', and a particularly aggressive propaganda campaign in its favour was launched by some of the clergy, led by Bishop Laud, who issued a set of 'Instructions' to preachers to deliver sermons in support of the loan, emphasising the subject's duty of obedience.[51]

It is worth considering from whom, at this point, Charles was receiving advice: Laud and Neile were appointed to the Privy Council in April 1627 and it is no accident that the Loan came to be presented and defended as a device not merely politically expedient but also theologically justified.[52] The backing given to Montagu against charges of heresy at the York House conference was being repaid by some trenchant support for the Loan. Some seem to have accepted the royal justification, as Lord Montagu of Boughton: 'What cause can be greater than the defence of the realm. . .I stand with my duty and religion cheerfully to yield in this to the king's desire'.[53] The loan was successful in purely financial terms, raising £243,000 of the hoped-for £300,000, but it was politically hugely controversial.[54]

While some areas of the country appear to have complied with payment of the Loan without complaint, elsewhere there was resistance, including in Montagu's own county of Northamptonshire, where '22 principal gentlemen, who drew after them more than half the shire', had to be disciplined at the behest of the Privy Council.[55] At a national level, several prominent figures opposed it, notably the Archbishop of Canterbury, George Abbot, who considered that 'there is neither Law nor Custom for it in the Kingdom of England', and was suspended from his archiepiscopal functions for refusing to licence a sermon that defended the loan.[56] Meanwhile the Lord Chief Justice was 'downgraded' and replaced by a client of Buckingham, and others of the judges were reported to 'go softly, adapting themselves'.[57] Over one hundred of the gentry were imprisoned for their refusal to pay. This was not itself unusual – indeed James I had imprisoned viscount Saye and Sele for refusing (and outspokenly criticising) the benevolence of 1622. In this case, however, five refusers decided to sue for a writ of habeas corpus in order to force the king to state his reasons for imprisoning them, and thereby, they hoped, challenge the legality of the loan itself in the courts. In the event the judges upheld the king's right to

58 Patriot king (1625–29)

imprison subjects without showing cause in an emergency.[58] The manner in which they did so, however, was ambiguous, and led to later charges that the Attorney-General had turned what was merely an interim judgement, remanding the prisoners in custody, into an official judgement against them in the King's Bench records which could serve as a precedent in future. While the legal argument became a political one later when the issue was raised by John Selden, one of the counsel for the five knights, in the parliamentary session of 1629, for now it is sufficient to note that, as Mark Kishlansky has shown, the imprisonment of the loan-refusers was intended to be temporary, for the duration of the collection of the loan, rather than an extended attempt to have the Crown's power to imprison by special command tested by the courts.[59]

A British 'Union of Arms'?

Amidst this domestic political and legal drama, it is sometimes easy to overlook the purpose for which the king was prepared to suffer it, namely the continuation of the war, and the level of political capital he had invested in it. By now, England was at war with France, a rupture arising from a combination of Charles's treatment of his wife's French entourage (which the French took as an infringement of the marriage treaty) and especially Buckingham's clumsy diplomacy. A tit-for-tat seizure of ships signalled a drift toward war.[60] This widening conflict prompted radical suggestions at the centre of government regarding the British military and naval forces. In a royal proclamation issued within six weeks of his accession, Charles had announced his intention to achieve 'one uniforme course of Government, in, and through Our whole Monarchie'. Now, in 'A Proposition for the Setling His Majesties Affairs', Secretary Coke outlined how foreign powers such as the Catholic League, France and Spain had sought to integrate and co-ordinate their respective military machines. He noted that the Catholic League, by uniting its forces, 'hath apparently subdued & ranged al Germanie to an absolute obedience to the house of Austria', while the French 'by uniting their land and sea forces into a new corporation', had defeated 'the discontented Princes' and were in a strong position to enlarge their trade. The most significant example, however, was Spain, which, 'by a late Union or Association haue ioyned al their

Patriot king (1625–29) 59

remote Prouinces for mutual defence', which, crucially, allowed to 'raise thereby great forces for the enlarging of their Monarchie both by Land and Sea'. He was referencing here the count-duke of Olivares's scheme for a 'Union of Arms' which required all of the Spanish Crown's provinces and territories to contribute meaningfully to funding and fighting in the king's armies. Coke went on to conclude that 'My proposition therefore is to learn Wisdom of our Enemies, and by uniting all our partie abroad & at home', to achieve 'more prosperous success to our affaires'. In the short-term, this meant a more meaningful co-ordination of Protestant war effort with England's allies on the continent, chiefly Denmark, Sweden and the Dutch, but also, in order to assist at La Rochelle, closer co-operation with the French Huguenot forces, the Swiss Cantons, and well-disposed Catholic states such as Savoy, Lorraine and the Republic of Venice.[61] This is a further indication of Charles's willingness to emulate continental European models such that it was clearly informing the deliberations of his councillors. Its implications would also be evident in the king's policy towards Scotland and in Strafford's government of Ireland in the 1630s.

La Rochelle

The expedition that ensued was intended to give relief to the besieged Huguenot city of La Rochelle and in order to do so it was necessary to take possession of the island of Ile de Rhé which guarded it. Charles personally superintended preparations for the fleet at Portsmouth in June, reviewing the troops and reportedly finding them 'well disciplined and in good condition'.[62] He also examined fortifications at Southampton and the Isle of Wight, while Buckingham, as Lord Admiral, commanded the ensuing naval expedition.[63] Unfortunately for him and for Charles, it was a complete disaster. An ill-prepared expedition with ladders that were too short to scale the walls was badly beaten by the French, 'with no little dishonour to our nation, excessive charge to our treasury, and great slaughter of our men'.[64] After a three-month long attempt to relieve the Huguenots, the expedition returned ignominiously to England, Buckingham having lost over half of the force of around 7,000 with which he had started (the official figures suggest just under

60 *Patriot king (1625–29)*

3,000 returned alive), and prompting much recrimination and soul-searching at home and highlighting the dissonance between the aggressive blaming of Buckingham in popular print and the steadfast support for him shown by the king.[65] While acknowledging Charles's genuine desire to assist the Huguenots, Simonds D'Ewes recorded a scathing verdict on Buckingham's role:

> So as the King of Great Britain, contrary to his own sincere and real intention to have succoured the French Protestants and the town of Rochelle, was the main cause, through the Duke of Buckingham's miscarriage (if not through his treachery) of ruining them.[66]

Coupled with this, the king's situation seemed worrying for another reason: he had a large body of troops under arms in the southern counties of England in preparation for further military action, troops who were billeted on civilians and frequently guilty of significant disorder, causing widespread discontent. The opportunity to air such grievances would be provided by the summoning of another Parliament, though as the expedients resorted to in the previous two years would suggest, this was by no means an easy decision. Indeed the Privy Council was divided between 'moderates' (such as the Lord President of the Council, the earl of Manchester, Lord Keeper Sir Thomas Coventry and the earl of Pembroke) who favoured a Parliament as the proper method of raising taxation and 'hardliners' (such as Bishop Laud, the earl of Dorset and the duke of Buckingham) who feared the likely backlash against recent royal policies in church and state and preferred to stick with financing the Crown by prerogative revenues.[67] In the end the moderates prevailed: Charles was persuaded that not only would a Parliament, if properly managed, be the only enterprise capable of yielding the necessary funds, but also that it would help to heal the political wounds caused by the Forced Loan. On 20 February 1628 the king agreed to issue writs to that effect.

1628 and the Petition of Right

As the Parliament convened, Charles was described as 'in earnest for present supply, in regard of the exceeding great danger the state

Patriot king (1625–29) 61

of Christendom is in': he had clearly not yet shed the mantel of the 'Patriot King'.[68] The Parliament began in an unexpectedly positive fashion, with a grant of five subsidies by the House of Commons, which, when Charles heard about it, he greeted with the warm, almost child-like air of a man who claimed to have always liked parliaments (really): 'At the first I liked parliaments, but since (I know not how) I was grown to distaste of them. But I am now where I was. I love parliaments. I shall rejoice to meet with my people often'.[69] Charles was even reported to have wept for joy when he heard the news that the grant was passed unanimously.[70] Unfortunately, his joy was not to last. When the Commons held back the subsidy until their grievances, which mostly related to the Forced Loan and its consequences, had been redressed, he found himself back to square one. More than this, in the wake of the Five Knights' Case, several members of the Commons had now got their teeth into the issue of the king's treatment of those who had refused to pay the Loan, which had included billeting troops on them, and which Charles promised to address if they would trust to his word as a king.[71] Trust was precisely the issue. Around this time, a letter was written to the House of Commons in the name of Joseph Hall, Bishop of Exeter, urging them to 'fear not to trust a good King, who after the strictest law made must be trusted with the Execution'.[72] They did not appear to agree.

Soon the Commons took up more telling legal question of the king's right under the royal prerogative to imprison his subjects without showing cause and to confiscate their goods without consent, and produced a set of propositions demanding that Charles declare Magna Carta and its six confirmatory medieval statutes still to be in force. Eventually they decided to proceed by means of a Petition of Right, a medieval device by which, rather than legislate on the matter, Parliament could extract an answer from the king to assuage their concerns. While Charles was willing to offer assurances that Magna Carta was still in force, he was horrified by the wider implications of the Petition. The document reflected the sources of discontent produced by the military preparations of the previous year, objecting not only to the Forced Loan and the imprisonment of those who refused to pay but also to the billeting of troops on civilians and the imposition of martial law. Charles declared on 12 May that he would commit himself not to imprison

62   Patriot king (1625–29)

subjects for refusal of loans in future, but he would not give up his power to imprison without showing cause as this would 'soone dissolue the very frame and foundacion of our Monarchie'.[73] This was a prerogative power in which Charles clearly believed passionately. He pointed out that in cases where such powers need to be exercised, 'it often happens that should the cause be shown the service itself would thereby be destroyed and defeated'. The Gunpowder Plot was an example frequently invoked by Charles's defenders, and in the course of his defence of the king at a parliamentary conference of 17 April, the Attorney-General, Robert Heath, had cited Catholic plotters from Elizabeth's reign who were imprisoned without charge while the ringleaders of the plot were searched out. In short, Charles could not concede this power without impairing the 'safety of our peoples' and 'without overthrow of sovereignty'.[74]

Such sentiments were further reflected in a draft declaration of May 1628, authored by Heath, though never published, in which the Commons' willingness or unwillingness to grant supply was presented as a test of loyalty and which alluded to the same ideas of a 'popular' conspiracy which is found in other official pronouncements (such as Laud's sermon at the opening of the 1626 Parliament).[75] Charles was here articulating a coherent, albeit contested, view of the importance of the royal prerogative within the constitution, and of the primacy of public safety over liberty. The post-Enlightenment mind (as reflected in Benjamin Franklin's pithy attack on such sentiments) is not generally well-disposed to these arguments, but it should be remembered that they sat within a venerable tradition of ancient and medieval political thought. Ideas of royal 'absolutism' and ideological conflict more generally are sometimes seen as absent from the parliamentary debates of the period and it has been fashionable of late to suggest that there existed an ideological consensus around the limitation of the royal prerogative, as expressed, for example, by the contemporary lawyer and parliamentarian Sir Edward Coke. Charles's utterances, backed up by Laud's and Heath's advice, would suggest that the picture is a little more complicated.

When, in the end, the king did issue an answer to the Petition, it was deemed unsatisfactory. On 2 June Charles gave a qualified answer:

The King willeth that right be done according to the laws and customs of the realm, and that the statutes be put in due execution, that the subject may have no just cause to complain of any wrong or oppressions contrary to their rights and just liberties, to the preservation whereof he holds himself in conscience as well obliged as of his prerogative.[76]

Failing directly to address any of the substance of the Petition, the qualifications to the usual formula 'let right be done' appeared capable of undermining the whole content of the document. The Commons refused to revive the subsidy bill until he gave a satisfactory answer, which he duly did on 7 June when he used the words employed for the assent to a private bill in parliament: '*soit droit fait comme est désiré*'. Even then, however, Charles managed to stand some of his earlier ground, stressing that this did not in any way imply a change of attitude to that embodied in his first answer, and stating that 'you neither mean nor can hurt my prerogative'.[77] He could also not resist delivering a warning, that 'I have done my part, wherefore if this Parliament have not a happy conclusion the sin if yours: I am free of it'.[78] Just as over the conduct of the war, Charles was here pinning all of the blame on his parliamentary critics for the recent divisions and the sense that he was preparing to wash his hands of parliamentary proceedings entirely is unmistakeable.

The king's second answer to the Petition of Right did not assuage the Commons' anger entirely, however. Having failed to impeach Buckingham in 1626, and having seen him conduct another failed military expedition the following year, they were determined once again to demand his removal from the royal counsels. Having composed a Remonstrance on the ill-government of the kingdom, they attributed all to the continued place of Buckingham in the royal counsels. In attack on 'the growth of the Arminian faction – Protestants in show, Jesuits in practice. . .[who were] not wanting friends near your Majesty', the Commons made clear their elision of their political and religious grievances.[79] Charles's initial response when it was presented to him was to upbraid the Commons for having 'fallen upon points of state which belongs to me to understand better than you, and I must tell you that you do not understand so much as I thought you had done', before ostentatiously giving Buckingham his hand to kiss in front of them.[80]

64   *Patriot king (1625–29)*

It might be thought this, as with the impeachment proceedings of 1626, merely represented an attack upon Charles's cherished royal favourite and presumption in trying to remove one of his councillors. All of this was true but, interestingly, in the more formal, extended reply to the Remonstrance which Charles had Laud draft for him (a process which Charles himself may have overseen directly, but in any case a sign of his increasing dependence on Laud as an adviser in political as well as religious matters), the most telling line is one reflective of wounded honour: 'what doth it make us to all our people while it proclaims that we can be led up and down by Buckingham. . .doth it mean to persuade our people we have lost our judgement, or have none to lose'.[81] Charles clearly saw this as an attack on his competence as well as his dignity as king.

Furthermore, he explicitly blamed Parliament for the failure of his foreign policy through their refusal to grant adequate supply: 'shall a Remonstrance turn that as a fault to us which is their fault that did not supply us?' Defending the Loan, he said that 'we doubt not but out Loving People will understand that Necessity was then our law: That the Course might have been prevented, if in the Parliament before supplies had been given in the ordinary way'.[82] The recent failure of parliaments, complained of in the Remonstrance, is of course blamed on the parliaments themselves as by 'forgetting their ancient, and faire way of Proceeding [they] have swelled, till they break themselves'. He also articulated again the sentiment implied in some of his statements of 1626, namely that parliaments were conditional upon their good behaviour, a claim underpinned by latent threat: 'we would be glad to see such moderate parliaments that we may love them and make them more frequent'. Even now, however, he was prepared to continue to try to work with parliaments. He decided not to publish this fiery response to the Remonstrance (a decision a clearly disappointed Laud attributed to the influence of his rival, Sir Richard Weston) and rather than dissolving Parliament as he had done in 1626 when faced with an attack on Buckingham, he instead prorogued it until 20 October.[83] However, in what might appear to have been a signal of his contempt for his parliamentary critics, he pardoned Richard Montagu and promoted him to a bishopric (of Chichester) over the summer and raised Laud to the bishopric

Patriot king (1625–29)

of London. He also began to backtrack on the Petition of Right, publishing it with his first, unsatisfactory answer, and appearing thereby to undermine the agreements already reached.

The death of Buckingham

While Parliament was in abeyance during the summer, the Lord Admiral prepared to lead another expedition to aid the Huguenots, further testimony, if any were needed, of the depth of his and Charles's commitment to the policy agenda they had first espoused back in 1624, championing embattled foreign Protestants against the might of Catholic Europe. Prior to doing so, he set about wooing some of his former enemies, including the earl of Arundel and Sir Thomas Wentworth.[84] In the event, however, Buckingham, who wished additionally to salvage his own severely tarnished reputation as a naval commander, would never get the chance: he was assassinated by a disgruntled former soldier, John Felton, on 23 August at Portsmouth. The fact that Felton, who despite opportunities to escape allowed himself to be captured, was found in possession of a copy of the Commons Remonstrance against Buckingham of 17 June, ensured that Charles would interpret his parliamentary critics as complicit in this most wounding personal bereavement. Though the king maintained his poise, continuing with his prayers at chapel after the news was delivered to him, according to Sir Francis Nethersole he then retired to his apartments and collapsed in grief, taking news of 'the Duke's death very heavily, keeping his chamber all that day', while 'the base multitude in this town drink healths to Felton'. The rest of the country rejoiced (except for Laud, for whom it was 'the saddest accident that ever befell him', and who was the only person to come close to the level of the king's distress).[85] Buckingham's body was not only buried in Westminster Abbey, but in Henry VII's chapel, where traditionally only kings could be interred, a further sign of the depth of Charles's grief.

It would be a mistake to see the death of Buckingham as marking some sort of transition for Charles from puppet to ruler. In fact, as Cust has pointed out, there had been plenty of instances in which Charles had asserted his own wishes above those of Buckingham, notably in pardoning Cranfield, appointing Pembroke to his inner

66 *Patriot king (1625–29)*

council for foreign affairs, and denying Buckingham the level of control over the bedchamber that he had enjoyed under James.[86] Nevertheless, it did open the way for some significant changes. First, on a personal level, it brought a dramatic improvement in Charles's relationship with his wife, with whom he was reported to be spending far more time. Second, in political terms, it led Charles to abandon the model of governing through a personal favourite, and, as Secretary of State Dorchester commented, Charles resolved 'not to discharge himself so much of affairs upon any one: but to take the main direction to himself, and leave others, every man to the duty of his charge'.[87] In addition, it opened the way for political reconciliation with former opponents of Buckingham as well as an attempted pacification of the religious climate.

To assuage the fears of the anti-Arminian MPs in the Commons, Charles issued a warning to Montagu, through Attorney-General Heath, 'that the Court of parliament may peradventure call things past into question notwithstanding your pardon' and that now, as a bishop, it was incumbent upon him to 'review' his book and to promote the peace and quiet of the church' by avoiding 'occasions of strife and contention', since in relation to 'controverted questions [issues surrounding predestination]. . .a sober ignorance may be safer & more seasonable than an over ruinous knowledge'.[88] Admittedly Heath was less sympathetic to Arminian doctrines than either Laud or Charles I but he shared their fear of 'popularity' and their determination to uphold royal authority, and was frequently used by the king as a draftsman of important documents in which he faithfully articulated his royal master's views.[89] By December 1628 Abbot was received back into favour at Court, kissing the king's hand and being invited back to the Council table, and a resolution made to have both parties 'restrained from preaching', while Montagu issued a recantation of his Arminianism. Reconciliation with the earl of Arundel, a leading opponent of Buckingham's among the nobility, was demonstrated by a royal visit to Arundel House on the Strand.[90]

1629 and dissolution of Parliament

The parliamentary session of 1629 was in many ways a great missed opportunity. With Buckingham dead, the source of so

Patriot king (1625–29)   67

many of the grievances and discontents of the previous years was removed. Former opponents of reconvening parliament, such as the earl of Dorset, were now brought round to it. Having quietened the religious controversy, Charles might also have good reason to hope for a less highly charged atmosphere in the Commons. The international climate was also more favourable to peace initiatives after the surrender of the Huguenots at La Rochelle the previous autumn, while both the French and the Spanish were now distracted by the war of the Mantuan succession in northern Italy. Peace negotiations would result in a treaty with France in April 1629 (an agreement with Spain following the year after). Charles's willingness to meet Parliament again might therefore be seen as evidence of his determination to try to work with the institution despite the earlier tensions, while practical necessity demanded that he seek a legal grant of tonnage and poundage, denied him at his accession (having been given it for only one year) and attempt to address the wider financial problems of the Crown.[91] Indeed the latter clearly rankled with Charles, who had noted in the draft response to the Commons Remonstrance that its collection 'without an Act of Parliament it can be no fault in us, but must lie upon them, who should have granted it to us, as it hath been usually granted to all our Royal Progenitors'.[92] Nevertheless he sought to placate his opponents by seeking parliamentary sanction for his continued collection of the duties:

> . . .supposing the agitation thereof would in time breed much distaste, and hinder the most important affairs, most graciously to prevent all further question, made a declaration to the same House, that he did not claim the said tonnage and poundage in any right of his own; but did desire that the Act of Parliament which was to be passed for it, might be confirmed unto him, as well what he had already received, as that which he should hereafter take.[93]

Why then did the session fail so drastically? To begin with, having witnessed the promotion of Neile (to Winchester), Laud (to London), and Montagu (to Chichester) and the pardoning of Montagu and Mainwaring (who had preached aggressively in support of the Forced Loan) since the end of the preceding

68 *Patriot king (1625–29)*

session, the Commons could not resist continuing with their attack on Arminianism, which, despite Charles's efforts, several MPs clearly saw as an existential threat to the doctrinal integrity of the Church of England. They proposed statutory confirmation of Calvinist statements of religious doctrine (including the Thirty-Nine Articles, which had recently been reissued with an ambiguous preface susceptible of a pro-Arminian reading) and attacked alleged Arminian evil counsellors such as Laud and Neile. This in itself might not have been terminal, but Charles responded to these attacks by declaring, on 23 February, that any actions by Crown officials should be assumed to have been carried out on his express orders, thereby removing the possibility of defusing tensions by sacrificing his advisers.[94] Though arguably an admirable display of personal loyalty, this was fatal in the context of parliamentary politics, and stunned the Commons, while the king adjourned Parliament until 2 March. As the Commons continued to attack Arminianism, which they now linked explicitly to perceived arbitrary policies within the state, such as the collection of tonnage and poundage without parliamentary sanction, a dramatic sitting saw the speaker held down in his chair while three resolutions were passed against these perceived abuses.[95] In anger and frustration, Charles dissolved the Parliament.

After the dissolution, Charles issued two royal proclamations justifying his actions. That he felt the need to do so suggests that he recognised the enormous implications of the failure of the session. The first proclamation emphasised Charles's increasingly adversarial view of the political universe, distinguishing between those 'who have shewed good affection to Religion and Government, and those that have given themselves over to Faction'. The second echoed the conditionality Charles had expressed in previous public utterances, notably his speech of 29 March 1626 making the continuance of parliaments conditional upon whether their 'fruits' were 'good or ill' and his more optimistic declaration in March 1628 that he had recovered his love of parliaments now that they were appearing to offer supply before redress of grievances (how wrong this assessment proved to be). Of course a year later the message was negative, admonishing members of Parliament to amend their behaviour: 'Wee shall bee more inclinable to meete in Parliament againe, when Our People shall see more cleerely into Our Intents and Actions'.[96]

Patriot king (1625–29)   69

Once again there was a vituperative, scolding tone and the sense that his people just did not 'get it': they had failed to understand that he was acting in their best interests in prosecuting the war with such vigour, and they had refused to play the parliamentary game by his rules by presuming to demand redress of grievances before voting supply. Having gone to such lengths to quieten controversy in the autumn and winter of 1628, this rancorous ending to the session was not inevitable, but the failure of the Commons, in Charles's mind, to respond favourably to his efforts at conciliation, and his own insistence on hitching his own honour and reputation to the actions of his servants, ensured a rupture and one that was arguably the turning point of the reign.[97] Another Parliament would not be summoned for eleven years.

While it has been fashionable of late to remove ideological conflict from the politics of the 1620s and instead suggest that the failure of the parliaments of the later 1620s was due to long-term structural weaknesses in the royal finances, exacerbated by Charles's personality traits and misguided policies, it is arguable that in fact the sources of conflict were more deep-rooted. Charles clearly conceived of Parliament as an institution which existed to serve the needs of the Crown, and its meetings were entirely conditional on its fulfilling these needs. Piqued at the Commons' refusal, in his mind, to honour the commitments it had made in 1624 to finance military intervention on the continent, and determined to uphold his own sense of honour in assisting his sister and later his uncle in their hour of need, he came to view it as an obstacle rather than as a help. When they added insult to injury by exploiting the Crown's need of them in order to seek the destruction of the royal favourite, Charles's view hardened, as demonstrated by the strident nature of his utterances to Parliament in 1626, in many ways the key Parliament of the decade. Its failure led Charles to seek to try alternative means of financing his wars in the shape of the Loan of 1627. This in turn produced another confrontation, one in which the power of the Crown, under its prerogative, to levy such loans and to imprison those who refused without showing cause, became the totemic legal and constitutional issue of the day and which produced the Petition of Right and Charles's attempts to frustrate it. When religious grievances also came to the fore, in the wake of the Montagu controversy and

70 Patriot king (1625–29)

the king's show of support for him through Buckingham at the York House conference, the parliamentary atmosphere became the more rancorous, as shown in the bitter sessions of 1628–29. In many ways the failure of the parliaments of 1625–29 can be reduced to two related issues: honour and trust. Honour, in the dynastic sense that impelled Charles to pursue his interventionist foreign policy so vigorously despite the financial and political obstacles, and in the personal sense that he came to feel his regal dignity threatened and traduced by the parliamentary attacks on his favourite and on his prerogative; trust, in the increasing lack of good faith evident in the Commons' dealings with the king, as shown by their persistent refusal to take Charles's promises of amendment of government seriously and insistence on framing their grievances in a Petition of Right and securing an answer sufficient to make it legally enforceable. The combination of Charles's sense of wounded honour and the Commons' unwillingness to trust their king proved fatal to the conduct of an effective relationship between Crown and Parliament by the end of the decade.

Notes

1 *CSPV, 1625–1626*, pp. 2–3.
2 Thomas Birch, *Court and Times of Charles I* (2 vols, London, 1848), I, p. 8; *CSPV, 1625–1626*, pp. 10–1.
3 *CSPV, 1625–1626*, pp. 2–3.
4 Birch, *Court and Times of Charles I*, I, p. 22.
5 Conrad Russell, *Parliaments and English Politics, 1621–1629* (Oxford, 1979), p. 204.
6 Samuel R. Gardiner, *History of England from the Accession of James I to the Outbreak of the Civil War, 1603–1642* (10 vols, 1883–4), V, pp. 325–6, 330–3.
7 Birch, *Court and Times*, I, pp. 29, 31.
8 Simonds D'Ewes, *Autobiography*, I, pp. 272–3.
9 John Hacket, *Scrinia Reserata: a Memorial Offer'd to the Great Deservings of John Williams* (1693), II, p. 4.
10 *HMC Report on the MSS of the Duke of Buccleuch and Queensberry* (1899), I, p. 260.
11 Birch, *Court and Times of Charles I*, I, pp. 35–6.
12 Maija Jansson and William B. Bidwell (eds.), *Proceedings in Parliament 1625* (New Haven and London, 1987), pp. 28–30.

Patriot king (1625–29) 71

13 *CSPV, 1625–1626*, p. 97.
14 Russell, *Parliaments and English Politics*, pp. 225–9.
15 Ibid., p. 218; Cogswell, *Blessed Revolution*, pp. 317–8.
16 *CSPV, 1625–1626*, pp. 97–8, 107.
17 Russell, *Parliaments and English Politics*, pp. 229–33.
18 *CSPV, 1625–1626*, pp. 141–3.
19 *Proceedings in Parliament 1625*, pp. 132–3.
20 *CSPV, 1625–1626*, pp. 141–3.
21 Ibid., p. 143.
22 *HMC Kellie and Mar*, p. 232.
23 *CSPV, 1625–1626*, p. 146.
24 Simonds D'Ewes, *Autobiography*, I, p. 279.
25 David L. Smith, *A History of the Modern British Isles, 1603–1707*, p. 69.
26 Hacket, *Scrinia Reserata*, II, pp. 16–18, 22, 67–9.
27 David Cressy, *Charles I and the People of England* (Oxford, 2015), pp. 67–9.
28 Birch, *Court and Times of Charles I*, I, pp. 77–8.
29 *HMC Buccleuch and Queensberry*, III, p. 265.
30 Simonds D'Ewes, *Autobiography*, I, pp. 292–3.
31 Cressy, *Charles I*, pp. 73, 78–9.
32 Mark Kishlansky, *Charles I: An Abbreviated Life* (London, 2014), p. 29.
33 Laud, *Works*, I, pp. 66–7.
34 *CSPV, 1625–1626*, p. 327.
35 *Proceedings in Parliament 1626*, I, pp. 20, 25.
36 *CSPV, 1625–1626*, p. 380.
37 Ibid., p. 385; Russell, *Parliaments and English Politics*, p. 292.
38 Birch, *Court and Times of Charles I*, I, p. 92.
39 William B. Bidwell and Maija Jansson (eds.), *Proceedings in Parliament 1626, Volume I: House of Lords* (New Haven and London, 1991), p. 398.
40 Birch, *Court and Times of Charles I*, I, pp. 103–04.
41 *CSPV, 1625–1626*, pp. 380, 416.
42 Kishlansky, *Charles I*, p. 28.
43 *Proceedings in Parliament 1626*, I, p. 637.
44 Birch, *Court and Tims of Charles I*, I, p. 101.
45 Barbara Donagan, 'The York House Conference Revisited: Laymen, Calvinism and Arminianism', *Historical Research*, 64 (1991), pp. 312–30, at p. 312.
46 Ibid., pp. 312–30.
47 *CSPV, 1626–1628*, p. 41.
48 *HMC Buccleuch and Queensberry*, I, p. 263.

72 Patriot king (1625–29)

49 Richard Cust, *The Forced Loan and English Politics, 1626–1628* (Oxford, 1987), pp. 36, 40–3; Russell, *Parliaments and English Politics*, p. 331.
50 Cust, *Forced Loan*, pp. 48–9.
51 *HMC Buccleuch and Queensberry*, I, p. 264; Cust, *Forced Loan*, pp. 62–3.
52 *CSPD, 1627–1628*, p. 154.
53 *HMC Buccleuch and Queensberry*, I, p. 265.
54 Richard Cust, *Charles I: A Political Life* (2005), pp. 64–5.
55 *CSPD, 1627–1628*, pp. 15–6.
56 John Rushworth, *Historical Collections of Private Passages of State* (8 vols, London, 1721–22), I, p. 437.
57 *CSPV, 1626–1628*, p. 137.
58 Birch, *Court and Times of Charles I*, I, pp. 294–5.
59 Russell, *Parliaments and English Politics*, p. 335; this charge of an intentional perversion of the court record on the king's orders is given its fullest exposition in J.A. Guy, 'The Origin of the Petition of Right Reconsidered', *Historical Journal*, xxv (1982), pp. 289–312, though it has been refuted strongly by Mark A. Kishlansky, 'Tyranny Denied: Charles I, Attorney-General Heath and the Five Knights' Case', *Historical Journal*, xlii (1999), pp. 53–83.
60 Russell, *Parliaments and English Politics*, pp. 328–9.
61 C.S. Bingham, *British Royal Proclamations Relating to North America, 1603–1783* (1911), p. 53 ('A Proclamation For Settling the Plantation of Virginia', 13 May 1625; SP 16/527/104, 'A Proposition for Setling His Majesties Affairs', 1627. I am grateful to Professor Geoffrey Parker for these references prompted by his discussion of this issue in Geoffrey Parker, *Global Crisis: War, Climate Change & Catastrophe in the Seventeenth Century* (New Haven and London, 2014), p. 562.
62 *CSPD, 1627–1628*, p. 222.
63 Birch, *Court and Times of Charles I*, I, pp. 237, 244.
64 Ibid., p. 286.
65 *CSPD 1627–1628*, p. 454; Cressy, *Charles I and the People of England*, pp. 127–8.
66 Simonds D'Ewes, *Autobiography*, I, p. 367.
67 Cust, *Forced Loan*, pp. 69–70.
68 Birch, *Court and Times of Charles I*, p. 334.
69 Cust, *Forced Loan*, p. 72.
70 Birch, *Court and Times of Charles I*, p. 337.
71 Ibid., pp. 345–6.
72 BL Add. 44848, f. 230.
73 TNA, SP 16/103/68.

Patriot king (1625–29) 73

74 Russell, *Parliaments and English Politics*, pp. 362–3, 366.
75 Richard Cust, 'Charles I and a Draft Declaration for the 1628 Parliament', *Historical Research*, 63 (1990), pp. 143–161.
76 Russell, *Parliaments and English Politics*, p. 377.
77 Ibid., p. 383.
78 Birch, *Court and Times of Charles I*, pp. 361–2.
79 *Proceedings in Parliament 1628*, eds. Robert C. Johnson et al. (6 vols, New Haven and London, 1977–83), IV, pp. 340–1.
80 Birch, *Court and Times of Charles I*, p. 366.
81 Laud, *Works*, VII, p. 636; Kevin Sharpe, *The Personal Rule of Charles I* (New Haven, CT, 1992), pp. 42–3, 147–8.
82 TNA, SP 16/108/66-7.
83 For which, see the endorsement of the manuscript, TNA, SP 16/108/66-7.
84 Cust, *Charles I*, p. 75.
85 *CSPD, 1628–1629*, pp. 268–9.
86 Cust, *Forced Loan*, p. 78.
87 *The Correspondence of Elizabeth Stuart, Queen of Bohemia*, ed. Nadine Akkerman (2 vols, Oxford, 2011), I, p. 710.
88 TNA, SP 16/118/33, Attorney-General Heath to Bishop Montagu, 7 October 1628.
89 On Heath's role see Cust, 'Charles I and a Draft Declaration', pp. 145–6.
90 Birch, *Court and Times of Charles I*, p. 451.
91 Russell, *Parliaments and English Politics*, pp. 394–9.
92 TNA, SP 16/108/66-7.
93 Simonds D'Ewes, *Autobiography*, I, p. 402.
94 Ibid., pp. 402–03.
95 Birch, *Court and Times of Charles I*, II, p. 12.
96 *Stuart Royal Proclamations*, ed. James F. Larkin (2 vols, Oxford, 1983), ii, pp. 224, 226–7.
97 Richard Cust, 'Was there an alternative to the Personal Rule? Charles I, the Privy Council, and the Parliament of 1629, *History*, 90 (2005), pp. 330–52.

3   Imperial monarch (1629–40)

Personal rule

Charles did not forgive or forget his experience of 1629: having imprisoned the members he considered to be the ring-leaders of the opposition, he released only those who were willing to acknowledge their fault and seek pardon, leaving the intransigent Sir John Eliot, whom he called 'an outlawed man, desperate in mind and fortune', to die in the Tower in 1632 and denying his relatives their request to transport his body to his native Cornwall to burial.[1] Vindictive? Perhaps, but testimony to his genuine disdain for the man who had once implicitly compared him to the Emperor Tiberius. To others, Charles showed himself conciliatory, and adept at talent-spotting potential servants, as several former opponents of royal policies in the Parliaments of the 1620s were taken into royal service: Thomas Wentworth, one of those MPs excluded in 1626, had become Lord President of the Council of the North at the end of 1628 and would be sent to Ireland as Lord Deputy in 1632, while William Noy, one of the counsel for the defence in the Five Knights' Case and a vocal supporter of the Petition of Right, succeeded Heath as Attorney General in 1631. Charles does not often get enough credit for this, given the provocation he had suffered, being 'remarakably patient, and even principled, in trying to incorporate diverse points of view in his new, post-parliamentary form of government', an approach which, as Michael Questier points out, would have been unthinkable to his Tudor predecessors.[2]

Views of the ensuing period of government without Parliament have been significantly polarised: the old Whig

Imperial monarch (1629–40) 75

narrative used the emotive term 'The Eleven Years Tyranny' to suggest something unnatural about a prolonged absence of parliaments, while revisionists have generally preferred the less loaded term 'The Personal Rule'.[3] By denying the existence of serious ideological conflict in the 1620s, revisionists have tended nevertheless to see the Personal Rule as crucial in explaining the outbreak of the Civil War. Kevin Sharpe has done most to try to revise negative judgements of the 1630s, arguing that it was a time of peace and prosperity and of effective conciliar government and vibrant court culture, only undermined by the impact of foreign affairs and the Scottish crisis after 1637.[4] More recent, interdisciplinary work has highlighted the limitations of the term 'Personal Rule' as excessively privileging the role of the king and the political elite at the centre of power, and preferring instead 'the 1630s' as a more neutral-sounding description of the decade. By implying that the absence of parliaments was the defining feature of the decade, it also overlooks the fact that parliaments were, in Russell's famous phrase, 'an event, not an institution', and, by appearing to ignore the Parliaments which met in Scotland in 1633 and 1639 and in Ireland in 1634, suggests Anglocentrism.[5] These interdisciplinary approaches have taken further the emphasis on the richness of Caroline court culture, focusing on Charles as a patron of the arts and imitator of continental models of kingship, as well as considering what literature and print culture can tell us about the period. This has been very useful in highlighting much about Charles's image-making and self-fashioning that served as a conscious adjunct to his policies and those of his leading councillors (notably Wentworth and Laud) in Church and State. The work of Richard Cust has emphasised Charles's revival of the chivalric ethos and the centrality of his relationship to the aristocracy to understandings of his regime. More negative judgements survive in the work of David Cressy, who, from the perspective of an analysis of popular culture and public opinion argues that this same court-centred cultural efflorescence was both exclusive and reclusive, the Personal Rule representing an out-of-touch and unpopular regime.[6] The recent growth of interest in print and popular politics has undoubtedly

76 Imperial monarch (1629–40)

proved a fruitful source of new insights and perspectives, notably by moving away from a narrow focus upon the politics of the aristocratic and clerical elites represented at court or on the Privy Council. Yet while this widening of our understanding of early Stuart politics has been hugely valuable, it should not be allowed to prevent our seeing the Personal Rule on its own terms and attempting to understand what Charles and the other key figures of his regime were trying to achieve by the structures, images, and policies that they sought to create.

The end of parliaments?

It has been argued, notably by John Reeve, that conciliar debate on the possible resummons of Parliament continued between 1629 and 1632 and that only in 1632 did Charles decide definitively not to intervene to help the increasingly successful Swedish forces in the Thirty Years War.[7] While undoubtedly such debates took place, Charles's actions immediately after the dissolution of Parliament in 1629, including the strong words used in his public justifications of his actions, suggest that he had set himself quite firmly against summoning another Parliament in the near future. There were clearly practical advantages, notably in relation to foreign policy: the end of the Parliament allowed Charles the space in which to conclude peace negotiations with France (the Treaty of Susa) in April and to pursue a similar treaty with Spain (the Treaty of Madrid), finally completed in November of the following year. It is also worth pointing out that periods without the meeting of a Parliament were by no means unique or even unusual: Charles's father's reign had seen a seven-year period of 'personal rule' (between 1614 and 1621) without the summoning of a parliament, and given that the Parliament of 1614 (the so-called 'Addled Parliament') met for only a few weeks and passed no legislation, it was arguably an even longer period without a meaningful parliamentary session. Charles, though, was adamant that if and when another Parliament did meet, it would do so upon his terms. His proclamation of 27 March, echoing his words to the Parliament of 1626, reflected his view of the conditional nature of parliaments:

Imperial monarch (1629–40) 77

And whereas for several ill ends the calling again of a Parliament is divulged, however we have shewed by our frequent meeting with our people our love to the use of Parliaments; yet the late abuse having for the present driven us unwillingly out of that course, we shall account it presumption for any to prescribe any time unto us for Parliaments, the calling, continuing, and dissolving of which is always in our own power, and we shall be more inclinable to meet in Parliament again when our people shall see more clearly our intents and actions, when such as have bred this interruption shall have received their condign punishment, and those who are misled by them and by such ill reports as are raised in this occasion, shall come to a better understanding of us and themselves.[8]

In punishing his opponents from the 1629 session, notably Eliot, Valentine and Holles, he clearly felt he had laid down a marker regarding acceptable conduct by MPs. A year later, Charles's new Secretary of State, Viscount Dorchester (formerly Sir Dudley Carleton, who had warned the Parliament of 1626 of the king's likely recourse to 'new counsels'), wrote to England's ambassador in Switzerland as if another Parliament might in future be summoned, providing recalcitrant MPs learned their lesson:

Since his departure time has bred no small alteration, all to the better, in settling the disquiet of men's minds after the heats kindled by the disorders of the last Parliament. Three of the chief authors are fined and imprisoned in the King's Bench for refusing to answer; whereby the world sees that Parliament men must be responsible for their words and actions in other courts, and so they will be more moderate hereafter, and the King may meet his people with assurance that they will never transgress in the point of due respect and obedience.[9]

Interestingly, however, the Crown displayed sensitivity to charges that it was seeking to fundamentally alter the nature of government in England. When in November 1629 a 'certaine discourse or proposicion. . .pretended to be wrytten for his Majesties service' reached the king, consisting of two parts, 'one to secure your estate, and to bridle the impertinencie of Parlamentes; the

78 Imperial monarch (1629–40)

other to increase your Majesties Reuenue much more then it is', Charles had it read out at a meeting of the Privy Council. His anger was at 'the meanes propounded in this discourse', which 'are such as are fitter to be practised in a Turkish State, then amongst Christians, being contrarie to the justice and mildnesse of his Majesties government, and the synceritie of his intentions'. A critic might suggest that the king protested rather too much, but given that 'Turkish' was a byword for despotic tyranny, he was clearly at pains to refute the suggestion that he was bent on the creation of an arbitrary government. The document was condemned as 'a most scandalous invention, proceding from a pernitious desseign both against his Majestie and the State', particularly as those responsible were alleged to have circulated it among their friends. The chief culprit was held to be Sir Robert Cotton, the celebrated antiquary whose house (in which Charles would later be kept during his trial) in Westminster was consequently sealed up, and who, along with and those with whom he was alleged to have co-operated, chiefly the earls of Clare, Somerset and Bedford, was detained pending a summons before the Court of Star Chamber.[10] This episode therefore not only illustrates the Crown's concern to cultivate a public image of adhering to traditional forms of government rather than practising any innovation, but also the way in which Star Chamber, which comprised members of the Privy Council and judges sitting as a prerogative court outside of the common law, and dealt particularly with criminal offences involving breaches of public order, came to be a key instrument for policing the political nation during the period of Personal Rule.

Caroline politics and government

The increased prominence of the Privy Council was nevertheless perhaps the most noticeable immediate consequence of the break with Parliament. Soon after the dissolution, the Venetian ambassador noted that 'The Council sits everyday for three or four hours, the king always being present. Nothing else is thought of, as this matters most of all', while despite calls for a fresh Parliament, the king's councillors would not have it, 'because they will run the risk of ruin'.[11] The greater role played by the

Imperial monarch (1629–40) 79

Council increased the centrality of the king to government and administration. Charles was more assiduous in his attendance at Council meetings than his father had been and as the business of the Council increased during the Personal Rule, and its functions became more specialised through the reliance on a regularised system of committees of the Council, Charles's role in the policy-making process increased accordingly.[12]

As the last chapter showed, the financial weakness of the English Crown had been one of the chief obstacles to effective government in the later 1620s and helped to explain the difficult relations Charles had with his parliaments. Without any parliaments sitting, and with the total royal debt having increased to £2 million due to the burdens of the recent wars, boosting the financial resources of the Crown was a priority. The work of Jonathan Scott has emphasised the extent to which, during the 1630s, Charles I was engaged in a form of 'state-building', overcoming the Crown's financial weakness by strengthening the central state and eliminating dissent by authoritarian methods, an approach that brought confrontation with the revolutionary forces of English Puritanism. Although the suggestion of an attempt to imitate continental models of 'absolutist' rule is not without difficulties given the diversity of structures and experiences across seventeenth century Europe, it is in some ways a useful paradigm through which to view Charles's agenda. Indeed some detected an ambition in the use of prerogative finance to give the Crown an 'advantageous position over his subjects' and 'that independent dominion over affairs, where he has been restrained by the ancient institutions of the realm'.[13] Additionally, as Malcom Smuts has pointed out, the influence of political ideas popular in Europe, notably those of Justus Lipsius focused around the importance of 'Force, love, and authority', help to explain some of the attitudes of Charles's councillors in certain contexts. Charles's own emphasis on family life and wider court culture, the so-called 'image of virtue', reflected the 'affective bonds' he sought to create between himself and his elite subjects, while the importance of the use of force was very clearly illustrated both by the authoritarian nature of Wentworth's government in Ireland and by the regime's response to the perceived threat posed both by the English Puritans and later the Scottish Covenanters.[14]

80 *Imperial monarch (1629–40)*

In many ways the Crown's financial policies during these years, far from being radically new, relied upon medieval precedents and traditions which had long fallen into abeyance. In this he was asserting his 'regalian rights' in a similar way to Philip IV and Olivares in Spain. As a consequence, however, they appeared innovatory and aroused anger and resentment. The chief agent of this 'fiscal feudalism' was the Lord Treasurer, Sir Richard Weston. A former Chancellor of the Exchequer, and a crypto-Catholic, he proved adept at rediscovering ways for the Crown to raise revenue. One such policy was the imposition in January 1630 of fines on those subjects who owned land or rents worth £40 per annum but who had failed to come forward to receive knighthoods at the time of the royal coronation in 1626. Sheriffs were to enforce the policy in the counties.[15] Secretary Dorchester presented this as a successful expedient to fund the Crown in peace-time, but hinted that parliamentary subsidies might be resorted to again in future:

> . . .his Majesty finds some help in the country, for the business of no-Knights goes roundly forward, no man disputing the legality of it in general; so as by this and other lawful but extraordinary ways some good sums are likely to be raised, till his Majesty shall see his own time to help himself again by subsidies.[16]

Hoping to raise up to £100,000, the government saw this as a tax which fell mainly on the wealthy, and might have noted that in earlier times the threshold for payment had been set much lower. There was, however, some resistance to this 'distraint of knighthood'. It was said that 'most men look't upon [it] as illegall, because it seem'd antiquated; not considering that former Parliaments had laid it asleep by the free supplies from time to time towards the Crown's necessities', though with no money forthcoming from Parliament of late Charles was forced 'towards supplies for his own subsistence'.[17] In particular counties resistance was more pronounced: for example in Kent, where some of those fined made excuses such as that they were not worth £40 per annum or that they were exempt as residents of the Cinque Ports. Charles's response to such resistance was to have his right to these fines declared by the Court of Exchequer and to declare that any

Imperial monarch (1629–40) 81

who refused to pay be referred to the Privy Council.[18] The fines were financially successful, bringing in around £170,000 by 1635, the equivalent of nearly three subsidies, and while this could never be a long-term source of revenue, it did help to address the immediate financial crisis in which the Crown found itself.[19]

In the absence of Parliament and with continued financial difficulties, it was said of Charles in June 1632 that 'he taxes his ingenuity for all sorts of inventions, which they call here vexations upon the people'. Several such 'vexations' were devised by the impressive new Attorney General, William Noy, whom Charles had brought into royal service, and who

> invented a way of obtaining a conservable yearly contribution, based on ancient laws, but which have fallen into desuetude and oblivion, whereby those who have houses in the country, even without rent, or on the banks of the Thames, are bound to pay a certain sum yearly, as his Majesty claims that this property has been usurped by those who cannot produce the royal investiture in writing.[20]

From 1634, landowners were also fined for having encroached on the royal forest. What may have begun as a power-play by the earl of Holland against Lord Treasurer Weston, whom he accused of violating royal woodland in the Forest of Dean, or indeed as a worthy attempt to prevent the decay of woodland more generally, became a convenient means of squeezing money out of the gentry and aristocracy. The sums the fines brought in, however, were relatively small (the Exchequer received only £25,000 between 1636 and 1638) given the hostility aroused. In the county of Essex, for example, forest fines were described as being 'a most heavy and fatal blow'.[21] Meanwhile urban areas were also affected by the Crown's search for new revenue streams: in London a commission was established to look into the extent of compliance with a proclamation from early in James's reign regarding the building of new houses in the City of London and to fine those found to have contravened it.[22]

As well as this 'fiscal feudalism', Charles was also presented with more innovative projects for the raising of money, some of which had less basis in law or precedent, and thereby 'crept in divers monopolies and projects probably less warrantable'.[23]

82 *Imperial monarch (1629–40)*

The creation of new, corporate monopolies such as that for the manufacture of soap, brought in additional revenue. Monopolies were unpopular owing to the scandals surrounding them in the Parliament of 1621 and James I had assented to a Monopolies Act in 1624 banning the creation of new monopolies to individuals. A corporate monopoly, however, circumvented the letter, if not the spirit of the Act, and Charles hoped to benefit from the sale of the patent and the £4 payable to the Crown for every ton of the soap sold. Despite arousing the hostility of the traditional soap-makers, particularly as the new company comprised several Catholics, and the resultant rumours that the soap had been adulterated and even blistered the washers' hands, eventually a compromise settlement brought the Crown a tidy sum by the end of the decade.[24] The overall picture was encouraging. By Weston's death in 1635 the financial health of the Crown had been substantially restored, the debt almost halved and the budget balanced.

The king enjoyed perhaps his greatest financial success, but also created the highest level of controversy, with the levying of Ship Money from 1634. Although it had been imposed before within recent memory (by James I in 1619), and Charles himself had attempted to impose it in 1628, the novelty lay in its being levied year after year and being extended to inland counties over and above the usual port towns.[25] Charles's justification for this, and, once again, it is noteworthy that Charles did offer a lengthy defence of the policy, was 'to provide for the defence of the kingdom, safeguard of the sea, security of our subjects, safe conduct of ships and merchandises' against the threat posed by ' thieves, pirates, and robbers of the sea'. Again Charles conceived of this, or at least sought to present it, in terms of his honour and reputation, given that 'we, and our progenitors, kings of England, have been always heretofore masters of the aforesaid sea, and it would be very irksome unto us if that princely honour in our times should be lost or in any thing diminished'.[26] Financially it was a great success: It brought in £200,000 a year, the equivalent of three parliamentary subsidies, and the money was used to improve the navy to good effect. The political fall-out, though, was considerable, notably in John Hampden's celebrated legal challenge. Sir Simonds D'Ewes, admittedly not a favourable witness, referred to the 'great and dreadful wound inflicted by this levy of Ship

Imperial monarch (1629–40) 83

Money upon the subject's liberty', indeed 'the most deadly and fatal blow it had been sensible of in five hundred years' on account of the prospect of its becoming a permanent charge such that 'no man was, in conclusion, worth anything'.[27] The Venetian ambassador, Anzolo Correr, albeit he had only recently arrived in England, observed within a month of the king's proclamation of the levy, in November 1634, that it 'has greatly stirred and exasperated the people here, especially as they see all signs of the speedy convocation of parliament recede into the distance'. The City of London offered opposition: the mayor and aldermen consulted lawyers who advised the levy was illegal unless confirmed by parliament, something to which Charles reacted angrily, summoning the mayor before the Privy Council for a dressing down from Lord Treasurer Weston. Weston pointed to the king's expectation of the 'loyalty and devotion of his subjects in the carrying out of his orders' and warned that they would 'repent of what they had done' if they persisted: eventually the mayor gave way and the City paid up (to the tune of £36,000). In many ways the ambassador hit the nail on the head regarding perceptions of Ship Money among elites, when he suggested that even 'If the result be not contrary to the laws of the realm in every part, as many contend, it is certainly repugnant to the uses and forms observed by the people up to the present time'. Yet while he reported some evasion of the levy among the gentry, within a few months he was saying that the 'extraordinary rigour' shown in collecting it had ensured that the contributions were 'practically all paid', with people increasingly ready to 'consent to it. . .in the hope that this will avail to establish the sovereignty of the sea'. When the levy was made permanent in its extension to inland counties towards the end of 1635, resentment seems to have been lessened by familiarity, bearing it 'more easily than they did last year'.[28] Laud defended the policy in a letter to Wentworth, explaining that the king's rationale in extending the levy to inland areas was to spare the ports the burden, 'so the Navy may be full, and yet the Charge less'.[29] He was dismissive of Hampden as illustrative of 'how unwilling the People are to contribute to any [work], be it never so honourable or necessary for themselves', but this unwillingness seems to have been confined to a relative minority among the king's elite subjects while the 'lesser folk, who have least power agree to pay fairly readily'.[30] Not for

84 *Imperial monarch (1629–40)*

the last time, opposition to one of Charles's policies was largely confined to elites, while the popular reception was at least quiescent, if not enthusiastic.

Reform of local government

England suffered a significant economic downturn in the late 1620s and early 1630s. Due to bad harvests in 1629 and 1630, the price of wheat rose from 38 shillings per quarter to 54 shillings while unemployment rose, especially in the textile industry. Coupled with regular outbreaks of epidemic disease, there was a general feeling of socio-economic hardship which produced a spate of disorder and vagrancy. In response the regime sought to address social problems by the issue of a new Book of Orders to Justices of the Peace (JPs). Issued in January 1631, the new Book of Orders required regular reports from JPs to the Privy Council, and can thus be seen as part of the centralising impulse that characterised Caroline government during the period of the Personal Rule. Charles was particularly concerned for the proper enforcement of laws enacted in previous reigns:

> . . .for the charitable relief of aged and impotent poor people. . .and for the training up of youth in honest and profitable trades. . .as also for the setting to work of idle persons, who [. . .] either wander up and down the city and country begging, or which is worse, maintain themselves by filching and stealing; and for the punishment of sundry rogues and vagabonds, and setting of them to work; and for suppressing of that odious and loathsome sin of drunkenness. . .

Given that the failure to implement such good laws was blamed on 'the neglect of duty in some of our justices of the peace and other officers', the purpose of the Books of Orders was to compel local magistrates into more vigorous enforcement of the statutes, particularly relating to poor relief, the punishment of vagrancy, the regulation of alehouses and combating famine and disease.[31] While a worthy attempt to alleviate the suffering of the population, the Book of Orders was hardly innovatory and instead largely represented a tightening-up of existing practices and directives. Some JPs resented the perceived interference from central government and the enforcement of the policy varied depending on the assiduity of local officials in particular areas. It does, however, suggest that the imagery Charles favoured of a kingdom at peace under a benevolent monarch was reflected in a paternalistic approach to welfare and the relief of poverty.

In addition, efforts were made to improve the quality of the armed forces whose inadequacy had been demonstrated by the campaigns of 1625–30. Through the Privy Council, Charles had ascertained that 'both the Armes are defective and the Trayned Bands not so well exercised in the use of their Armes as were necessary for the defence and securitie of the Realme'.[32] Charles wrote to the earl of Suffolk in September 1629, complaining that previous instructions for the 'reformation' of the trained bands were not being executed, a serious matter since the militia was 'so essential a part of the strength and safety of the kingdom'. In future they were to be 'well chosen, well armed and well disciplined'.[33] Instructions therefore went out in December 1629 to all Lords Lieutenant of the counties for the appointment of muster-masters in each county to be responsible for ordering and training the militia. Each one was not only to have prior experience of training the militia at home but also to have been 'a Practick Souldier and expert in the warres abroad'. They were then to ensure that only fit and able-bodied men were chosen for the trained bands and that their weapons were in good condition and were their own rather than borrowed. The muster-masters were to reside in their respective counties so that they would be ready when called upon.[34] Meanwhile deputy-lieutenants of the counties were instructed to maintain beacons and magazines, both of which were important for resisting invasion. Provision was also made for the regular inspection of armaments and ordnance at the behest of the Privy Council. These reforms appear to have produced some success and the equipment and condition of the militia seems to have improved, though when called upon to fight against the Scots in 1639–40 they did not prove as effective as hoped.

The royal court

One clear consequence of the death of Buckingham had been a growing closeness between the king and his wife. They began to

86 Imperial monarch (1629–40)

sleep together more often and, when she went into premature labour at Greenwich in May 1629 the Venetian ambassador noted that when told that either mother or child could be saved, Charles, still at this stage without an heir, 'said he could have other children, please God, and he would rather save the mould than the cast, showing by this and his constant attendance at the bedside, the great love he bears her'.[35] The ambassador further speculated that the continued importance of dynastic concerns and their international implications, namely Elizabeth of Bohemia and her children, would result in the resummons of a Parliament, but the birth of a healthy son almost exactly a year later, 29 May 1630 at St James's Palace, not only provided for the succession but also began Charles's projection of himself as a family-man.[36] Henrietta Maria's role at court has recently been re-emphasised. While the marriage was 'as politically disastrous as it was personally successful', Henrietta Maria in many ways fulfilled the role of consort impressively, promoting a cosmopolitan court culture, remodelling her palaces at Greenwich and Somerset House and sharing in her husband's encouragement and patronage of artists.[37] Her role in the commissioning and performance of court masques was also considerable: the Venetian ambassador noted in February 1635 that the court had been 'fully occupied' with 'dances, comedies and other pleasant diversions', in particular one masque which 'the queen has repeated three times, set out with the most stately scenery, machines and dresses'.[38] She also played a key role in court appointments and the arrangement of aristocratic marriages.[39] In addition, she performed a more widely recognised role in the politics of court faction, particularly in the promotion of a pro-French foreign policy, which, given France's active support for the Protestant cause in the Thirty Years' War after 1635, attracted many of the Puritan peers at court (such as the earls of Warwick and Holland) who favoured renewed English involvement on the Protestant side.

The structure and organisation of Charles's court also came to be more clearly defined during the Personal Rule. Having exhibited a negative reaction to aspects of his father's court culture, notably the ease of access to the monarch and the atmosphere of moral laxity, and having been impressed by the dignity and ceremony he had witnessed in Spain (whose use as a model was now

Imperial monarch (1629–40)   87

more feasible as hostilities came to an end), Charles was described soon after his accession as presiding over a court that was 'kept more strait and private than in the former time'.[40] One of his earliest measures in this regard was to banish petitioners who used to hang around the precincts of royal palaces in the hope of speaking to the king. The period after 1629 saw him develop this new court culture more fully, restricting access to his person and using this increased control and space to elevate the mystery and dignity of the monarchy.[41] In January 1631 he issued 'Orders. . .for the reformation of certain irregularities in the Court':

> 1.That precedency be duly observed in going to and coming from Chapel; 2. That none wait upon the King to Chapel in boots and spurs, or enter booted into the presence or privy chamber; 3. That no man come into the inner closet under the degree of a baron; 4. That no man come upon the degrees where the chairs of the King and Queen are placed, but such as are licensed to come into the inner closet; 5. The like distance to be observed when either the king or Queen eats in public; 6. Ladies about the Queen to keep their places as orderly as the lords are to do; 7, That both noblemen and their ladies use great distance and respect to the royal persons, as also civility one to another.[42]

Notable is the concern with precedence and hierarchy, a sign of Charles's increased interest in the status of the nobility as well as that of the Crown, and the fact that the queen is mentioned so frequently, a reflection perhaps of the growing regard Charles now felt for his wife as well as to her status.

Charles was very interested in reviving the culture of chivalry surrounding the monarchy, a further example of what is sometimes termed his 'medievalism'. More than that, it can also be seen as part of his 'Elizabethanism', as he sought to revive the partnership between Crown and nobility which had characterised her reign and which, to some extent, had been lost under James. In many ways, James I was seen as having cheapened nobility, sometimes literally by his sale of titles (even inventing the new rank of baronet for the purposes of selling it to raise money for the Crown) but also by his promotion of relatively low-born royal

88   *Imperial monarch (1629–40)*

favourites (such as Somerset and Buckingham) who were regarded as upstarts by many of his leading nobles. One of Charles's first actions (though of course he had maintained Buckingham in his position of eminence), had been to restore the lustre of the ancient nobility by ordering an end to the sale of honours and restoring to Lords Lieutenant their right to appoint their own deputies. The earl of Arundel as Earl Marshal was at the forefront of this campaign, and while his disfavour in the period 1626–28 due to his conflict with Buckingham saw the sale of titles revived at the favourite's behest, his death in 1628 saw Arundel return to favour and the curbing of the practice once again. Between 1631 and 1641 only three baronetcies were sold and the total number of peers actually declined during the Personal Rule.

Charles himself was very much in control of appointments and promotions within the ranks of the nobility, even refusing Wentworth when he requested an earldom in 1634.[43] Arundel himself came to embody the status and dignity of the revived ancient nobility, as reflected in the impressive Rubens portrait painted of him in 1629.[44] Another feature of the resurgence of the nobility was the revival of the Order of the Garter. Charles himself had been elected to the Order when Duke of York in 1611 and he took his role as head of it extremely seriously. Foreign observers noted this as a feature of the Personal Rule, the Venetian ambassador remarking in April 1632 that St George's Day was celebrated at Windsor with particular ceremonial splendour and was preceded by a procession, revived by Charles in 1629, and followed by state banquet. Van Dyck was also commissioned to produce a fresco of Charles and the Garter Knights in procession for the Palace of Whitehall, and the surviving sketch of 1639–40 (when amidst the conflict with the Scots Charles might have wished to stress his martial qualities) emphasises the scale and grandeur of the occasion, one in which Charles features prominently.[45] The Garter also became central to the iconography of the Personal Rule: Arundel, who helped to champion it, had been portrayed wearing, and conspicuously toying with, his St George medal in a portrait by van Dyck (on the artist's visit to London in 1620–21); and Charles himself was meticulous in his wearing of the medal. Not only is it prominently displayed in the famous van Dyck portraits of the 1630s but Charles even had Rubens paint St George strangely

Imperial monarch (1629–40) 89

resembling him in his *St George and the Dragon*, purchased by Charles in 1635. This alludes to the increased religious significance attached to the Order during the Personal Rule, embodying as it did the ideal of Christian knightly service, chivalric and military as well as sacral. The military dimension has frequently been underestimated, but Charles, as has been seen, took military matters extremely seriously, linked as they were to his sense of honour and dignity as king.[46]

Linked to this elevation of noble rank was the restriction of access to the royal person. When Charles went hunting or out on royal progress, these rules continued to apply and those who might wish to see or even approach the king, such as petitioners and other suitors, found themselves turned away. David Cressy has gone so far as to suggest that Charles became an 'inaccessible' monarch, who was effectively invisible to most of his subjects and whose distance and aloofness created widespread discontent and resentment. But in many ways this misses the point: Charles did go on royal progresses, notably to Scotland in 1633 and to Oxford and its environs in 1636, on which he could be seen by at least some of his subjects, and as was seen over the dissolution of parliament in 1629 and again over the imposition of Ship Money in 1634, he frequently issued proclamations and declarations explaining or justifying his policies to the political nation. Royal servants responded to criticism, notably of Caroline religious policies, in print and so the lines of communication between ruler and ruled were far from closed.

Court politics

One other feature of Charles's court was faction: there was no chief minister, though some contemporaries, notably the Venetian ambassador, tended to see Lord Treasurer Weston as being the dominant councillor until his death in 1635. Weston certainly enjoyed clear signs of royal favour, including the king's personal attendance at the marriage of his son, Jerome, to Frances Stuart, sister of the duke of Lennox, to whom he gave a gift of 50,000 florins.[47] Weston was ultimately raised to the earldom of Portland in March 1633. William Laud, who disliked Weston intensely, and who after 1633 as Archbishop of Canterbury can certainly

90 Imperial monarch (1629–40)

be seen as the main voice in ecclesiastical affairs, was also a key councillor, though his supremacy in church matters has been challenged by historians such as Julian Davies and Kevin Sharpe who wish to see Charles as the driving force behind religious policy, preferring 'Carolinism' to 'Laudianism' as a characterisation of the direction of the Church of England in these years. In many ways, as Anthony Milton points out, such obsession with nomenclature misses the point: the relationship between Laud and the king was symbiotic, with no policy taking root without the king's approval, but with scope for his servants to 'work towards' him by devising and outlining policy ideas in their respective areas before securing his assent. Thomas Wentworth, Lord President of the Council of the North from 1629 and Lord Deputy of Ireland from 1632, was undoubtedly a key figure, notably in his extensive correspondence with Laud and their joint policy of 'Thorough', reflected in his forceful approach to Irish affairs, but his absence in Ireland until his recall in 1639 imposed limits upon his influence at the centre of power. Laud and Wentworth shared a hostility to Weston, whom they derisively termed 'Lady Mora'.[48] Their alliance was significant but should not be overstated: for example, Laud detested Francis Cottington, Chancellor of the Exchequer and a close ally of Weston's, while Wentworth carried on a fairly regular correspondence with him.

The three nevertheless shared a broadly pro-Spanish outlook in foreign affairs. After Wentworth became Lord Deputy of Ireland in 1632 and Laud was raised to Canterbury the following year, the two of them corresponded frequently about Irish affairs in particular, but also about the wider politics of the Personal Rule. Together, they claimed to be pursuing a distinctive approach to government, which they labelled 'Thorough', the precise meaning of which is slightly obscure. From their correspondence it is clear that it was in part a defensive concept: they saw themselves as embattled servants of the king having to overcome entrenched opposition, in particular the 'common lawyers', whom they appear to have seen as the 'blob' of their day. Laud expressed the hope to Wentworth in November 1633 that 'if the common Lawyers may be contained within their ancient and sober Bounds; if the word Thorough be not left out, (as I am certain it is). . .' then the government of the kingdom

Imperial monarch (1629–40) 91

would improve, though in August 1637 he was despairing that 'I have done expecting of Thorow on this Side'. They both saw themselves as carrying out the king's wishes, and Wentworth, who exercised a good deal of autonomy in Ireland but who used Laud as a convenient conduit to the king in London, suggested that their joint aim of 'reducing of this kingdom [Ireland] to a Conformity in Religion with the Church of England, is no doubt deeply set in his Majesty's pious and prudent Heart'. They had a clear sense of the British context of their policies, with Laud famously joking that having been obliged to write nine letters in one day to Scotland, 'I think you have a Plot to see, whether will be *Universalis Episcopus*'.[49]

When Weston died in 1635 the battle to succeed him as Lord Treasurer highlighted the extent to which Charles was able to assert himself above the divisions at court. The immediate decision on a successor was postponed, and for a time the Treasury was placed into Commission, an arrangement which does not seem to have suited many of its members. Cottington complained that 'In our Committee for the Treasury we manage our Business extreme ill, and so as if it continue, we shall soon spoil all', while Laud, who was also a member, complained that 'I never had so little Leisure in my Life, as I have had since I was a Commissioner of the Treasury', and expressed the hope that Charles would name a successor soon '[so] that our troublesome Commission were at an End'.[50] Both Cottington and Laud, who cordially disliked each other, were candidates to take the office, though Cottington seems not to have rated his own chances and to have assumed that Laud would get the job, and Laud to have hoped for the office for himself. When Charles finally chose William Juxon, Bishop of London, for the role, it is often assumed to have been both a victory for Laud and a sign of the growing (and in the minds of Puritans, malign) influence of the clergy in politics. Given Laud's own aspirations in that direction, however, it ought instead to be seen as a result of Charles's realisation that Laud and Cottington could not have worked together at the Treasury.[51] Juxon was very much Charles's choice: indeed he was reported as having 'assured the Lords' that Juxon 'was his owne election', and his treatment of the Treasury in the period 1635–36 illustrates his control of political appointments.[52]

92 *Imperial monarch (1629–40)*

Foreign policy

Foreign policy was perhaps the area of clearest factional division at the Caroline court. The making of peace with France and Spain in 1629–30 might be seen to herald a withdrawal into diplomatic isolationism. The Venetian ambassador suggested in January 1631 that England had been reduced to the status of a mere 'cipher' on the international stage, though he added that it was 'the will rather than the power [that] may perhaps be said to be lacking' as the kingdom enjoyed a period of 'universal quiet and peace'.[53] This would, however, be too simplistic. Foreign policy was an area in which Charles very clearly played a directing role, and he remained committed to trying to recover the Palatinate for his brother-in-law. The initial signs were that Charles's policy was to be pro-Spanish, and the Treaty of Madrid of November 1630, which was negotiated by his pro-Spanish councillor, Francis Cottington, was accompanied by a secret agreement to assist the Spanish in an invasion of the Netherlands in return for the restoration of Frederick and Elizabeth to their German territory.[54] There was a change of tack in the following year, however: Great interest was shown in the entry of the Swedes into the war against the Empire, leading to proposals for an alliance. Their victory at Breitenfield in September 1631 prompted the dispatch of an embassy led by Lord Craven and discussions about sending 'levyes here for his victorious Majestie' as well as the revival of calls for a Parliament, since 'All here beleeve that if wee send ayde to the King of Swede wee shall have a Parliament'.[55] This ran up against Charles's continued antipathy towards summoning the assembly: he declared that the very suggestion was 'derogatory to his authority and was equally remote from giving him satisfaction'. Nevertheless, he considered it 'very necessary to think about help for the King of Sweden, but not by such means' and 'he hoped they would find the means of supplying it to him without opening the gates to fresh scandals'.[56]

The death of Gustavus Adolphus at the battle of Lützen a year later reduced the incentive to take such political and financial risks. Instead Charles put renewed energy into diplomacy, with a broadly pro-Spanish policy holding until the middle of 1635, when the death of Weston (one of the leading Hispanophile

Imperial monarch (1629–40) 93

councillors) and the signing of the Peace of Prague (in which the Palatinate was awarded to Bavaria) reduced the appeal of Habsburg friendship. While the queen, incongruously aligned with the more aggressive Protestant councillors, promoted a French alliance, Charles persevered with the Habsburgs, dispatching the earl of Arundel (who relished the art-collecting opportunities of such assignments) to Germany as ambassador extraordinary in 1636 to try to achieve the restitution of the Palatinate at the emperor's behest. Although the Imperialists were pleased to receive such an envoy as proof of Charles's 'wholesome and princely intentions for them', the necessity of canvassing the views of the other Imperial electors at the Diet in Ratisbon as well as the fact that Frederick's electoral title had by now been transferred to the duke of Bavaria complicated matters and soon Arundel concluded that 'all faire means with Austria is in vaine for doing any good for the Elector Palatine'.[57] The negotiations were not helped by suspicion on the Imperial side about the role of the pro-French faction surrounding Henrietta Maria. In particular, they thought her Catholic courtier, Wat Montagu, who was 'addicted to France', was exerting an anti-Habsburg influence in Rome.[58] After Arundel returned empty-handed early in 1637, the pro-French faction appeared likely to win the day and the possibility of war with Spain grew. Robert Sidney, second Earl of Leicester, who was sent on an embassy to the French court, was in frequent correspondence with his wife back in England, and she reported the king's enthusiasm for the French negotiations in March 1637 and even suggested that Laud and Arundel were agreeable to such an alliance. She also relayed Henrietta Maria's wishes that 'the business in France' would 'goe well'.[59] Meanwhile in reply to a letter from Wentworth expressing fears of a war with the Habsburgs, Charles replied that he had misunderstood. It was not a question:

> whether I should declare war to the House of Austria or not, but whether I shall join with France and the rest of my friends to demand of the House of Austria my nephew's restitution, and so hazard (upon refusal) a declaration of war.[60]

Once again, the dynastic concern for the recovery of the Palatinate remained central to his considerations, rather than the wider fate

94   *Imperial monarch (1629–40)*

of international Protestantism that was pre-occupying some of his more forward councillors. He did though strongly imply that he was disinclined to risk such an outcome by promising to follow Strafford's advice in the matter. In November of that year, Laud was writing to Wentworth to the effect that, 'As for war with Spain, I can say no more of it yet, but I fear it may come thither at last'.[61] In the event, the outbreak of the Covenanter rebellion the following year distracted attention away from foreign affairs and subsequent events removed the possibility of intervention in the European war, though the assistance offered to Spain in 1639 and the hope for Spanish financial help against the Scots in return reflected the dominance of the pro-Spanish courtiers by the end of the decade. The earl of Northumberland, who favoured a French alliance, wrote of the controlling influence on policy of Laud, Strafford and Hamilton, who 'do absolutely gouerne' and whom he described as 'as much Spanish as Olivares'.[62] The presence from October 1638 of Marie de Medici, Henrietta Maria's mother, the dowager queen of France and, as an avowed enemy of Richelieu, a partisan of Spain, contributed to this sense of an increasing gravitation of the Caroline court towards the Habsburgs as well as feeding growing anti-Catholic hysteria in the capital.

The Caroline Church

Charles's personal religion is to some extent quite opaque. His commitment to the prayer book and the institution of episcopacy were constant as attested by his dealings with the Scots and later the negotiations for a settlement after the First Civil War, but he left little record of his own theological beliefs. Instead his personal religious life revolved around his devotions, and his conception of the Church around order and authority.[63] One slightly scandalised observer noted in 1637 the putting up of 'hangings over the altar in the Kings Chappell the likest a Crucifix that hath been seen there these fortie yeares', alluding to Elizabeth I's known preference for such adornments in her chapel.[64] In terms of his management of ecclesiastical affairs, he appears to have left much of it to William Laud. Laud became Archbishop of Canterbury in August 1633 following the death of Abbot. Described by Sir Simonds D'Ewes as 'a little, low, red-faced man, of mean parentage', he

Imperial monarch (1629–40) 95

became a lightning rod for all sorts of resentments, many of them religious but not all.[65] The latter remark, an unfair one given that Laud was the son of a moderately prosperous Reading clothier, in many ways reflects the anti-clericalism commonly aroused among the gentry and aristocracy by the involvement of prelates in affairs of state. Charles undoubtedly relied on him very heavily and given that his name has come to define the Church of England in this the period – 'Laudian' – it is tempting to see him as the prime mover in the making of religious policy. That appellation is, however, in some ways unhelpful, not least because many of its defining policies pre-date Laud's arrival at Canterbury and have their roots in the 1590s, and because it minimises the role of other clerics and of the king himself.

One key influence upon the king in religious matters was Matthew Wren, who had accompanied Charles as Prince of Wales on his journey to Madrid and had famously remarked to Lancelot Andrewes upon his return that Charles could be relied on to defend the Church of England better than his father had.[66] Wren's enjoyment of royal favour was shown by his promotions even after the death in 1626 of his patron, Andrewes: he became dean of Windsor in 1628, where he also served as Register of the Garter (from 1635) and in 1633 he accompanied Charles on his visit to Edinburgh for his Scottish coronation, perhaps planting in Charles's mind the idea of reforming the ceremonies and practices of the Scottish Church along English lines. He became Clerk of the Closet the same year, a role which gave him close access to the king, and was subsequently raised successively to the bishoprics of Hereford and then Norwich (both in 1635), becoming dean of the Chapel Royal in 1636 and then bishop of Ely in 1638, in which (particularly in the large diocese of Norwich, which he suggested to the king needed partitioning) he was an assiduous enforcer of Laud's and Charles's ecclesiastical agenda.[67]

Some historians, notably Kevin Sharpe and Julian Davies, have argued that in fact Charles was the principal instigator of ecclesiastical change and that the leading clergy, such as Laud, Wren and Neile, were merely his willing factotums. As a consequence they prefer the label 'Carolinism' to Laudianism. This may be taking things too far, though it is helpful to remember, as Laud undoubtedly did, the importance of Charles's views and preferences in

96   Imperial monarch (1629–40)

shaping religious policy in what remained, after all, a monarchical church. In some areas Laud appears to have been the driving force, notably for instance in relation to the altar policy (the moving of communion tables to the east end of the church and railing them off), which he had championed as early as 1617 when dean of Gloucester, and in the reissuing of the *Book of Sports* in 1633. In both cases, however, Laud had to tap into his royal master's anti-Puritanism to convince him. At the Privy Council meeting of November 1633 at which the policy was formally promulgated, Laud appears to have persuaded Charles of the need to insist that parish churches follow the lead of their local cathedral in order to guarantee order and obedience and overcome puritan recalcitrance about kneeling at communion. Likewise in 1633 he argued to the king that permitting recreations on Sundays after divine service would help to curb the growth of Puritanism, particularly in the north. Charles seems to have regarded bringing Puritans to heel as a central objective, and he was very directly involved in the suppression of puritan lectureships (such as that of Great Yarmouth) and in the wider attack on puritan preaching, which he associated with his wider fear (shared with Laud) of 'popularity' and the subversion of royal policy.[68]

The punishment of those who seemed to threaten to undermine the Church and its governance was often severe, and reflected the conviction of both Laud and Charles that threats against the Church amounted to threats against the State. One example was the fate of Alexander Leighton, a copy of whose book, *An Appeal to Parliament; or, Sion's Plea against Prelacy* (1628) fell into Laud's hands in February 1630. While not attacking the king directly, it was forceful in its condemnation of Buckingham and of the king's marriage to a Catholic, along with the state of the Caroline Church. Worse, however, was his invitation to Parliament to resist dissolution and effectively set itself up as a permanent body, a clear defiance of the royal prerogative. Proceeded against in Star Chamber, he was sentenced to a heavy fine and various corporal punishments, the severity of which signalled the increasing association drawn by the Caroline regime between Presbyterianism and political subversion.[69] This was further emphasised by the fate of William Prynne, who was punished for his book, *Historiomastix*, in 1634. While often seen

Imperial monarch (1629–40) 97

as a sign of the Caroline regime's intolerance, the prosecution of Prynne, led impressively by Attorney General Noy, paid relatively little attention to his religious criticisms (instead referring those to the Court of High Commission), or the attack on the queen for appearing in court masques, and instead demonstrated effectively that his work was politically seditious in its attack on the king: it sought to alienate the king's subjects from his affections by bringing him and the queen into disrepute, as well as fomenting disloyalty by directly commending the assassination of several Roman emperors and comparing Charles I to the Emperor Nero. As Mark Kishlansky has shown in an extensive examination of the trial, in many ways Prynne was fortunate to escape with the most lenient punishment recommended against him by the court.[70] Three years later, Prynne was again in trouble, along with two others, John Bastwick and Henry Burton, who were sentenced to have their ears cropped for attacking the institution of episcopacy (since Prynne had in fact already had his ears cropped for his first offence, he now had the remainder of his ears entirely removed). Laud's speech delivered in Star Chamber at their condemnation on 14 June 1637 sought to refute the claim they had made that the belief that bishops held their power *iure divino* was an implied diminution of the royal prerogative, and reiterated the conviction he shared with his royal master that there was an inextricable alignment between royal and ecclesiastical authority and that the intent of the Puritan opponents of royal policy was to rouse 'popular' unrest:

> No man can libel against our calling (as these men do), be it in pulpit, print or otherwise, but he libels against the King and the State, by whose laws we are established. Therefore all these libels, so far forth as they are against our calling, are against the King and the Law, and can have no other purpose than to stir up sedition among the people. . .[71]

Laud reinforced this when he wrote to Wentworth agreeing with the latter's assertion that Prynne, Burton and Bastwick 'do but begin with the Church, that they might after have the freer Access to the State', but lamented that after their stint in the pillory they received the acclaim of the people, a sign that many others did not

98 Imperial monarch (1629–40)

share their political vision of a stronger and more authoritarian monarchy, such that Laud commented he had 'done expecting of Thorow on this Side'.[72]

Even one of Laud's episcopal colleagues, John Williams, admittedly a long-time enemy on the bench, joined in the attack on the archbishop, publishing a book called *Holy Table, Name and Thing* (1637) criticising the altar policy. Indeed Williams was labelled 'the greatest opposer' of the moving of altars and was eventually sentenced by Star Chamber to a heavy fine and imprisonment in the Tower.[73] The penalties could therefore be heavy for presuming to criticise Laud's policies, which had such strenuous backing from the king, but so often it was the political implications of those religious criticisms that prompted the severity of the regime's response. Charles showed his favour to Laud repeatedly: when Lord Treasurer Portland died in 1635, Laud was included on the commission appointed to administer the Treasury until a new appointment. When a successor was chosen the following year, although Laud seems to have put himself forward as a candidate, the selection of another bishop, William Juxon, is further suggestive of Charles's desire to work closely with his archbishop in creating an even greater mutual dependency between Church and State. In August of that same year, 1636, Charles gave what was perhaps the ultimate sign of his favour: a personal progress to Oxford to be entertained by Laud (who was chancellor of the University) at his own college of St John's, and where Canterbury Quadrangle, with its statues of Charles and Henrietta Maria at either end, commemorates the importance of the visit.[74] Yet Laud's relationship with the queen was frequently tense: there is an irony to the fact that, while Laud was often accused by his opponents of conspiring to bring in popery, he himself was acutely sensitive to that charge and anxious to refute it. One thing which greatly concerned him was the number of conversions to Catholicism at court, usually of court ladies under the queen's (and the papal agent's) influence, and when Lady Newport converted in 1637, Laud spoke out in council about it to the king and secured a proclamation against any future such conversions, a move which 'highly displeased' Henrietta Maria.[75] That Charles was also receptive to his archbishop's case is a further reminder that he

Imperial monarch (1629–40) 99

too understood the danger posed to his ecclesiastical project by its being tainted with the imputation of crypto-popery.

Imperial monarchy?

In many ways the monarchy of Charles I during the 1630s can be seen as 'imperial' in character. This is reflected in the portraiture and material culture of his regime, in for instance representations likening him to a Roman emperor, the use of colour (imperial purple) in royal portraiture[76] and grand architectural projects (even if never realised), as well as in the manner in which he governed his territories, notably in attempts to enforce greater uniformity and conformity (especially of religious practice) across his three kingdoms. While many of the policies of the Personal Rule were drawn from and justified by English history (often from the Middle Ages), the iconography of the regime, including its art and architecture, was largely taken from neo-Roman models. John Peacock has highlighted the Roman imperial motif running through several of van Dyck's paintings of the king and which was common to the themes and scenery of court masques, the latter of which was frequently designed by Inigo Jones, premier champion of the neo-classical architectural style in England, as shown in his most notable contributions in the shape of the Banqueting House at Whitehall (in James's reign), the Queen's House at Greenwich (completed in 1635) and the new west portico of St Paul's Cathedral. Van Dyck's famous painting of *Charles I and M. de St Antoine* showed the king riding through a Roman triumphal arch, propped up against which was a shield containing the royal arms surmounted by an imperial crown, in case the message needed reinforcing. Others of his paintings referenced Titian's *Caesars*, while his *Charles I in Three Positions* was painted to provide the multiple angles from which Bernini could produce a sculpture of the king (lost in the Whitehall fire of 1698) which evoked the self-presentation of Roman emperors. The court masque *Albion's Triumph* (1632) saw Charles appear as the Romano-British Emperor Albanactus, in a costume and amidst sets all designed by Jones. As Charles had no military victories to celebrate, the imperial triumphs with which he was having himself associated appear to have been moral and abstract, rather than literal.[77]

100 *Imperial monarch (1629–40)*

Nevertheless, the Caesarean theme was clearly one with which Charles was pre-occupied, judging by his keen display of busts of emperors and by his purchase of the enormous series of nine monumental *Triumph of Caesar* canvases by Andrea Mantegna, amongst his other acquisitions from the Duke of Mantua's collection in 1627, having been persuaded of their artistic merit by his Flemish art broker, Daniel Nijs. Mantegna's paintings arrived in England in late 1630 and were probably moved to Hampton Court soon after.[78] Nor was the imperial theme only taken from the ancient world: van Dyck's second painting of *Charles I on Horseback* (c. 1637–8), also displayed at Hampton Court, was likely modelled on Titian's painting of *Charles V on Horseback*, a masterful depiction of the closest thing early modern Europe had seen to a Roman emperor after his decisive victory over the Schmalkaldic League at the battle of Mühlberg in 1547. Though van Dyck's Charles is a decidedly less warlike image, the king would have seen the Titian on his visit to Madrid in 1623, and he owned another image of the Habsburg Emperor, *Charles V with a Dog*, that had been gifted to him by his descendant, Philip IV, upon Charles's departure from Spain, and which was prominently displayed in the Bear Gallery in the Palace of Whitehall.[79]

Moreover, the equestrian bronze statue of Charles by Hubert Le Sueur, which now stands in front of Trafalgar Square, does evoke a more martial and chivalric image, depicting Charles in the armour of a tournament knight, lord of all he surveys. Although commissioned by Lord Treasurer Weston in 1633 for the garden of his house at Mortlake Park in Roehampton, it very much reflects the image Charles wished to present of himself and the fact this was being further projected by his leading courtiers and councillors. Le Sueur, who had produced miniature equestrian bronzes of Henri IV and Louis XIII of France, also made a marble bust of Charles (the latter pieces are now in the V&A) and bronze statues of the king and queen for Laud, which now adorn niches in Canterbury Quad at St John's College, Oxford. Meanwhile the grand plans for a new palace complex at Whitehall, an ambitious design of baroque splendour intended to emulate (and rival) the size and scale of the Escorial outside Madrid or the Louvre in Paris, drawn up by Inigo Jones and his pupil John Webb between 1637 and 1639 (but never realised due to the outbreak of the

Imperial monarch (1629–40) 101

Scottish crisis), further demonstrate both the extent of Charles's ambitions to transform the centre of power at the heart of his three kingdoms, as well as the influence of continental models.[80]

While one would not wish to draw too direct a link between portraiture and policy, the plentiful evidence of Charles's near-obsession with imperial neo-Roman and classical artistic forms would seem to chime very closely with his pursuit of uniformity and conformity, particularly in matters of religion, within his three kingdoms (particularly Scotland and Ireland), as well as his high view of royal authority and regal dignity more generally. While Charles's father had aspired to be, and had given himself the exalted title of 'King of Great Britain', he had been relatively uninterested in art and architecture (the building of the Banqueting House aside). His son, appearing to wish to fulfil his father's intentions in this as in much else, sought to remedy that, not only in the famous Rubens ceiling he commissioned to adorn James's Banqueting House at Whitehall, depicting his predecessor's 'apotheosis' as British king, but also perhaps go one better in adding a distinctly 'imperial' dimension to his own self-presentation as ruler of Great Britain. It is to Charles's policies in his two other kingdoms during the 1630s that we now turn.

Strafford and Ireland

When Thomas Wentworth was appointed as Lord Deputy of Ireland in 1632 he was seen as 'a strong champion for the King in all affaires', having demonstrated his capabilities as a fiercely efficient Lord President of the Council of the North in his native Yorkshire in the preceding three years.[81] The government of Ireland in the first years of the reign had been rather unstable: Lord Falkland, the previous Lord Deputy, had been removed in 1629 and Wentworth was supposed to whip the kingdom into shape, chiefly by addressing the shortfall in royal revenues made apparent by the recent expenditure on defence during the war with Spain, bringing the Irish Church into closer conformity with that in England (which would be assisted by his close co-operation with Archbishop Laud), and asserting royal authority over the Irish population. This latter goal was made more challenging by the combustible tripartite division of Irish society into Old English

102   *Imperial monarch (1629–40)*

(the descendants of the original English settlers of the Middle Ages, landowning and predominantly Catholic), the Gaelic or 'Native' Irish (the vast majority of the population, impoverished and overwhelmingly Catholic), and their frequent antagonists, the New English (more recent, post-Reformation arrivals who dominated political office and sought to enforce their Protestantism on the native population). The 'Plantation of Ulster' by James I had added an even more aggressively Protestant, Scottish Presbyterian contingent to the northern counties of the kingdom. Falkland had found himself obliged to make concessions to the Old English in order to extract sufficient revenues to defend the kingdom against the feared Spanish incursion in the period 1625–28, symbolised by his granting of the 'Graces' of 1628 which promised greater freedom from persecution for Catholics and protection of their land tenure.

These were, however, only provisional and contingent upon their confirmation by an Irish Parliament. As such, when Wentworth went over to Ireland in autumn 1633, after Charles's return from Scotland, his first task was to summon a Parliament for the following year to which he held out the carrot of the confirmation of the Graces in return for a substantial grant of subsidies. Not only did Wentworth fail to fulfil his part of the bargain, but he boasted, in a clear evocation of the 'imperial' frame of mind which built on traditional English conceptions of Ireland as a colony enjoyed by right of conquest, and as a testing ground for policies which might later be pursued in England, that Charles would be in Ireland 'as absolute here, as any Prince in the whole World can be'.[82] In many ways there was an echo here of the administrative and fiscal policies being pursued by Wentworth's Castilian contemporary, the Count-Duke Olivares, who had urged his royal master, Philip IV, to bring 'these kingdoms which comprise Spain into conformity with the laws and style of the government of Castile. . .which, if we could find the proper way to encompass it, would make your majesty the most powerful prince in the world'.[83] Wentworth's model of demanding supply from Parliament and promising redress of grievances in a deferred second session would be followed by Charles in relation to the Short Parliament in England in 1640. As Anthony Milton has argued, Wentworth's thinking about parliaments as submissive instruments of the royal will represent a variation upon continental absolutist ideas and demonstrate the more

Imperial monarch (1629–40)   103

innovatory aspects of the political thought of the Personal Rule.[84] He did succeed in increasing Irish revenues by about £80,000 per annum, mainly through reform of the customs, and this income was able to be diverted to England, a further sign of the fiscal dimensions of Charles's imperium.

While most of Wentworth's policies had precedents in the rule of previous lord deputies, the increased efficiency with which they were implemented caused particular disquiet. His de facto toleration of Catholicism (on the pragmatic basis that he did not see persecuting Catholics as a priority rather than from any sympathy with the Catholic religion) combined with his attempt to impose Laudian reforms on the Church of Ireland, aroused the suspicion of the aggressively Protestant settlers in the north and the Pale. Meanwhile his fiscal demands and his feuding with various Irish nobles, notably Lord Mountnorris, ranged powerful interest groups against him. His use of the Court of Castle Chamber in Dublin, which mirrored the functions of the Court of Star Chamber in London, was used to force through his policies and punish opposition, such as that which he faced to his scheme for the planation of Galway. He turned this into a strong instrument for the enforcement of his authority and its employment as an all-encompassing vehicle for the Lord Deputy's rule led one historian, with some justification, to describe this as an 'instrument of despotism as severe as that of Richelieu' and Wentworth's regime more generally as 'Study in Absolutism'.[85] While paying heed to differences of national context, these continental parallels can be fruitful: just as Olivares's policies in Spain are blamed for the revolts in Catalonia and Portugal in 1640, and the outbreak of the Fronde in France in 1648–49 is seen as a belated reaction against the ministerial absolutism of Richelieu and his successor, Mazarin, the outbreak of the Irish rebellion in October 1641 is often attributed to Wentworth's aggressive attempts to drive Ireland into greater conformity with England. Certainly he can be said to have exacerbated existing political and religious grievances, but his policies saw notable success on a fiscal and administrative level, and it is noteworthy that the rebellion broke out two years after his departure from Ireland when his strong hand and ruthlessness in the service of his royal master's imperial project was removed.

104 *Imperial monarch (1629–40)*

Scotland

As in Ireland, the term 'Personal Rule' is in many ways inapposite to describe Charles's government of Scotland, since a Scottish Parliament did meet in 1633 and again in 1639 (albeit in the second case not by the king's willing choice). Yet in other ways the policies he pursued there resemble his most aggressive efforts at upholding and extending the rights and prerogatives of the Crown. His Act of Revocation in the year of his accession had offended many among the Scottish nobility by its wide-ranging re-claiming of lands that had been sold off by the Crown and Church, backdated to 1542 to ensure maximum gains for the Crown, though in practice of limited success as its enforcement was administered by the same nobles it intended to dispossess. Charles did make some concessions but the final version of the Act, implemented in 1629, still required those who had acquired Church and Crown lands to give them up to him, before receiving them back upon less favourable terms. As Geoffrey Parker has pointed out, this was in some ways similar to the Edict of Restitution promulgated by Emperor Ferdinand II in the same year and likewise aroused resentment.[86] It further suggests that Charles was not operating in a vacuum and that both his aims and actions had continental parallels.

Nevertheless the associated fact of decisions relating to the kingdom being taken by a Scottish Privy Council dominated by a favoured coterie of nobles and bishops and which contained several Englishmen resident in London did not help in winning over his elite Scottish subjects. Moreover, while James had only re-visited Scotland once after his move south, in 1617, and had not been amongst the most popular of Scottish kings (not least for his efforts to re-impose episcopacy on the Scottish Church), he had at least been perceived as a native Scot who had spent his formative years amongst his own people. Charles, meanwhile, although born in Scotland, moved south as a three-year old boy and did not visit his northern kingdom until the summer of 1633, eight years after his accession to the throne. As such, while this was not entirely his fault, he was widely perceived as a distant, absentee monarch, whose priorities were always English rather than Scottish, a view only reinforced by his actions in the early part of his reign.[87] He governed

Imperial monarch (1629–40) 105

Scotland by letter and appeared insensitive to many of the concerns and priorities of his Scottish subjects.

Yet consideration of the Jacobean inheritance in Scotland once again produces something of a case in mitigation. As Laura Stewart has argued, James VI and I had pursued a policy of 'confessionalisation' in Scotland, entailing 'the harmonisation of ecclesiastical practices across Britain', culminating in his attempt in 1617 to enforce the Five Articles of Perth, which upheld private communion, private baptism, and episcopal confirmation, as well as requiring observance of the holy days of Christ's life and, most controversially, kneeling to receive holy communion.[88] Charles's primary purpose in visiting his northern kingdom in 1633 was to be crowned, though in addition, it was to address deficiencies he found in the Scottish Church, 'to make it more conformable to that in England', a policy that his father had also pursued in the latter part of his reign.[89] When Charles offended Scottish sensibilities by using the English Prayer Book and ceremonies for the service at Holyrood and had the Scottish Parliament confirm all previous acts concerning religion, the latter was essentially something James had tried to do on his visit in 1617 but had ultimately recoiled from. This backing down in the face of protest gave confidence to his Presbyterian opponents, a confidence that would later undermine Charles's efforts to continue with his father's project.

By contrast, when a protest was drawn up by some members of the Scottish Parliament against his religious policies, Charles refused to receive it, making clear his displeasure at the opposition to his will, and then decided to make an example of Lord Balmerino (who was found with a copy of the protest in his possession) by sentencing him to death for slandering the king. Though the unfortunate peer received a pardon the following year, the draconian verdict created a sense of injustice among the Scottish nobility and made some think united opposition was safer than individual protest.[90] Charles's decision to embark on a wider programme of reform of the Scottish Church by imposing new canons in 1636 and announcing the introduction of a new prayer book the following year is often seen as one of his greatest misjudgements: It provoked riots in St Giles's Cathedral in Edinburgh at its first use in July 1637 and then a full-scale rebellion following the

106 *Imperial monarch (1629–40)*

formation of a significant opposition group around the National Covenant of February 1638. Yet James's actions had, by the early 1620s, created a climate of protest and his concessions seemingly shown the city of Edinburgh's ability to defy the royal will over the Five Articles of Perth; fourteen of the town councillors who witnessed the prayer book riots of 23 July 1637 had been politically active during the final years of James's reign. In many ways, 'James left behind a potential time bomb in Scotland'.[91]

While the imposition of Charles's new Scottish prayer book is often blamed on Laud, the archbishop himself blamed the Scottish bishops for failing to explain the project effectively, (an approach which, he alleged, fitted 'his Majesty's disposition'), as well as Charles's failure to consult the Scottish Council more extensively before proceeding, and the earl of Traquair's mismanagement of the situation in Edinburgh.[92] Both he and Wentworth, however, advised Charles to be firm with the Scots rebels in order to succeed where his father had failed. Laud defended the king's Scottish policy as 'a great Service to the Crown as well as to God himself' and lamented the outbreak of Covenanter resistance as 'a great Blow as well to the Power as Honour of the King'.[93] Wentworth, still in Ireland in 1638, went so far as to advise the king to treat Scotland like Ireland: to subdue it, Anglicise it, and rule through a Lord Deputy.[94] It has been argued forcefully by Mark Kishlansky that Charles showed flexibility and a willingness to compromise in his dealings with the Covenanters, and that it was his opponents who compelled him to use force against them.[95] While it is undoubtedly true that Charles relied on information reaching England, often with a significant delay, and could only act upon what he heard, and that the Covenanters did widen their critique of the Church beyond the prayer book to include demands for the abolition of episcopacy, Charles's concessions were largely strategic from the start of the crisis and he did not intend to honour them.

As far as Charles was concerned the central issue was one of authority and the need to uphold it against this flagrant challenge. His correspondence with the marquess of Hamilton, whom he sent to negotiate with the Covenanters in June 1638, reflects his determination to use force against them. He insisted that he was determined to 'stick to my grounds, and that I expect not anything can reduce that people to obedience, but only force'. He was

Imperial monarch (1629–40) 107

also quite happy to deceive his opponents, allowing Hamilton 'to flatter them with what hopes you please, so you engage me not against my grounds', by which he meant his refusal to grant the Scots a Parliament or a General Assembly until they renounced the Covenant, 'grounds' which he would later abandon. He admitted that his immediate objective was 'now to win time, that they may not commit public follies, until I be ready to suppress them'. Above all, he was concerned that 'not only now my crown, but my reputation for ever, lies at stake', and declared that 'I will rather die than yield to these impertinent and damnable demands. . .for it is all one, as to yield to be no King in a very short time'.[96] Famously he declared that 'so long as this Covenant is in force. . .I have no more power in Scotland than as a duke of Venice, which I will rather die than suffer' and instructed Hamilton to 'shew the world clearly that my taking of arms is to suppress rebellion, and not to impose novelties'.[97] Here was Charles's characteristic association of opposition with disloyalty and his sense that compromise was incompatible with his position as king, along with a clear willingness to deceive. Despite efforts to present Charles as conciliatory, it is hard to sustain when his innermost thoughts as revealed in his correspondence seem to suggest that his concessions are false. He continually referred to the Covenanters as 'traitors' whose professions of religious motivations he regarded as a cloak for political rebellion.[98] He also failed to listen to Hamilton's considered advice in the early summer of 1638 that he should make more far-reaching concessions.[99] In many ways Charles's problem was that he had tried to both recover lands from the Scottish nobility and impose reforms on the Scottish Church without an apparatus of coercion with which to compel obedience. As such, while he was hindered by his father's legacy, it was his attempt to pursue an authoritarian end without authoritarian means which, not for the last time, would undermine his entire policy.

Meanwhile a further dimension of the Scottish crisis that provoked suspicion of the king was the involvement of the Catholics. Scottish Catholic aristocrats (such as the marquis of Huntly) were conspicuously loyal to the king during the crisis, while the papal agent at the English court, George Con, a Scot himself, whose presence had already begun to cause disquiet in the capital, and who saw the Covenanters as an anti-Catholic movement, urged Charles

108 *Imperial monarch (1629–40)*

to take firm action. He encouraged, along with Hamilton, a scheme to bring over the Catholic earl of Antrim (whose countess was Buckingham's widow, Lady Katherine), with an Irish force to use against the Scots and sponsored a collection among English Catholics towards the king's war effort.[100] While this scheme never came to fruition, and subsequent Covenanter claims that Charles had raised a 'popish' English army against them were vastly overstated, the fact that the king chose the earl of Arundel as commander-in-chief of his forces contributed to this perception. Arundel was widely regarded as crypto-Catholic, as were Cottington and Windebank, two other keen advocates on the Privy Council of a hard-line policy towards Scotland. When Arundel was seen to use Con's coach, emblazoned with the papal arms, to drive to Council meetings at court, suspicions of a Catholic conspiracy only increased.[101]

The first Bishops' War

Charles was implacable in his attitude towards the Scottish rebels and determined upon their destruction. As war loomed in February 1639, he continued to regard the Covenanter rebellion as essentially political, having been instigated, he told the earl of Suffolk, by 'some factious persons ill affected to monarchical government, who seek to cloak their too apparent rebellious deigns under pretence of religion'.[102] He was also convinced that they were being assisted by the French, and, while Richelieu was uninterested in offering such help, the overtures made by the diplomat, Bellièvre, fed such suspicions, even if they were unfounded. He also firmly rejected suggestions that he summon a Parliament, determining that he could finance the war by the Crown's existing resources.[103] His *Large Declaration* of March 1639, prepared by Walter Balcanquhall, Dean of Rochester, compared the Scottish Covenanters to Jesuits in their lack of respect for kings, and insisted that the Covenant was incompatible with monarchy:

> . . .they did and doe pretend Religion, yet nothing was or is lesse intended by them, but that they having received from Us full satisfaction to all their desires. . .yet their persisting in their rebellious and tumultuous courses, doth demonstrate to the world their weariness of being governed by Us and

Imperial monarch (1629–40) 109

> Our Lawes. . .That these men who give themselves out to be
> the onely Reformers of Religion, have taken such a course
> to undermine and blow up the Religion Reformed, by the
> Scandall of Rebellion and Disobedience. . .it will plainely
> appeare that their Maximes are the same with the Jesuits.[104]

As Tim Harris has recently emphasised, the fact of Charles's commissioning this defence of his actions, with his own name written
on the title page, and choosing Balcanquhall, a Scot and a moderate in religion, to write it, attests to the attention he paid to
government propaganda.[105] Just as in 1629 when he had felt the
need to justify his dissolution of Parliament and explain why he
was disinclined to summon another in the future, he now sought
to maximise support for his campaign against the Scots by asso-
ciating them in the public mind with rebellion and disobedience.
Amidst widespread sympathy for the Scots' religious grievances,
it suited Charles's interests to present their actions as politically
motivated rebellion. Though it might be advanced that a ruler
who felt compelled to justify his actions so stridently must be
insecure in his authority, and Charles would indeed subsequently
waver in his resolution, this was one instance in which his world-
view actually served his political advantage.

As for the military campaign, Charles hoped to bring troops over
from Ireland, having been promised forces by the Catholic earl of
Antrim and separately by Wentworth, but these hopes quickly
evaporated by early April such that Wentworth even advised
postponing the campaign until the following year. Requests for
money to fund the raising of troops were made to leading nobles
and to the judges, though it also proved necessary to levy coat
and conduct money in the localities for the equipping of recruits;
noblemen who were too old or infirm to attend the king in person
in the north were obliged to give a cash payment or provide horses
instead.[106] Nevertheless the king, having left London on 27 March
1639 and reached York three days later, where he had summoned
the nobility of the realm to meet him, remained resolute. A sign
of his fury was the proclamation drafted early in April which, in
the initial draft, placed a bounty on the heads of several named
Scottish noblemen. This licensing of political assassination demonstrated that Charles and Hamilton, who continued to advise

110 *Imperial monarch (1629–40)*

him on Scottish affairs, genuinely regarded the Covenanters as irredeemable traitors. The king was, however, persuaded by horrified Scottish councillors, notably Sir Lewis Stewart, to amend the proclamation lest he inflame the situation further, and so told Hamilton that he would not 'set prices upon the declared rebels' heads, until they have stood out some little time' but rather 'offer some things of favour to those that shall repent'.[107] Meanwhile his English nobles were also being cajoled into backing his campaign. While at York, a modified oath of allegiance, the 'army oath', composed in consultation with Windebank, Arundel and Con, was tended to the peers on 21 April with the intention that even Catholics would be able to swear it. Binding those who took it to fight for the king 'to the utmost hazard of their life and fortunes', it led to fears in some quarters that Charles would demand their whole property, and while most peers consented, two, Lords Saye and Brooke, refused and were briefly placed under arrest. Charles moved to Durham on 1 May and issued a proclamation a fortnight later undertaking not to invade Scotland provided that his Scottish subjects offered civil and temporal obedience and promised in their turn not to invade England. If they approached within ten miles of the border they would be attacked as traitors and invaders. By 28 May the king was at Berwick and there, contrary to expectations (the Venetian ambassador had predicted that 'the royal forces will be very feeble on this occasion'), the rank and file soldiery of the army appeared to be in good spirits and enthusiastic for the fight against the king's enemies.[108] In fact the king's army, totalling between 16,000 and 20,000 men, was a strong force, comparable in size to Parliament's Civil War New Model Army, and the king's resolution 'to treat no more where he ought to be obeyed' seemed far from misplaced.

In many ways the ensuing campaign was a missed opportunity: the English forces were the stronger and when the earl of Holland moved with a reconnaissance force of 4,000 men to face the Scots at Kelso on 4 June, the prospects were good. Deceived by the Scots' deployment into thinking he was outnumbered, however, Holland chose to negotiate, and the king's best opportunity to defeat his Scottish adversaries was lost.[109] The resulting Pacification of Berwick saw Charles recover his Scottish fortresses (including Edinburgh Castle) but forced him to concede the meeting of a

Imperial monarch (1629–40) 111

General Assembly and a Scottish Parliament, both of which were likely to make religious demands unacceptable to the king. As such, the treaty represented a truce rather than a settlement, as was suggested by Charles's parting shot at the end of the document:

> And as we have just reason to believe that to our peaceable and well-affected subjects this will be satisfactory, so we take God and the world to witness, that whatsoever calamities shall ensue by our necessitated suppressing of the insolencies of such as shall continue in their disobedient courses is not occasioned by us, but by their own procurement.[110]

At the beginning of August Charles arrived back in London, where, to the consternation of moderates like Northumberland, he became increasingly reliant on the advice of Laud, who shared his fears for the future of monarchical as well as episcopal government, and Hamilton. He was seemingly reluctant to communicate regarding Scottish affairs to his other councillors, beyond ordering that the Covenanters' latest publication be burned by the public hangman.[111] In this same vein, the king wrote to Archbishop Spottiswoode of St Andrews, to explain that any concessions in Church or government he made were only 'for the present. . .[and] we shall not leave thinking in time how to remedy both'.[112]

When the General Assembly met on 12 August Charles once again chose to make his grounds political rather than religious. He gave the earl of Traquair instructions only to consent to the demand for the abolition of episcopacy for the satisfying of the people and settling of disorders and not to concede that it was unlawful or wrong in principle. He was particularly concerned that any declaration that government of the Church by bishops was unlawful would have implications for the Churches of England and Ireland, and he therefore characteristically left himself wriggle room by stating that he would not be bound by anything Traquair agreed in his name. As such Charles was angered when Traquair appeared to permit a declaration that episcopacy was unlawful according to the constitution of the kirk and ordered that the forthcoming Scottish Parliament not be allowed to confirm this Act unless the word 'unlawful' was removed.[113] The Parliament which convened in Edinburgh on 31 August was less easily managed than Scottish

112   *Imperial monarch (1629–40)*

parliaments traditionally had been: owing to the absence of the bishops, the steering committee, the Lords of the Articles, had to be remodelled and the resultant increase in influence for the Covenanters saw an Act proposed to declare episcopacy unlawful within the Scottish Kirk. Unable to stomach this defiance of his will, Charles decided to adjourn the Parliament, a resolution which Northumberland feared the Scots would defy and thus make renewed war inevitable. In the end they accepted Traquair's prorogation on 14 November until the following June, albeit under protest, while Charles proceeded to reward those peers who had supported him with titles and honours.[114] The enmity between Charles and his Scottish opponents was to continue.

The end of Personal Rule

The key moment in bringing the Personal Rule to an end was arguably the recall of Wentworth to England in September 1639. Resolved as he was to mount a second campaign against the Scots to enforce their obedience to his royal will regarding the Church, the hard-line Wentworth was to be Charles's chief adviser for the next fourteen months, and he dominated the committee for Scottish Affairs formed in early November, comprising leading privy councillors, and including Laud, Hamilton, Cottington and Windebank. Wentworth advised that Scotland should be ruled directly from England, and that in order to coerce the Scots into obedience it would be necessary to summon an English Parliament, which he proposed at a meeting on 5 December in a move supported by both Laud and Hamilton. Charles agreed, having first secured the promise of loans from his councillors in case the parliament should founder.[115] It was summoned to meet on 13 April, and Wentworth was to go to Ireland first in order to demand financial support from an Irish Parliament. In anticipation, he was elevated to the earldom of Strafford in January 1640, the rank he had once sought from Charles but had been denied earlier in the decade. Again, Charles was taking a British approach to the resolution of his difficulties in his northern kingdom and he would later seek help from continental Europe when the Parliament failed.

At this point, of course, Charles envisaged making use of Parliament to strengthen his rule by facilitating the restoration

Imperial monarch (1629–40)   113

of his authority in Scotland. He was not to know that it would instead end in rancour and, when he failed in his subsequent second military campaign against the Scots, the recall of parliament from a position of unparalleled weakness. He had ruled his English kingdom for over a decade without recourse to a parliament and, in many ways, had done so successfully. He had made peace with England's enemies abroad though he had not withdrawn from the networks of European international relations, as his continued diplomatic efforts to achieve the restoration of the Palatinate to his nephews, involving an array of European powers, Catholic as well as Protestant, attest. He had maintained close connections with Europe in other ways, notably through his and his wife's enthusiastic patronage of the arts and the promotion of a cosmopolitan court, one which was also characterised by the kind of order and civility conspicuously absent from that of his father. He had also revived the culture of chivalry, for instance through the renewed emphasis upon the Order of the Garter, and successfully promoted a partnership between Crown and nobility which evoked the Elizabethan era and before. At the same time, he had encouraged a British model for the government of his three kingdoms, continuing his father's efforts at greater homogenisation and unashamedly making this about conformity to his vision of political, fiscal and ecclesiastical administration. The levying of prerogative taxation, rooted in medieval precedent and contributing, along with a decade of peace, to the halving of the royal debt, could be considered a notable financial success, particularly Ship Money, with which the navy was substantially expanded.

The Church, too, had been revitalised and, working closely with Laud, he had developed a vision of a Protestant ceremonialism, distinctive within Reformed Europe, which had led to the architectural regeneration of many parish churches (in addition to St Paul's), as well as the removal of obstructive gentry pews and the permitting of lawful Sunday recreations after divine service, all of which seem to have been popular in vast swathes of rural and provincial England. On a personal and dynastic level, Charles and Henrietta Maria had provided abundantly for the succession and produced a model of domestic harmony to present to the country. And yet none of this (perhaps apart from the latter, and even then with increasing disquiet, as the decade wore on,

114 *Imperial monarch (1629–40)*

at his wife's patronage of Catholics at court), was uncontested. His lack of action in foreign affairs as existential conflict raged in Europe between Protestant and Catholic, and his gravitation towards Spain, caused rumblings of disquiet. His religious reforms produced angry Puritan polemic against the drive for conformity to the king's narrow view of English Reformed Protestantism, while the assertion of his regalian rights, notably the fiscal demands of prerogative taxation, and particularly those involving the revival of obscure charges that had long fallen into desuetude, elicited firm, if isolated, protest.

Above all, his efforts at establishing a British imperial model of governance across his Scottish and Irish kingdoms had stirred up religious and cultural tensions which Charles insisted on regarding as narrowly political. His reasons for doing so were firmly rooted in his personality, particularly in his tendency to view all opposition as disloyalty masquerading as dissent, and in his experience as king in the 1620s, when support taken for granted was withdrawn and royal policies as well as royal servants were attacked. He could not look on the Covenanters and see loyal dissent when he watched them draw up wide-ranging demands, disobey his instructions and challenge a religious and political dispensation much of which he had inherited from his father. Charles can be criticised for the nature of the Personal Rule, both for his policies and the means of their enforcement, but they were internally coherent and represented a distinctive approach to the problem of governing three different kingdoms. While he may have achieved more in the presentation of himself as a commanding ruler with imperial aspirations than in the implementation of the policies which underpinned this vision, his attitudes, aspirations and methods were in many ways understandable in the light of his inheritance, his character and his early political formation.

Notes

1 *CSPD, 1629–1631*, p. 71; Samuel R. Gardiner, *History of England from the Accession of James I to the Outbreak of the Civil War, 1603–1642* (10 vols, 1883–4), VII, p. 81.
2 Michael Questier, *Dynastic Politics & the British Reformations, 1558–1630* (Oxford, 2019), pp. 454–5.

Imperial monarch (1629–40) 115

3 For a detailed discussion by one of its leading exponents of Revisionism and its impact, see John Morrill, 'Revisionism's Wounded Legacies', *Huntington Library Quarterly*, 78 (2015), pp. 577–94.
4 Kevin Sharpe, *The Personal Rule of Charles I* (New Haven and London, 1992).
5 Julie Sanders and Ian Atherton, 'Introducing the 1630s: questions of parliaments, peace and pressure points', in Ian Atherton and Julie Sanders (eds), *The 1630s: Interdisciplinary Essays on Culture and Politics in the Caroline Era* (Manchester, 2013), pp. 1–27.
6 David Cressy, *Charles I and the People of England* (Oxford, 2015).
7 L.J. Reeve, *Charles I and the Road to Personal Rule* (Cambridge, 1989).
8 Quoted in Gardiner, *History of England*, VII, pp. 81–2.
9 *CSPD, 1629–1631*, p. 203.
10 *Acts of the Privy Council, May 1629–May 1630* (HMSO, 1960), p. 177; see also *CSPD 1629–1631*, pp. 95–7.
11 *CSPV, 1629–1632*, p. 8.
12 Kevin Sharpe, *The Personal Rule of Charles I* (New Haven and London, 1992), pp. 263–5, 269.
13 *CSPV, 1632–1636*, p. 315.
14 Malcolm Smuts, 'Force, Love and Authority in political culture', in Atherton and Sanders (eds), *The 1630s*, pp. 28–49.
15 *APC, May 1629–May 1630*, p. 272.
16 *CSPD, 1629–1631*, p. 203.
17 Sir Philip Warwick, *Memoires or Reflexions upon the Reigne of King Charles I* (London, 1701), p. 49.
18 *CSPD, 1629–1631*, pp. 174–5, 321, 340–1.
19 Sharpe, *Personal Rule*, p. 116.
20 *CSPV, 1629–1632*, p. 630.
21 Simonds D'Ewes, *Autobiography*, II, p. 137.
22 Birch, *Court and Times*, II, pp. 233–4.
23 Warwick, *Memoirs*, p. 49.
24 Sharpe, *Personal Rule*, pp. 122–3; Birch, *Court and Times*, II, p. 231.
25 Harris, *Rebellion*, p. 295.
26 Sir Charles Petrie (ed.), *Letters of King Charles I* (London, 1968), pp. 92–4.
27 Simonds D'Ewes, *Autobiography*, II, pp. 129, 136.
28 *CSPV, 1632–1636*, pp. 299–300, 314–5, 334–5, 433–4, 470.
29 Knowler, *Strafford Letters*, I, p. 438.
30 Ibid., II, p. 132; *CSPV, 1632–1636*, p. 325.
31 J.P Kenyon, *The Stuart Constitution: Documents and Commentary* (Cambridge, 1966), pp. 497–501.
32 *APC, May 1629–May 1630*, p.213.
33 Petrie, *Letters of Charles I*, pp. 83–4.
34 *APC, May 1629 – May 1630*, p. 213.
35 *CSPV, 1629–1632*, p. 70.
36 *CSPD, 1629–1632*, pp. 268–9.

116 *Imperial monarch (1629–40)*

37 Caroline Hibbard, 'Henrietta Maria in the 1630s: perspectives on the role of consort queens in *Ancien Régime* courts', in Sanders and Atherton (eds), *The 1630s*, pp. 74–91, at p. 93.

38 *CSPV, 1632–1636*, pp. 334–5.

39 Hibbard, 'Henrietta Maria in the 1630s: perspectives on the role of consort queens in *Ancien Régime* courts', pp. 74–91.

40 Birch, *Court and Times of Charles I*, I, p. 8.

41 See Judith Richards, '"His Nowe Majestie" and the English Monarchy: The Kingship of Charles I before 1640', *Past and Present*, 113 (Nov. 1986), pp. 70–96, at p. 80.

42 *CSPD, 1629–1631*, p. 478.

43 Knowler, *Strafford Letters*, I, pp. 301, 331–2.

44 Richard Cust, *Charles I and the Aristocracy, 1625–1642* (Cambridge, 2013), pp. 58–61, 67–70.

45 *CSPV, 1629–1632*, p. 617. The sketch is now in the Ashmolean.

46 For all of this see Cust, *Charles I and the Aristocracy*, pp. 119–39.

47 *CSPV 1629–1632*, pp. 626, 628, 637.

48 Hugh Trevor-Roper, *Archbishop Laud* (London, 1962), p. 212.

49 William Knowler (ed.), *The Earl of Strafforde's Letters and Dispatches* (2 vols, London, 1739), I, pp. 155–6, 187–8, 271; II, pp. 99–102.

50 Knowler, *Strafforde Letters*, I, pp. 430–1, 438.

51 Brian Quintrell, 'The Church Triumphant? The emergence of a spiritual Lord Treasurer, 1635–1636' in J.F. Merritt (ed.), *The Political World of Thomas Wentworth, earl of Strafford, 1621–1641* (Cambridge, 1996), pp. 81–108, at p. 99–103.

52 *HMC Report on the MSS of the Earl of Denbigh* (HMSO, 1911), V, p. 22.

53 *CSPV, 1629–1632*, p. 463.

54 Cust, *Charles I*, p. 126.

55 *HMC Denbigh MSS*, V, pp. 8–9.

56 *CSPV, 1629–1632*, pp. 573–4.

57 *HMC Denbigh MSS*, V, pp. 26, 30, 35, 42, 46–7.

58 Ibid., p. 25.

59 *HMC Report on the MSS of the Right Honourable Viscount De L'Isle* (6 vols, HMSO, 1966), V, pp. 92, 100.

60 Knowler, *Strafford Letters*, II, pp. 59–60; Petrie, *Letters of Charles I*, p. 99.

61 Ibid., pp. 132–3.

62 Arthur Collins (ed.), *Letters and Memorials of State* (2 vols, London, 1746), II, pp. 617–8.

63 On Charles's personal religious practice, see Kevin Sharpe, *Personal Rule*, pp. 279–81; on his beautification of the chapels royal, see Simon Thurley, 'The Stuart Kings, Oliver Cromwell and the Chapel Royal 1618–1685', *Architectural History*, vol. 45 (2002), pp. 238–274, at p. 242.

Imperial monarch (1629–40) **117**

64 *HMC De L'Isle*, p. 99.
65 D'Ewes, *Autobiography*, II, pp. 100–01.
66 *Parentalia: or Memoirs of the Family of the Wrens*, ed. Christopher Wren (London, 1750), pp. 45–7.
67 Nicholas W.S. Cranfield, 'Wren, Matthew (1585–1667)', *ODNB*.
68 Cust, *Charles I*, pp. 138–40.
69 Gardiner, *History of England*, VII, pp. 144–51.
70 Mark Kishlansky, 'A Whipper Whipped: The Sedition of William Prynne', *The Historical Journal*, 56 (2013), pp. 603–27, at p. 624.
71 Kenyon, *Stuart Constitution*, p. 166.
72 Knowler, *Strafforde Letters*, II, pp. 99–102.
73 *HMC Denbigh MSS*, pp. 49–50.
74 *The Works of the Most Reverend Father in God, William Laud, D.D. Sometime Lord Archbishop of Canterbury*, eds. William Scott and James Bliss (7 vols, Oxford, 1847–60), III, pp. 226–7.
75 Laud, *Works*, III, pp. 229–30.
76 I owe this point to John Adamson, who is currently working on a study of colour in the seventeenth and eighteenth centuries.
77 For much of the above, see John Peacock, 'The image of Charles I As Roman emperor', in Atherton and Sanders (eds), *The 1630s*, pp. 50–73.
78 Barbara Furlotti and Guido Rebecchini, '"Rare and Unique in this World": Mantegna's "Triumph" and the Gonzaga Collection', in *Charles I: King and Collector* (London, 2018), pp. 54–9.
79 Desmond Shawe-Taylor, 'The "Act and Power of a Face": Van Dyck's Royal Portraits', in *Charles I: King and Collector*, pp. 126–47; Per Rumberg and Desmond Shawe-Taylor, '"The Greatest Amateur of Paintings Among the Princes of the World' in *Charles I: King and Collector* (2018), pp. 17–25, at p. 22.
80 David L. Smith, *A History of the Modern British Isles, 1603–1707* (Oxford, 1998), pp. 84–5.
81 *HMC Denbigh MSS*, pp. 8–9.
82 Knowler, *Strafford Letters*, I, p. 344.
83 Quoted in R.A. Stradling, *Philip IV and the Government of Spain, 1621–1665* (Cambridge, 1988), pp. 83–4.
84 Anthony Milton, 'Thomas Wentworth and the Political Thought of the Personal Rule', in J.F. Meritt (ed.), *The Political World of Thomas Wentworth, Earl of Strafford, 1621–1641* (Cambridge, 1996), pp. 133–56.
85 Hugh Kearney, *Strafford in Ireland, 1633–1641: A Study in Absolutism* (Cambridge, 1989), at pp. 73–4.
86 Geoffrey Parker, *Global Crisis: War, Climate Change and Catastrophe in the Seventeenth Century* (New Haven and London, 2014), p. 332.
87 David Stevenson, *The Scottish Revolution: The Triumph of the Covenanters, 1637–1644* (Newton Abbot, 1973), pp. 15–6, 35–41.

118　*Imperial monarch (1629–40)*

88　Laura A.M. Stewart, *Rethinking the Scottish Revolution: Covenanted Scotland, 1637–1651* (Oxford, 2016), pp. 10–1; idem, 'The Political Repercussions of the Five Articles of Perth: A Reassessment of James VI and I's Religious Policies in Scotland', *The Sixteenth Century Journal*, 38 (2007), pp. 1013–36, at pp. 1013–5.

89　D'Ewes, *Autobiography*, II, pp. 100–01.

90　Stevenson, *The Scottish Revolution*, pp. 43–4.

91　Stewart, 'Political Repercussions of the Five Articles of Perth', pp. 1035–6.

92　Stevenson, *Scottish Revolution*, p. 100.

93　Knowler, *Strafford Letters*, II, p. 264.

94　Stevenson, *Scottish Revolution*, p. 100.

95　Mark Kishlansky, 'Charles I: A Case of Mistaken Identity', *Past and Present*, 189 (2005), pp. 41–80, at pp. 74–9.

96　Petrie, *Letters of Charles I*, pp. 106–07.

97　Gilbert Burnet, *The Memoires of the Lives and Actions of James and William, Dukes of Hamilton* (Oxford, 1852), p. 76..

98　Petrie, *Letters of Charles I*, pp. 109–10.

99　See Julian Goodare, in Clive Holmes, Julian Goodare, Richard Cust and Mark Kishlansky, 'Charles I: A Case of Mistaken Identity (with Reply), *Past and* Present, 205 (Nov. 2009), pp. 175–237, at p. 198.

100　Caroline Hibbard, *Charles I and the Popish Plot*, pp. 90–8, 101–02.

101　Hibbard, *Popish Plot*, pp. 99–102.

102　Petrie, *Letters of Charles I*, p. 111.

103　*CSPV, 1636–1639*, 575, 8 Feb. 1638/9 and 576, 11 Feb. 1638/9.

104　Hibbard, *Popish Plot*, pp. 111–2.

105　Tim Harris, 'Charles I and Public Opinion on the Eve of the English Civil War', in Stephen Taylor and Grant Tapsell (eds), *The Nature of the English Revolution Revisited: Essays in Honour of John Morrill* (Woodbridge, 2013), pp. 1–25.

106　*HMC Buccleuch and Queensberry*, I, pp. 276–7, 282, 284.

107　Stevenson, *Scottish Revolution*, pp. 141–2; Burnet, *Memoirs of the Dukes of Hamilton*, pp. 152–3. [II, 191–2, 195].

108　Gardiner, *History of England*, ix, pp. 11, 16, 22; *CSPV, 1636–1639*, p. 504 18 March, 605, at https://www.british-history.ac.uk/cal-state-papers/venice/vol24/pp501–515.

109　John Adamson, 'England Without Cromwell: What if Charles I had avoided the Civil War?' in Niall Ferguson (ed.), *Virtual History: Alternatives and Counterfactuals* (1997?), pp. 91–124, at pp. 98–9.

110　Burnet, *Memoires of the Dukes of Hamilton*, p. 179. [II, 240].

111　*HMC De L'Isle MSS*, p. 182.

112　Quoted in Gardiner, *History of England*, ix, pp. 48–9.

113　Stevenson, *Scottish Revolution*, pp. 162–4, 166.

114　*HMC De L'Isle MSS*, v, p. 201; Gardiner, *History of England*, ix, p. 55.

115　Laud, *Works*, III, p. 233.

4   Royalist-in-chief (1640–42)

Charles's role in the years after 1640 has been characterised as that of a 'party leader': in a decidedly backhanded compliment, Conrad Russell once memorably observed that had Charles been as poor a king as Edward II or Richard II then he would have been deposed but he was ultimately skilled enough to raise a body of supporters and to fight a civil war.[1] Unable to be the unifying figure his office called him to be, he nevertheless became an adept leader of the royalist party, motivating his core supporters and sustaining a loyal and devoted following even in the case of adversity. This portrayal is not without merit and, as will be seen, Charles in these years, with the help of his advisers, crafted an image of himself as the defender of the mixed constitution and an episcopal national Church which appealed to a wide constituency. Yet there was more to royalism than this, and more to Charles's self-fashioning as royalist-in-chief. Demonising his opponents as the rebels and traitors he genuinely considered them to be, Charles was engaged not merely in raising a party and then an army to fight his cause in a civil war, but also maintaining a vision of monarchy in which he sincerely believed and through which he intended to re-unify his broken kingdoms.

Charles's decision to resummon Parliament after an eleven-year interlude was a momentous one. The cost of the impending second campaign against the Scots, of fielding an army of 35,000 foot, together with artillery and a fleet to patrol the northern coasts, was estimated at £1 million per year and, as Northumberland predicted, 'If the Parliament supplie not the King, God only knows how this money will be gotten'.[2] As the Privy Council loan had

120 *Royalist-in-chief (1640–42)*

yielded very little, and the City of London baulked at providing the requested loan of £100,000, Charles's financial hopes and needs really were staked on the meeting of his English Parliament. The king's approach to the assembly had been described by Secretary Windebank the previous December, writing that if it did not fulfil its 'duties' towards the Crown, he would be 'forced contrary to his own inclination to use extraordinary means' rather than 'by the peevishness of some few factious spirits to suffer his state and government to be lost'.[3] The adversarial tone was reminiscent of the words used to the parliaments of 1626 and 1629, and emphasised the extent to which Charles's constitutional attitudes, and those of his advisers, continued to be influenced by those bitter experiences.

Wentworth, newly created Earl of Strafford as well as Lord Lieutenant of Ireland, was the key to the enterprise. He left for Ireland on 16 March, intending to cajole the Irish Parliament to a generous grant towards the king's Scottish war, and thereby present a model for the conduct of its English counterpart. In this he was successful: a Parliament dominated by the native Irish, who naturally feared the triumph of the aggressively anti-Catholic Scots Covenanters, 'opened auspiciously', responding enthusiastically to the demand for four subsidies (around £250,000) and left open the prospect of more.[4] Strafford also anticipated the raising of an Irish army, 9,000 strong, loyal and motivated, which would be deployed against the recalcitrant northern kingdom. Meanwhile, as the elections were held for the parliament in England, Charles came into possession of a letter from the Covenanters to Louis XIII, addressed '*au roi*', which he hoped would serve as positive proof to the Commons that his Scottish enemies were out-and-out traitors.

The Short Parliament

The Parliament was opened on 13 April, after a sermon by Bishop Matthew Wren (another sign of the favour in which he was held during the Personal Rule) by the new Lord Keeper, Sir John Finch, who had replaced the recently deceased Coventry and who had been the speaker of the Commons at the time of the dramatic dissolution of Parliament back in 1629. Since then he had shown himself as a judge to be a reliable upholder of the king's right to

Royalist-in-chief (1640–42)   121

levy Ship Money and so was associated in the minds of many MPs with support for prerogative taxation.

Finch laid it on thick regarding the disobedience of the Scots and the necessity for 'bringing them to their duty by force', placing their rebellion within a British context by suggesting theirs was the one kingdom yet to be brought firmly under royal authority.[5] He promised that if they were prompt in voting the much-needed supply for the war, then their grievances would be redressed, if necessary in a second session of parliament later in the year.[6] At the king's behest, the newly discovered evidence of Covenanter correspondence with Louis XIII was introduced in an attempt to generate hostility to the Scots, and was followed up by Windebank in the Commons three days later, but it met with a decidedly muted response. Already at this early stage in the session, Northumberland wrote that his soundings suggested 'it will be a hard matter to please them. Their jealousies and suspitions appeare upon every occasion, and I feare they will not readily be perswaded to beleeve the faire and gratious promises that are made them by the King'.[7] Likewise the Venetian ambassador reported that 'No one believes that parliament is disposed to give satisfaction before recieving it'.[8] They were to be proved right.

Instead of prompt supply, on 17 April Pym began a lengthy statement of the Commons' grievances, outlining the accumulated resentments of the Personal Rule. He began by complaining of the attack on parliamentary privilege represented by the manner of the dissolution in 1629 and the absence of parliaments in the following years, before proceeding on to innovations in religion, particularly the ceremonialism favoured by Laud and the punishment of those who objected. His main thrust, however, was the political grievances represented by prerogative taxation during the Personal Rule, notably Distraint of Knighthood, Forest Fines, monopolies and, of course, Ship Money, as well as the means used to raise money for the campaigns against the Scots, notably coat and conduct money which, in many quarters, was a notably heavier burden than Ship Money.[9] As hopes for prompt supply receded, on 21 April Charles summoned the two Houses to Whitehall and had Finch remind the Commons of the urgency of the situation holding up the recent Irish Parliament as an example to follow, exactly the model of parliamentary pliability that

122 *Royalist-in-chief (1640–42)*

Strafford had pioneered there since 1634. What followed was an appeal to the Lords, the chamber in which Charles invariably felt better supported. Again at Whitehall, three days later, Charles this time spoke to the Lords alone, expressing his frustration at the dilatoriness of the Commons and their putting grievances before supply, or 'the cart before the horse' as he saw it:

> The necessity of calling this parlement makes me to come this day contrary to expectation. You remember what the Lo[rd] Keeper said concerning the meeting and. . .the H[ouse] of C[ommons] have taken it into their Consideration but they have in a manner concluded the contrary. . .and soe putt the cart before the horse. If they will not trust me first all my business is lost.[10]

The reference to 'trust' was surely significant: the fundamental cause of the growing tensions between Charles and his parliament, or sections of it, was a perceived breakdown of trust on both sides. While Charles increasingly saw the delay in voting him the money with which to wage a second campaign against the Scots as evidence of sympathy, if not collusion, with his Scottish enemies, Pym had in the Commons begun to articulate the fears of those who suspected that the king's disregard for the privileges of parliaments, his support for innovations in the Church and his novel fiscal expedients meant that the constitutional, religious and legal frameworks to which they were attached were not safe in Charles's hands without some formal limitations being imposed upon his prerogative.

Nevertheless, Charles's appeal to the Upper House was superficially effective: by a vote of 61:25 the Lords backed him in a resolution that supply ought to come before the redress of grievances.[11] Yet it proved self-defeating in two ways: first, among those twenty-five opponents were peers such as Brooke, Saye and Sele (who had both refused the army oath at York the previous year), Bedford, Essex and Warwick, who were becoming increasingly consistent critics of the king's policies and would, before long, be engaged in treasonable co-operation with the Scottish Covenanters; second, and more important in the short-term, was the affront given to the Commons in presuming to invite the Lords

Royalist-in-chief (1640–42) 123

to pronounce on supply, a matter traditionally the preserve of the Lower House. This resulted in a formal complaint of breach of privilege and a second vote in the Lords which, while it continued to back the king, did so with a significantly reduced majority.

The final attempt to gain supply from the Commons came on 4 May, when the Secretary of State, Sir Henry Vane the Elder (who had replaced Sir John Coke earlier in the year), offered on the king's behalf that the Crown would be willing to give up Ship Money in return for a grant of 12 subsidies. It became clear, however, that while this gained some support within the chamber, the mood was much more in favour of the abolition of military charges such as coat and conduct money, which many counties found more burdensome, while Pym began to plan to petition the king to come to terms with the Scots, something Charles had absolutely no intention of doing. The well-informed Venetian ambassador was already reporting that Charles 'has intimated clearly that if the members remain so obdurate he will dissolve the assembly without more ado', and that he would 'use the royal authority alone to compel the people to pay the taxes required to meet the expenditure for present emergencies'.[12] As such, with Vane telling him 'plainly, that it was in vain to expect longer, or to make any other overture to them. For no Money wou'd be had against the Scots', Charles called a meeting of the Privy Council at the unusually early hour of 6 o'clock in the morning on 5 May.[13] Having consulted his leading councillors, he decided to dissolve the Parliament, a move supported by all except for Northumberland and Holland. Later that day, a further meeting, this time of the eight-man committee for Scottish Affairs, considered what was to be done next in relation to the continued problem of the Covenanters. This was the occasion on which Strafford famously advised the king that, to 'reduce them by force', he was 'loosed and absolved from all rules of government' and, therefore, 'reduced to extreme necessity. . .everything might be done that power might admit', even bringing over an Irish army 'to reduce this kingdom'. His rationale, clearly designed to appeal to Charles's obsession with his regal dignity, was that otherwise the king risked 'loss of honour and reputation'. Backed by Laud, who argued that supply was due by 'the law of God' and Cottington, who suggested that Charles could

124 Royalist-in-chief (1640–42)

claim to be acting in self-defence, as the Scots were in 'leagues abroad' with foreign powers and 'the Lower House are weary both of King and Church', Strafford finished by telling Charles that 'In reason of state you have power' to raise money and troops on his own prerogative.[14]

It is easy to dismiss these arguments as expressive of paranoia, but it in the context of his bitter disappointment at the conduct of the recent Parliament and the atmosphere of suspicion and mistrust which pervaded it, the stance taken at the committee meeting makes some sense. Charles's perception that, as his kingdom faced a crucial military campaign against a determined foe, his leading subjects were unwilling to support him, in many ways echoing his experience of his early parliaments in 1625, 1626 and 1628–29, left him with few available options than to raise what extra-parliamentary revenue he could and then stake all on a decisive engagement against the Scots. In a letter to Viscount Conway, who would command the royal troops in the campaign against the Scots in the coming war, Secretary Windebank hinted at the increasing suspicion within court circles that members of Parliament were in league with the Scots, liking 'their courses so well that they would contribute nothing towards their suppression'. The king's offer to give up Ship Money 'has left them inexcusable', and so he had no choice but to 'resort to other counsels and ways for the preservation of the monarchy, which if they become more burdensome to them they may thank themselves'. Charles would be resolute in 'pursuing vigorously the war', despite the attempts of 'his ill-affected and refractory subjects' to put obstacles in his way, risking his 'honour and safety both at home and abroad'.[15]

This was borne out by Charles's public justification of the dissolution, written by Lord Keeper Finch, though edited by himself, and a further sign of his willingness to engage in the public-relations battle with his opponents.[16] He began by referring to the legacy of the years 1625–29, a reminder of how formative those were for the king's political consciousness: those 'Discouragements he hath formerly had, by the undutiful and seditious Carriage of divers of the Lower House in preceding Assemblies of Parliaments', which had, he admitted, 'made him averse to those antient and accustomed ways of calling his People together'. In a damning assessment of those early parliaments, which in many

Royalist-in-chief (1640–42) 125

ways summed up his attitude to Parliament as an institution, he blamed their failure on the lack of 'dutiful Expressions towards his Person and Government', instead of which 'they vented their own Malice and Disaffections to the State; and by their subtil and malignant Courses endeavour'd nothing more than to bring into Contempt and Disorder all Government and Magistracy' There, writ large, was the conspiracy theory that had gradually evolved in Charles's mind to explain the failure of parliaments, and which had been substantially reinforced by his recent experience. And yet, he said, he had attributed this misconduct to a minority and so had been prepared to try again in the Short Parliament, because the threat from the Scots was so serious, given that they were, he claimed, in league with foreign powers and aiming at the 'Ruin and Overthrow of this famous Monarchy'. And so when the Commons had put grievances before supply, he had had no choice but to appeal to the Lords. In what amounted to a defence of the Personal Rule, he marveled at the Commons' conduct, given that never 'did this Kingdom ever so flourish in Trade and Commerce, as at this present, or partake of more Peace and Plenty in all kinds whatsoever'. Above all, 'ill affected' elements within the Commons had forgotten the duties of subjects and

> introduced a way of bargaining and contracting with the King; as if nothing ought to be given him by them, but what he should buy and purchase of them, either by quitting somewhat of his Royal Prerogative, or by diminishing and lessening his Revenues,

behaviour that was 'repugnant. . .to the Duty of Subjects'.[17] Familiar, defensive themes were present here, of threats to monarchy and prerogative, and the perversion of otherwise benign constitutional instruments by a wicked minority. Charles appreciated the importance of public justifications for his actions, one might almost say of 'propaganda' in a very early guise, and while it is hard to know how such arguments were received, that he made them and made them in the way that he did, says much for the continuities visible between 1640 and 1629. In addition, his suspicion that his opponents within the Commons were in league with the Scottish rebels was shown by the fact that he had several of them, notably the earl

126   *Royalist-in-chief (1640–42)*

of Warwick, Lord Saye and Sele, Lord Brooke, Sir Walter Earle, John Pym and John Hampden, arrested and their papers taken, partly 'to discover what Scotch papers or remonstrances were in their hands, to see whether any correspondences were held between the Covenanters and any members in Parliament'.[18]

The failure of the Short Parliament was widely seen as a watershed moment in Charles's reign thus far. In some quarters it was speculated 'that England will not see parliaments for a long while, and that the king, throwing aside all respect for the ancient laws, will lay fresh taxes on his people'.[19] Northumberland, who had opposed the dissolution, and whose sister, the countess of Carlisle, thought that his having done so 'will mutch rest in the king's thoughts',[20] expressed his dismay at 'the unhappie Breache of the Parlement', predicting that 'the King intends vigorously to pursue his former Designes' but, the question was, how? After all, in the absence of a parliament, he could not think 'by what Meanes we are certaine to get one Shilling, towards the defraying this great Expence'.[21] One source of revenue was the clergy who were gathered in Convocation which, controversially, continued sitting after the dissolution. The straightforward rationale for this was that the king did not want to lose out on the clergy's grant, secured by Laud on 22 April, of six subsidies over six years, which, while at £20,000 were scarcely comparable to parliamentary subsidies, could hardly be disregarded in the circumstances. Critics of Laud's religious policies, however, saw the extended sitting as much more about passing a controversial new set of Canons which, among other things, upheld the divine-right of kings, the Crown's entitlement to parliamentary supply, and required the swearing of an oath, the infamous 'et cetera' oath, to all clergy to uphold the government of the Church was it currently was, and implying that this meant the Laudian establishment and who knew what else.[22] Laud had been the subject of popular protest in south London on the night of 11–12 May after libels had been posted in the City and a mob of apprentices, the most easily roused and manipulable constituency in early Stuart London, had attacked Lambeth Palace while hunting 'William the Fox', but Laud had escaped to his shelter in his apartment across the river at Whitehall Palace.[23] Showing how seriously Charles took these disturbances, in his own hand he directed the Lieutenant of the Tower, Sir William Balfour, to use

Royalist-in-chief (1640–42) 127

the rack on one of the ring-leaders, John Archer, the last recorded instance of an English monarch authorising the use of torture in the interrogation of a suspect.[24]

The Second Bishops' War

The Crown was now preoccupied other attempts to find sources of funding. So desperate were the Crown's financial straits that a debasement of the currency was even considered.[25] A request for a loan of £200,000 from the City was rejected on the grounds that 'the grant of money ought to depend on the judgement of parliament alone', while the king summoned the mayor and aldermen, four of whom were imprisoned, to upbraid them for refusing to give names of inhabitants of their wards who were wealthy enough to contribute.[26] Strafford explored the possibility of a loan from the Spanish Crown. In December 1639 he had met Philip IV's envoys in London to ask for a loan of £100,000 and now, in May 1640, he sought the larger sum of £300,000 in return for an Anglo-Spanish military alliance against the Dutch and permission for the Spanish to recruit 3,000 men from Ireland to serve in the Spanish armies, while the English navy would likely have been offered for use to keep the Dutch from harassing Spanish supplies to Flanders. Had this come to pass, and combined with the promise of subsidies Strafford expected from the Irish Parliament, this could have funded the subsequent Scottish campaign. The scheme was wrecked, however, by the outbreak of the Catalan Revolt in June, which left Philip without the funds to assist his fellow monarch.[27]

The raising of funds was problem enough, the raising of troops was more difficult still, and more difficult than it had been a year previously. When the Privy Council sent out requests to the lords lieutenant to inform them of the progress in this regard, the response was mixed. In Kent, the earl of Pembroke received a report from his deputy lieutenants that 'in short, we find a confusion; some will not go beyond the colours, others will not go into Scotland. . .They all hope to be relieved by pressed men if they can be found',[28] while in Lincolnshire, the deputy lieutenants complained of 'the mutinous and rebellious ill-affected people already pressed'.[29] Likewise from Wiltshire it was reported that 'we find many [so] obstinate [as] to refuse

128 *Royalist-in-chief (1640–42)*

payment of the coat and conduct-money we are doubtful what mutinous courses these armed men may take', highlighting what a grievance the payment of the extra tax had become.[30] By contrast, the earl of Suffolk reported from Cambridgeshire and Suffolk that 'the men are weekly mustered at their several rendezvous according to my former directions' and that coat and conduct money, 'of which they conceive the whole or most parts levied accordingly. . .they hear not that any do deny payment of it'.[31] Similarly, the earl of Huntingdon and Lord Hastings, Lords Lieutenant of Leicestershire and Rutland, reported that 'all the men are impressed, except two or three, and the conduct money is ready, the coats are made'.[32] The overall commander, the earl of Northumberland, was not optimistic, however: he wrote to Conway to the effect that 'We have engaged the King in an expensive occasion without any certain ways to maintain it',[33] while complaining that the troops 'run away so fast that scarce half the numbers will appear at the rendezvous in the North'.[34] Indeed he went so far as to say that those that remained were so mutinous that they would be 'readier to draw their swords upon their officers than against the Scotts'.[35] Northumberland himself pleaded illness as reason for not joining the army and this, coupled with the stories of indiscipline and disorder on the part of the troops, which had initially led Charles to authorise the imposition of martial law in July, also made him resolve by mid-August to journey north to lead his army in person. Prior to his departure he issued a rallying cry to the lords lieutenant of the northern counties:

> The rebellion in our kingdom of Scotland is now grown to that height that they have not only taken arms and committed sundry acts of hostility against us there, and have likewise levied a powerful and numerous army. . .The great and imminent danger to our person, crowns, and dignity, and to our loving subjects, whose safety and preservation we tender as our own. . .hath drawn a necessity to us to repair in person to our army in the northern parts. . .our true hearted English subjects. . . [will] spare neither their persons nor means to assist us in this common danger, who do and will most cheerfully expose ourself and all we have for their preservation.[36]

Royalist-in-chief (1640–42)   129

Charles's genuine equation of the Scots actions with an assault on his royal dignity, his presentation of this as a just fulfilment of his responsibility to defend his subjects and his determination to crush the rebellion, should not be underestimated.

He arrived at York on 22 August. The king's arrival appeared to have a positive effect and saw more of the Yorkshire gentry flock to the cause, Vane noting with only a touch of hyperbole that 'the person of a King is always worth 20,000 men at a pinch'.[37] Yet the persistent difficulties in assembling and paying for the army suggest that by the time of this second campaign, public support for war against the Scots had lessened considerably, while the generally poor condition of the troops boded ill for the likely success of any military action against the Scots in the field. And so it proved. In response to the Scots' crossing the Tweed into England, a development that had been rumoured in London for several weeks, and determined to protect Newcastle (and with it, London's coal supply) the royal army moved to engage the Scots force at Newburn. The result was a military disaster, the evacuation of Newcastle and its occupation by the Scots.

The Great Council of Peers

On the very same day as the defeat at Newburn, the 28 August, an equally important political development took place: 12 noblemen submitted a petition to the king, demanding the summons of a parliament. While the petition was couched as a response to 'the great distempers and dangers now threatening the Church and State and your royal person', the boldness of the gesture illustrated the extent of disillusionment among a section of the king's leading subjects and their perception of Charles's weakening position, while the complaints listed reflected the increasing coalescence of religious and political grievances. In addition to the 'sundry innovations in matters of religion' (including the recent canons) and the 'great increase of Popery' (notably the inclusion of Catholics in the army), it attacked Ship Money and the recent prosecution in Star Chamber of those sheriffs who refused to collect it, as well as heavy duties on trade. Above all, however, the peers complained of 'The great grief of your subjects by the long intermission of Parliaments' and the abrupt dissolution of the Short Parliament, urging him to

130 Royalist-in-chief (1640–42)

summon a new parliament in order to air grievances and, impose 'condign punishment' upon those councillors responsible.[38] The peers were going to get their chance to present their views to the king in person as Charles had already summoned a Great Council of Peers, an assembly of the nobility, to meet at York the following month, a meeting that would last from 24 September until 28 October.[39] When it met, its first resolution was to recommend the calling of a parliament. Charles knew that, having been beaten by the Scots and being in a weak financial and military position, any parliament would be able to demand significant concessions from him in return for money. There was, as Clarendon later pointed out, an irony to the fact that having sought to justify levying prerogative taxation in the 1630s on the basis of an apparent emergency, the fact of which many doubted, now that there was indisputably a real emergency in the shape of a foreign army occupying his northern territories, Charles was having to appeal to Parliament for funds. Given that he had exhausted every other available avenue, 'it was visible enough he must resign very much to their affections and appetite'.[40] He agreed to the summons, with the writs to be sent out immediately and the assembly to meet on 3 November. This helped to create a positive mood at the opening of the Great Council, and exemplified the skill with which Charles handled the assembly.

In many ways the decision to summon it reflected Charles's medievalism and fitted in with his revival of chivalric tradition during the Personal Rule. Indeed his speech at the opening referenced the historic convention among his predecessors that the peers were summoned when the realm was threatened by invasion.[41] There was some surprise among contemporaries: the earl of Leicester, resident ambassador in Paris, was told the news by a correspondent who suggested (wrongly) that this was 'such a Counsell as hath not been called since K. Edward the first time'.[42] The other issues were the negotiations with the Scots and the need to find money with which to pay the troops until Parliament met. In relation to the first, commissioners were sent to Ripon to negotiate and Charles was eventually persuaded to accept the peace terms, which included payment of £850 per day towards the cost of maintaining the Scottish army occupying northern England. Charles himself, according to one account, told the Council that 'If you raise money

Royalist-in-chief (1640–42) 131

to pay these rebels, it must be besides Parliament', but the problem of raising that money without 'plundering' the already severely burdened northern counties preoccupied the king and the peers in their discussions. Charles sought to use the impending parliament as a prop against the Scottish demands, undertaking to 'To send the rebels word, that they would nothing but with a Parliament'. Those nobles who had been in sympathy with the Scottish rebels, such as Lord Brooke, were unreceptive to suggestions that the Scots be asked to reduce the size of their army in order to reduce the cost, while when Strafford was put on the spot by the earl of Bristol as to the state of the English army, he was apprehensive whether it could effectively resist any but 'small parties', and 'he would not answer the success'.[43] Overtures were made to the City of London to advance money urgently, but it was only persuaded to loan the king £50,000, rather than the hoped-for £200,000, and so the king's financial dependence on the forthcoming Parliament was only increased.

The Long Parliament

Charles continued to negotiate with the Scots and concluded the Treaty of Ripon with them on 21 October, agreeing to pay them £850 per day until formal terms were agreed and confirmed by the English Parliament. This was hugely significant in weakening the king's position: financially beholden to the forthcoming Parliament, he was now unable to dissolve it as he had done the Short Parliament earlier in the year, and any concessions they demanded in return for supply would be almost impossible to decline. He returned from York in time for the opening of Parliament on 3 November and it was noted that he opened it with less ceremony than usual, travelling to the Palace of Westminster by barge.[44]

In accordance with the traditional doctrine of 'evil counsel', it was widely expected that the parliament would quickly turn its attention to attacking Charles's leading advisers. While Charles had resisted the bitter attacks on Buckingham in 1626 and 1628, and on Laud and Weston in 1629, circumstances now were very different. As Northumberland wrote to Leicester, 'such are the kings necessities that he will not be any way able either to defend those men or helpe himself, be their

132 Royalist-in-chief (1640–42)

proceedings never so distasteful to him'.[45] The two chief targets were Strafford and Laud, but it was the former against whom Pym and his allies moved first, testament to the genuine fear with which they regarded him, as the only one of Charles's advisers who might be sufficiently bold, powerful and ruthless to destroy them and perhaps the parliament too by instituting a military government. There were still, after all, troops under arms in Strafford's native Yorkshire, where he had been with them as Lord-General, and there was the army in Ireland which, as his enemies were soon to discover, he had advised could be used to buttress the king's authority in his other kingdoms. While some MPs, such as Sir Edward Dering, wanted to begin with religion, Pym was determined to neutralise Strafford first, and on 11 November he presented charges of high treason against the earl. Laud was impeached on a charge of high treason on 18 December, having been denounced by the Scots as an incendiary, and imprisoned in the Tower, though he would not ultimately stand trial until 1644.[46] Others of Charles's leading councillors, including Lord Keeper Finch, who had been one of the judges supportive of Ship Money in 1638, and Sir Francis Windebank, whose Catholic sympathies made him a prime target, fled to the continent. Furthermore, the first 'Root and Branch' petitions for reform of the Church reached parliament (though they would not be debated until February), demanding a total overhaul of the ecclesiastical establishment. This would prove to be a help to Charles in raising a royalist party around defence of the episcopal Church of England, as would become clear over the following months.

It was in this context, and from a position of political weakness, that Charles made a lengthy speech to the Lords on 25 January 1641. He condemned those who made no distinction 'betwixt reformation and alteration of government', and lamented that 'divine service is irreverently interrupted, petitions tumultuously given, and much of may revenue detained or disputed'. At the same time, and demonstrating both his Elizabethanism and an ability to pitch for the centre ground which would in time serve as the basis for the royalist party he formed in 1642, he undertook to 'reduce all matters of religion an government to what they were in the purest time of Queen Elizabeth's days'. Moving to particulars,

Royalist-in-chief (1640–42)   133

he promised to 'lay down' any 'parts of my revenue [which] shall
be found illegal or grievous to the public', an indication that he
was prepared to make concessions over issues of finance. He was
much less prepared to make concessions, however, over issues of
religion. He conceded that 'bishops may have overstretched their
power, or encroached upon the temporal; which if you find, cor-
rect and reform the above, according to the wisdom of former
times, so far I am with you'. Yet he steadfastly refused to

> consent for the taking away of their voice in parliament,
> which they have so anciently enjoyed, under so many of my
> predecessors, even before the Conquest, and ever since, and
> which I conceive I am bound to maintain, as one of the fun-
> damental institutions of this kingdom.

In resting his case on history and tradition, he was signalling
what would become one of the hallmarks of his appeal for support from among the political nation, but it was also an argument
which fitted comfortably with the medievalism he had repeatedly
demonstrated consistently during the Personal Rule.

In relation to the proposal for more frequent parliaments,
which took legislative shape in the form of the Triennial Bill, he
was more circumspect. He expressed approval of the principle of
more frequent parliaments but was loathe to surrender his freedom to summon parliaments as and when he, as king, thought fit:

> The thing I like; that is to say, to have often parliaments;
> but to give power to sheriffs and constables, and I know not
> whom, to do my office, that I cannot yield unto. . .I am con-
> tent you shall have an act for this purpose, but so reformed, it
> neither trench on mine honour, nor on that inseparable right
> of my crown concerning parliaments. . .I ingenuously confess
> that frequent parliaments is the best means to preserve that
> right understanding between me and my subjects which I so
> heartily desire.[47]

In many ways the speech embodied Charles's strong attachment
to the royal prerogative, his keen sense of honour, but also the
streak of political pragmatism that would be visible time and

134 *Royalist-in-chief (1640–42)*

again in his responses to the political difficulties which he faced over the succeeding months and years. And yet Charles was forced by need for money to consent to the Triennial Bill on 16 February, a hugely significant move which represented the surrender of a crucial prerogative power, the enormity of which was captured by the Venetian ambassador, albeit in hyperbolic fashion, when he suggested that he now had nothing 'left to him but the title and the naked shows of king'.[48]

Charles knew that his position would continue to be weak while the Scottish issue remained unresolved. Hamilton had made significant progress in the negotiations, such that the previous December Charles had confirmed measures passed by the Scottish Parliament and soon the financial terms of the Scots army were settled too. While continuing to seek a more permanent peace settlement, the Scots, conscious of the strength of their position, made it clear that they would not rest until Strafford had been put to death.

In relation to Strafford's fate, the king was determined to save his servant's life. He made a point of attending the trial (sitting behind a screen) in order to demonstrate his support while he even showed willingness to take Strafford's leading opponents such as the Earl of Bedford, Oliver St John, and even John Pym, onto the Privy Council in return for saving the earl's life. Indeed Bedford undertook to try to save Strafford from the death penalty in return for this mooted remodelling of the government.[49] At the same time, the marriage of Charles's daughter, Princess Mary, to the Dutch Prince of Orange, after several months of negotiations, was designed to burnish Charles's Protestant credentials and perhaps make up for his reprieve of the Catholic priest, Goodman, earlier in the year.[50] As the trial of Strafford unfolded and charges of treason proved remarkably difficult to prove against the earl (the effectiveness of his defence being largely due to the fact that he was manifestly not guilty, and his exposure of the trial as the political ploy which it undoubtedly was) the Commons found themselves forced to proceed by attainder. Unfortunately for Charles, all efforts at compromise were foiled by two damaging developments. The first was the revelation of his complicity in the so-called 'Army Plot' (initially two distinct plots which gradually merged), a scheme to rescue Strafford from the Tower

Royalist-in-chief (1640–42) 135

by means of a military coup, one which ultimately collapsed and which discredited him in the eyes of many parliamentarians, who now doubted the genuineness of his willingness to make concessions. Though his direct involvement was difficult to prove, and indeed Charles had initially expressed scepticism about the proposals concocted by several of the queen's counsellors, notably Henry Jermyn, Sir John Suckling and Henry Percy, to take control of the army in the north (possibly placing a sympathetic colonel, George Goring at its head), and bring it south buttress the king's authority, it needed little to substantiate such suspicions in the febrile atmosphere of the capital in April 1641.[51] A letter from Henry Percy, in whose lodgings the conspirators met, to Charles and Henrietta Maria, made it seem 'as if they knew more than was expressed'.[52] After going to the House of Lords on 1 May to appeal in person for Strafford's life, pleading that his conscience would not allow him to sign the bill of attainder for treason and asking that the charge be lessened to one of misdemeanour, a misjudgement that appeared to harden the Lords' resolve, Charles did approve a plot involving one Captain Billingsley to seize control of the Tower with a body of armed men on 3 May, while Suckling had been seen in the City with a troop of sixty soldiers. The lieutenant of the Tower refused to let Billingsley in, and revealed what had happened to the House of Lords, who at that point were considering the attainder against Strafford.[53] The revelation of the king's involvement in what amounted to a military coup to undermine parliamentary proceedings was a red rag to the Puritan bull. In the eyes of Pym and his supporters in the Commons, all of this appeared to vindicate their wildest conspiracy theories about a 'Popish Plot' based on underhand political dealing backed by military force, the alleged popish element only reinforced by the involvement of so many of the queen's counsellors, and by the king's recent pardoning of a Catholic priest, John Goodman, earlier in the year, reputedly at the queen's behest.[54] As such, on the very same day, 3 May, a Protestation was drawn up by the Commons, which required that all adult males take an oath to defend the Protestant religion against the threat of popery, while Pym revelled in outlining the full details of the plot to shocked Commons chamber two days later. Charles was also forced to agree on 10 May to an act

136 Royalist-in-chief (1640–42)

against the dissolution of the Parliament without its own consent, further limiting his freedom of manoeuvre.

The second significant development was the death of the earl of Bedford on 9 May, removing the possibility of the remodelling of the Privy Council in return for sparing Strafford's life. Charles's conscience was genuinely troubled. He had promised Strafford by letter on 23 April, just after the passage of the attainder by the Commons, that 'I cannot satisfy myself in honour or conscience without assuring you. . .that upon the word of a king you shall not suffer in life, honour or fortune', and he now summoned a group of bishops in order to consult them as to whether he could in conscience now renege on this promise.[55] Williams, characteristically, suggested that there was a difference between private and public conscience which would justify his abandonment of the earl. It was not this, however, but the threat of violence from rampaging anti-Straffordian mobs in the capital, who he feared would otherwise 'pull down White-Hall', and in particular the attendant fears for the safety of his wife and children, that prompted Charles to give way and to sign the death warrant, with tears in his eyes, on 10 May.[56] Even now, however, Charles sought to save Strafford's life, by making one last appeal to the Lords, sending the ten-year old Prince of Wales to deliver a message asking for the sentence to be commuted to life imprisonment.[57] The appeal was to no avail, and Strafford was executed on Tower Hill on 12 May. The story that upon learning of his impending execution he uttered a wry comment upon Charles's earlier promise to save him, by quoting from Psalm 146, 'Put not your trust in princes', is almost certainly apocryphal.[58] After an episode which once again revealed the centrality of considerations of honour and conscience to Charles's decision-marking, he never forgot or forgave those who he blamed for bringing him to this, and indeed would express contrition for his actions when he himself stood upon the scaffold eight years later. Aside from the personal torment it had inflicted upon the king, the destruction of Strafford had deprived him of one of his most effective (and feared) political advisers. Indeed, Cardinal Richelieu was supposed to have remarked upon hearing news of Strafford's death that 'The English Nation were so foolish, that they would not let the wisest head among them stand upon its own shoulders'.[59] As a reflection on Charles's own role

Royalist-in-chief (1640–42)   137

in succumbing to the pressure to execute him, however, the most telling assessment was that of Laud, who wrote that Strafford's misfortune was to have 'served a mild and a gracious prince, who knew not how to be, or be made great'.[60]

Following Strafford's demise, Charles gave in between late June and early August to further demands for the dismantling of his prerogative powers. An act was passed to permit the collection of tonnage and poundage but only for a period of two months at a time, thereby further guaranteeing Parliament's continued existence for the purposes of the act's renewal. Further measures included the abolition of the Courts of Star Chamber and High Commission, the Councils of Wales and The North, knighthood and Forest Fines, and Ship Money. He did this reluctantly, particularly his assent to abolish the two prerogative courts, as this amounted to a substantial surrender of royal authority. An even bolder assault on Charles's freedom of action was contained within the Ten Propositions, which Pym introduced into the Commons on 23 June, and which included demands that he get rid of his 'evil counsellors' and replace them with men of whom Parliament approved, and even demanded that the queen be placed under guard and denied the service of British-born priests and that the education of the royal children be entrusted to Protestants.[61] Charles's position must have appeared weak, particularly as Pym began, over the following weeks, to be known by the sobriquet 'King Pym', a further, humiliating sign of the king's dwindling authority.

Charles's visit to Scotland

The real king's more immediate hopes, however, lay in his impending visit to Scotland, which parliament had consistently tried to delay out of fear as to what he might do while so far from their oversight. Their fears were not without foundation, as Charles saw the trip as an opportunity to try to build a royalist party from among the Scottish peerage.[62] He departed for his northern kingdom on 10 August and arrived in Edinburgh four days later to a warm reception, though a sour note was sounded when the Scottish Parliament rejected his offer to perform the traditional ceremony of assent to its recently passed acts by touching

138   *Royalist-in-chief (1640–42)*

them with his sceptre, suggesting rather that these acts were valid without his assent. Equally unwelcome were the lengthy Presbyterian sermons to which he was obliged to listen when he attended church. Ironically he was forced to attend 'prayers and preaching the Scottishe way', featuring 'ex tempore prayers and singeing of psalmes' in St Giles's Kirk, scene of the infamous riots against the Scottish Prayer Book back in 1637.[63] While he was away in Scotland, Charles relied on Sir Edward Nicholas, recently given the signet formerly belonging to Windebank (who had fled to the continent) and soon to replace the latter officially as Secretary of State, for information from London.[64] Nicholas kept up a steady stream of correspondence with the other Secretary of State, Sir Henry Vane, who had accompanied Charles to Scotland, and with the queen, who was one of the commissioners left in charge in London, but was in effect at their head. Vane was able to report in late August that Charles and the Scottish Parliament were well-advanced in their negotiations for a peace treaty, but a less optimistic analysis reached Nicholas from Endymion Porter, who had also joined the king in Scotland. Porter, who had accompanied Charles and Buckingham to Spain in 1623 and whose family had long-standing Hispanophile and Catholic connections (his wife having been converted by the papal agent, George Con, and he himself resisting conversion only for political reasons), complained that in Scotland 'the publick applause opposes monarchie, and I feare that this Iland before it bee long will be a Theater of distractions. . .wee are like to see lamentable times'.[65] In many ways this was a prescient observation.

Charles's efforts to sway certain of the former Covenanters to his side, were undermined by revelations of his involvement in a violent plot to strike against his enemies. The key figure in this was William Murray, a childhood friend of Charles's (though sometimes falsely termed his schoolroom 'whipping boy'), who, like Porter, was a Groom of the Bedchamber who had also travelled to Scotland. Murray, in conjunction with Montrose, then a prisoner in Edinburgh Castle, turned the king against Hamilton, whom he had formerly regarded as his principal servant in Scotland but who had of late been making independent overtures to the leading Covenanters, and organised a plot to arrest the earls of Argyll and Lanark, as well as Hamilton. It was even suggested by one of

Royalist-in-chief (1640–42)   139

Murray's co-conspirators, the Catholic earl of Crawford, that the three earls be killed, possibly by having 'cut their throats in the King's withdrawing chamber'.[66] After one of the soldiers involved in the plot revealed all to General Leslie, this 'Incident' was discovered and Charles, despite denouncing the plot and denying all knowledge of it, suffered huge reputational damage in his northern as well as his southern kingdom. Given Murray's closeness to the king, it seems likely that the latter's denials were disingenuous at best. Even if he did not have any significant part in it, his attempt to prevent the accused from being examined by a Scottish parliamentary committee rather than a full parliament, a point on which he was later forced to concede, did nothing to avert suspicion. Indeed an account attributed to Hamilton's brother, Lord Lanark, reflected the views of many when it said that 'he [the king] injures himself much, in striving to protect those that are accused'.[67] In a further blow to Charles's public image, particularly among those in the south who remembered the scandal of the earlier Army Plots, news of the Incident had reached the English Parliament by 5 November and it further discredited him in their eyes.[68] The breakdown of trust in the king, which was one of the proximate causes of the outbreak of the Civil War in England in 1642, was significantly exacerbated by this episode.

The other consequence of the furore surrounding the Incident was that it succeeded in delaying Charles's return to England, though the king was by now 'as weary of Scotland as he had been impatient to go thither, finding all things proposed to him as to a vanquished person, without consideration of his honour or interest'.[69] His main aim had been to try to build a following, and having failed in his efforts to construct a Scottish royalist party, and having further aroused fears of his untrustworthiness and susceptibility to schemes for the use of military force, his visit had hardly been a success. Meanwhile in England, Parliament had proceeded to chip away at the royal prerogative, such that Henrietta Maria urged Nicholas to issue, in the king's name, a 'declaration against the orders of Parliament which are made without the King'.[70] Increasingly suspicious of what was happening in London in his absence, before Charles left Scotland he was also told that it was being reported in England that he intended to import the Scottish Presbyterian model upon his

140   *Royalist-in-chief (1640–42)*

return, a report which he was swift to deny, urging Nicholas, to quash such rumours by once again proclaiming his attachment to the Church of England as he had inherited it from 'Queen Elizabeth and my father', and his resolution (in the end a prophetic one), 'to live and die in the maintenance of it'.[71] Despite his travails, Charles's return to London was greeted with widespread popular rejoicing; the City put on a grand reception as well as a dinner at Guildhall, the hope being that signs of love and affection towards the king would 'conduce much to settle his affairs', testimony to the fact that at this stage a swift restoration of political stability was eagerly anticipated and expected.[72] In a meeting with his Privy Council on 25 November, Charles tried to accentuate the positive. As the king told them, he had achieved his main objective in journeying north, namely to ratify the treaty and finally bring the Second Bishops' War to an end. He had made concessions, or, as he put it, 'not had his way in everything', but insisted that 'the power he has parted with in Scotland will be no precedent for others to expect [the like] elsewhere'.[73] He proceeded to Hampton Court, where he intended to spend the winter.

The Irish rebellion and the Grand Remonstrance

If Charles thought that his reception upon his return heralded a new atmosphere of deference and co-operation, however, he was to be sadly mistaken. Unfortunately, the main obstacle to the calm and mature resolution of the political tensions between king and parliament was the increasingly lurid news coming out of Ireland, where a rebellion had broken out the previous month. Rumours abounded in London of massacres and atrocities totally out of proportion to the true numbers of killed and wounded, while some alleged that the rebellion had been 'contrived or fomented by the King, or at least by the queen, for the advancement of Popery', the substance of which was only enhanced by the rebels' own claims to be acting with the king's authority and approval against the 'diverse great and heinous affronts' done to them by 'the English Protestants, especially the parliament there'.[74] It was in this context that Pym finally presented the 'Grand Remonstrance' that he had been working on for several weeks. As William Montagu wryly

Royalist-in-chief (1640–42) 141

observed, parliament 'posted as fast to dispatch the Remonstrance as the king did to dispatch his journey but I fear it will not please him so well as the City's entertainment'.[75] The Remonstrance had, however, revealed significant divisions within parliament, passing the Commons by only 11 votes.[76] Hostility to the document was reflected in the speech by Sir Edward Dering, the MP who had introduced the Root and Branch petition the previous year, who said that he 'did not dream that we shou'd remonstrate downward, tell Stories to the People, and talk of the King as of a third Person'.[77] It was finally presented to the king on 1 December at Hampton Court, accompanied by a petition from the Commons which emphasised the threat of popery and its recent manifestation in the Irish rebellion, as well as making demands for the reform of religion and the removal of evil counsellors. Proceeding to substance, the 'root of all this mischief' was alleged to be 'a malignant and pernicious design of subverting the fundamental laws and principles of government', singling out the 'Jesuited Papists' and the 'bishops, and the corrupt part of the clergy', as well as 'councillors and courtiers. . .[who] have engaged themselves to further the interests of some foreign princes or states'.[78]

Charles's response to the petition accompanying the Remonstrance, made on 23 December provides a good indication of his approach to the opposition he now faced, namely a desire to uphold his prerogative while at the same time wrapping himself in the mantle of political and constitutional moderation. For instance, he began by expressing outrage at the 'Disrespect' implied by the publication of the petition (echoing Dering's sentiments), but went on to promise 'all due Satisfaction to the Desires of Our People, in a Parliamentary way', even if the petition itself he regarded as 'Unparliamentary'. Denying that he had employed 'Wicked and Malignant' councillors (otherwise he would have removed them), the lengthiest section of his answer was concerned with religion. He defended the right of bishops to sit in Parliament, 'grounded upon the Fundamental Law of the Kingdom, and Constitution of Parliament', using his opponents' language against them. He cited his abolition of the Court of High Commission as evidence that he had 'moderated' the perceived 'Inordinate Power of the Clergy' of which the petition complained, and then, proceeding to religious doctrine and practice, he promised 'That for any Illegal

142 Royalist-in-chief (1640–42)

Innovations, which may have crept in, We shall willingly concur in the Removal of them', agreeing to consider a 'National synod' to examine the state of the Church should Parliament advise it. He insisted, however, that

> no Church can be found upon the Earth that professeth the true Religion with more Purity of Doctrine than the Church of England doth, nor where the Government and Discipline are jointly more beautified and free from Superstition, then as they are here Established by Law.

That stance upon legality again was clearly designed to appeal to moderate opinion, and he went further by invoking the Elizabethan notion of the via media, promising to defend the Church of England 'not only against all Invasions of Popery, but also from the Irreverence of those many Schismaticks and Separatists, wherewith of late this Kingdom and this City abounds', neatly turning round their complaints by requesting Parliament's 'timely Aid and active Assistance in this'. There may have been more than a hint of irony here, given the Commons' passage of an order for the removal of images in September 1641 which had led to a wave of iconoclasm. In secular matters, he reminded them that he had sacrificed councillors to public trial (i.e. Strafford and Laud) as evidence 'that there is no Man so near unto Us in Place, or Affection, whom We will not leave to the Justice of the Law', but he also insisted upon his freedom to choose his own councillors, as an 'undoubted Right of the Crown of England', the removal of which would be 'to debar Us that Natural Liberty all Freemen have', while promising to choose persons of 'Abilities and Integrity'. Finally, he turned to Ireland, linking the suppression of the rebellion there to 'the Glory of God in the Protestant Profession, the Safety of the British there, Our Honour, and that of the Nation', the latter point an astute linkage of Charles's abiding sense of personal honour with that of the country at large.[79]

More generally, the king's answer embodied his increasingly concerted attempt to pitch for the political and religious centre ground. It is at this point that the emergence of a royalist party can really be identified. Clarendon, who, as Sir Edward Hyde was central to this emerging party, later wrote that when

Royalist-in-chief (1640–42)   143

the king returned to Whitehall from Hampton Court he found 'both his Houses of Parliament of much better temper than they had been', with indignation at the king's treatment having prompted the formation of a group 'zealous for the preservation of the law, the religion, and the true interest of the nation [and] zealous to preserve the King's honour from any indignity and his regal power from violation', all of which would suggest that the line taken by Charles in his answer to the petition was bearing fruit in the growth of support for his new brand of 'constitutional royalism'.[80]

The attempted arrest of the Five Members

Throughout December 1641 London was in a febrile state of protest and tumult, fed above all by the increasing fears of a 'popish plot' induced by the news from Ireland. In the City a new Common Council was elected which was dominated by men sympathetic to Pym and his supporters. Much of the popular unrest surrounded hostility to the episcopate, with crowds of citizens, who had grown 'very tumultuous', being seen to 'flock by troops daily to the Parliament', crying 'No Bishops!'[81] On 27 December the bishops were forcibly prevented by an angry mob from entering Parliament, with John Williams (by now raised to the archbishopric of York) having his robe torn in the scuffle, and together with disturbances in the City this prompted Charles the next day to order the Lord Mayor to 'forthwith cause so many of the train bands to be raised as you shall think fitting, well-armed and provided to supress such tumults and disorders'.[82] The bishops overreached themselves, however: led by Williams, on 30 December they made a formal protest at their exclusion, claiming that any parliamentary business transacted in their absence was invalid. This in turn, being both grist to the mill of anti-episcopalian sentiment in the Commons and an offence to the lay peerage in the Lords as a breach of privilege, led to their impeachment and imprisonment in the Tower.[83] While religion was central to this increasing division, another crucial issue was the control of the militia. As Parliament contemplated its response to the Irish rebellion, the question of who should command the army sent to repress it arose in debate. At this stage, a committee was proposed to prepare a bill with the

144   *Royalist-in-chief (1640–42)*

intention of placing the militia under the control of Parliament, something which alienated those who thought that control of the armed forces naturally belonged to the king.

Meanwhile the queen, Henrietta Maria, became a focal point for protests and was alleged to be behind the Irish rebellion as well as all manner of domestic popish threats. Fearing that his wife would be impeached, Charles decided in the new year to act to pre-empt this: first he offered Pym the chancellorship of the exchequer in the hope of neutralising him, and, when Pym rejected the offer, he instead appointed two of the emerging constitutional royalists, Sir John Culpeper and Viscount Falkland, as Chancellor and Secretary of State respectively. Charles further resolved to strike against his leading opponents, using official parliamentary procedure against them, by issuing articles of impeachment against Pym and others of his leading critics (Holles, Strode, Hampden and Hazelrigg in the Commons, and Viscount Mandeville in the Lords). His case, rooted above all in the treasonable dealings several of these men had had with the Scots during the Covenanter rebellion, was in many ways a strong one.

It is worth considering at this point who was advising Charles in his actions. A key influence on the king was George Digby, recently raised to be Baron Digby of Sherborne, and a son of the earl of Bristol. Digby had once been a strong critic of royal policy: as one of the MPs for Dorset in the early months of the Long Parliament he had helped to manage the impeachment of Strafford and had also strenuously supported the Triennial Bill. When the impeachment failed and the Commons resorted to a bill of attainder, however, Digby became one of its sternest opponents, and henceforth vocal in his support of the king's interests. Elevated to the Lords to avoid censure from the Commons, he grew in influence over the king in the final months of 1641 and, while he had recommended to Charles the appointment Culpeper and Falkland, he also engineered the appointment of Colonel Lunsford as Lieutenant of the Tower, and it was he who would be employed in the attempted coup that followed. Digby, together with the queen, who feared her own potential impeachment, advised that Charles override parliamentary procedures (and privilege) by attempting to arrest his named opponents in Parliament at the head of a body of around 400 armed soldiers, commanded by Lunsford, on

Royalist-in-chief (1640–42) 145

4 January.[84] Although Charles would protest that he was 'more careful to maintain their privileges' than any monarch before him, 'but that in cases of treason no man had privilege', as it turned out the objects of this raid on Parliament had been forewarned and so absented themselves.[85] One account has it that it was the countess of Carlisle, formerly a supporter of Strafford's, but who had since transferred her allegiance to John Pym, who betrayed the plan.[86] Regardless, Charles was faced with the embarrassment of being told by the speaker that he could not reveal the members' whereabouts without the House's permission, and having to walk out of the Commons chamber to cries of 'Privilege'. Digby fled with Colonel Lunsford to meet disbanded army officers in Kingston and, suspected by the Commons of planning a further military coup, he fled abroad to the Netherlands under the king's warrant before the House was able to impeach him the following month. From the continent he corresponded with the king urging him against compromise, and re-joined his master later in the year, becoming a key adviser as one of his secretaries of State (after Falkland's death) during the Civil War.

As with the Army Plots and the Incident in Scotland, both of which represented a similar resort to violence, but on this occasion more immediately and more humiliatingly, Charles was suffering the worst of both worlds: allegations of tyrannical behaviour without the prize for which it was employed. The unpopularity of this abortive coup in London was demonstrated by his experience at Guildhall the following day, where he went to demand the City hand over the five members. He made a speech in which he said he wanted the six men to be handed over but guaranteed them a fair trial, distinguishing between Parliament as a whole and the traitors within it he sought: 'I have and will observe all privileges of Parliament, but no privileges can protect a traitor from a legal trial'.[87] He also professed that he would both 'throw down popery' and 'have the government as formerly in the Church', which would include suppressing separatists.[88] Charles's anti-puritanism had not left him. Though he was feasted by the sheriff, Alderman Garrett, his reception was otherwise lukewarm; the Common Council refused to hand over his enemies and there was a hostile reception from some of the crowds outside with reports of his coach being jostled and jeered. He issued a declaration further defending his

146   *Royalist-in-chief (1640–42)*

actions against the five members, insisting that 'neither our Crown nor our life shall be more dear to us than the constant preservation of all the just liberties of our people and Parliament'.[89] In response to this discovery that he lacked support within the City, and to fears for the safety of his wife and children, which, just as they had over Strafford's fate weighed heavily with him, Charles fled London on 10 January for Hampton Court and then for Windsor. The decision to abandon his capital has subsequently been seen as a huge tactical error, and, given its value as an asset to the parliamentarian side during the ensuing Civil War, it is easy to see why. However, given the hostile atmosphere he was by now facing there, and the success he was to have over the coming months in rallying support elsewhere in the country, it was perhaps not quite such a foolish move as it is sometimes presented.

The construction of a Royalist party

It has now become a commonplace to describe Charles as an effective 'party leader' (though by no means intended as a compliment, and indeed meant partially as an indication of his inadequacies as a king).[90] While this label perhaps understates Charles's aspiration to be a figure of unity and concord (even if he was only intermittently successful at achieving this), it nonetheless does reflect the skill with which he maximised his political capital and institutional assets in order to construct a sizeable and cohesive political and military grouping during the year 1642 and beyond.

He did not abandon conciliation but it was now barbed with the promise of a reckoning. From Windsor on 13 January Charles announced that he would waive proceedings and respect the privileges of Parliament, but that 'when the minds of men were composed, he would proceed against them [the five members] in an unquestionable way'.[91] Having then journeyed to Dover in February with Henrietta Maria to watch her take ship for France (in order to raise funds for the raising of a royalist force in England), he there finally gave his assent to the Bishops' Exclusion Bill, having been persuaded that it would help to preserve the Church or perhaps 'lest the queen should be thought a hindrance of it'.[92] In retrospect, though, it could be seen has having caused some of his natural supporters to doubt his resolve while achieving

Royalist-in-chief (1640–42)   **147**

little to weaken or divide his opponents. Indeed this was clearly the reaction of the queen, who had arrived at The Hague on 25 February. She wrote to the king in early March urging him against any further concession. In a startlingly blunt letter, she chided him for his past displays of weakness:

> A report is current here, that you are returning to London, or near it. I believe nothing of it, and hope that you are more constant in your resolutions; you have already learned to your cost, that want of perseverance in your designs has ruined you. [But] if it be so, adieu; I must pray to God, for assuredly you shall never change my resolution to retire into a convent, for I can never trust myself to those persons who would be your directors, nor to you, since you would have broken your promise to me.[93]

Charles was constant, however, in refusing his assent to the Commons' Militia Bill, which, by depriving him of control of his armed forces, would have effectively rendered him impotent in the face of his adversaries and represented the surrender of perhaps the most fundamental of royal prerogative powers. The Commons decided to pass it as an ordinance, without the royal assent, effectively claiming the power to legislate independently of the king. Charles was indignant, writing to the Lords to the effect that 'no ordinance of Parliament without his assent shall be of force to do anything in it'.[94] He then travelled north, heading for his northern capital, York. At Stamford on 16 March he issued a proclamation to magistrates and judges to enforce the Elizabethan laws against Catholics, thereby aiming to deflect accusations of being soft on popery and further burnish his credentials as the defender of the Church of England by law established. At York on 22 March he was 'received by the people there with demonstrations of the utmost joy', and, perhaps to emphasise the feudal obligations of the aristocracy to their king, he ordered lavish celebrations for the Order of the Garter to take place on St George's Day, which included the admission of the young duke of York to the order, another symbol of the emotional power of hereditary monarchy. When the earls of Essex, Leicester and Holland declined to attend him at York, they had their offices taken away

148   *Royalist-in-chief (1640–42)*

from them, though many other nobles, including some who had formerly 'supported the principles of the most seditious', in the words of the Venetian ambassador, did go to York to show obedience by the end of May.[95] There Charles issued a declaration enjoining noble subscription, and which represented a rallying cry to the peerage:

> Wee do declare, that we will require no obedience from you, but what is warranted by the known law. . .Wee will defend you all and all such that shall refuse any such commands [from Parliament]. . .We will defend the true Protestant religion, establish'd by the laws, the lawfull liberties of the subjects of England, and the just priviledges of all the three Estates of Parliament. . .And wee will not (as is falsely pretended) engage you in any war against the Parliament; except it be for our necessary defence against such, as do insolently invade or attempt against us and our Adherents.[96]

The matter of raising troops and arms was also pressing. From York Charles had written to Lord Keeper Littleton ordering him to prevent the earl of Warwick, one of his long-standing opponents within the peerage, from taking control of the navy as Parliament had instructed, while he also declared his own intention to lead troops to Ireland to crush the rebellion there, fear of which had prompted the passage of the militia ordinance the previous month and which was still the cause of consternation in Parliament at the extent to which this would strengthen the king's military position.[97]

Yet again, however, the queen had to stiffen Charles's resolve. Contemplating the seizure of the arsenal at Hull, the king prevaricated, anxious lest he should be seen as provoking war. Henrietta Maria argued that Charles's dilatoriness was weakening his cause, as 'the Parliament believes you are constantly expecting an accommodation', whereas taking Hull would show 'you in action' and then perhaps 'they would speak after another fashion. For you having Hull is not beginning anything violent, for it is only against the rascal who refuses it to you'. She continued to chide him for delay: if he waited for Parliament to declare war on him, he would forfeit the chance to raise other funds, and be 'reduced to do what the parliament shall please'. In that event,

Royalist-in-chief (1640–42) 149

she reiterated her threat to retire to a nunnery. She also expressed anxiety at rumours reaching her that Charles had promised to surrender control of the militia for one year, insisting that he must remain firm: 'My whole hope lies only in your firmness and constancy and when I hear anything to the contrary, I am mad'.[98] Once again Charles's tendency to waver having begun by appearing firm was infuriating his wife and further demonstrating the weakness of resolution that had contributed to the escalation of the crisis in which he had found himself since 1638.

Further to which, on 22 April Charles reached the gates of Hull, demanding entry in order to take control of the arsenal there. To his consternation the governor, Sir John Hotham, refused to obey, and this prompted a war of words between king and parliament, the former insisting on his right to his own property for the defence of the kingdom, the latter arguing, using a rather strained version of the theory of the king's two bodies, that they better represented the king's interests than Charles himself did. Denying Charles's claim that he had as much right to the towns and magazines of the kingdom as subjects did to their own property, they argued rulers were merely 'entrusted with their kingdoms, and with their towns, and with their people, and with the public treasure of the commonwealth'. Against the king's accusation of treason, they sought to separate his person from his authority, asserting that

> that treason which is against the kingdom is more against the King than that which is against his person because he is King; for that very treason is not treason as it is against him as a man, but as a man that is a king.[99]

Such strained reasoning attests to the increasingly difficulty in reconciling opposition to the king with the claim to be acting in his name against the king himself.

The widening divisions were becoming increasingly apparent. Edward Montagu noted on 8 June that 'the proceedings of the Parliament hath been very little of late, because the differences betwixt the King and them do daily increase'.[100] One source of this increase was the Nineteen Propositions drawn up by the two Houses as the basis for a settlement of their differences, and presented to the

150   *Royalist-in-chief (1640–42)*

king a few days previously. Not only did they require that Charles accept the militia ordinance and other erosions of the prerogative such as the Triennial Act, but he was also required to have his appointments to the Privy Council vetted by Parliament and those existing councillors of whom it disapproved were to be removed. If that were not enough, he was obliged to pardon the five members, enforce the laws against Catholics rigorously, and to allow a reformation of the Church along lines set out by Parliament. Agreeing to these terms would, in Charles's mind, have indeed seen him reduced to the kind of ceremonial 'Doge of Venice' to which he had once feared the Covenanters would lower him. The king once again now took the opportunity to respond to the radical political and religious demands of his parliamentary opponents with a manifesto of moderation. The work this time was done by Falkland and Culpeper, who couched the king's reply as a defence of the traditional, mixed constitution of king, Lords and Commons and of the established Protestant religion as embodied in the Elizabethan settlement. The Commons sat late considering the king's answer, finding the preamble 'full of aspersions'.[101] Intended as a rallying cry to the moderates, it clearly did not appease everyone.

The actual raising of troops now proceeded apace. The king had commanded those nobles who had joined him at York to ignore the parliamentary militia ordinance which had been sent out to lords lieutenant in the counties requiring them to raise forces on behalf of Parliament. Further, Charles had sought to counter Parliament's constitutional innovation with a resort to a medieval device for the raising of troops: Commissions of Array, which had first been employed by Edward I, were issued on 11 June. He subsequently issued a proclamation in defence of this measure, suggesting he was conscious of their perceived novelty. Beginning with a defiant statement that the right to control the militia was 'a most known and undoubted right and prerogative' and one which 'belonged in all times solely to ourself and our progenitors, kings of England', he invoked Magna Carta, an Act of Parliament from the reign of Henry IV, as well as a statute from the reign of Mary Tudor in order to prove that 'commissions of array have frequently been issued for prevention of danger either of enemies abroad or at home'. Adding a hint of menace, anyone disobeying or opposing the commissions was to be accounted

Royalist-in-chief (1640–42)   151

'unworthy of our grace and mercy and such as must expect that justice (how penal or capital soever it be) shall be done upon them according to their demerits'.[102] In any case, Charles was optimistic that the loyalty of his nobility would hold up. He had received his chief legal officer, the Lord Keeper, Littleton, at York on 3 June and repeated orders to him and to the assembled peers not to obey the Parliament's rival commands. The Venetian ambassador suggested that only around 16 peers remained in London to side with Parliament, one of whom, the earl of Holland, failed to get the county of Middlesex to obey the militia ordinance. By contrast, the earl of Derby, premier aristocrat in the north-west, was reported to have taken control of Lancashire for the king by the beginning of July.[103] Meanwhile Parliament had issued a declaration on 9 June announcing that the king, 'seduced by wicked counsel, intends to make war against his Parliament' and condemning his efforts to raise forces. Instead, again relying on a distinction between the king's person and his office, they planned to raise forces 'for the defence of the King and both Houses of Parliament from violence' as well as maintaining both the Protestant religion and 'the King's authority and his person in his royal dignity'. On 12 July, the Earl of Essex was appointed as Captain-General of the forces to defend the parliamentarian cause, which included 'preserving the safety of his Majesty's person'.[104] Charles concentrated his efforts on the midlands and the north: Secretary Nicholas was able to report on 27 July that the king had just returned from Leicestershire where, the previous week he had been received by 10,000 gentry and the 'better sort' who had shown conspicuous obedience, including to the commission of array. On 22 August he raised his standard at Nottingham against 'the late rebellion of the Earl of Essex', emphasising once again a medieval frame of mind to conceive of the impending conflict as in some sense a revolt of a faction of his nobility, something evident as early on as their assistance to the Covenanters.[105] Another telling component was that on Charles's banner was written 'Give Caesar his Due', redolent with various layers of meaning and emblematic of Charles's self-fashioning.[106] Not only did it allude to the Biblical arguments deployed in support of the king's prerogative taxes (from the Forced Loan through to Ship Money) and to the more general debt of obedience owed by subjects to sovereign, but it also picked

152 *Royalist-in-chief (1640–42)*

up on the imperial language and imagery of the Personal Rule from Van Dyck's portrayal of Charles riding through a triumphal arch to the policy of Thorough in Ireland. In many ways it captured so much about Charles's attitude and approach to the crisis he now faced. From Nottingham he issued further proclamations in support of his cause as a defence of the traditional constitution and the established Church, before moving first to Derby then to Chester and then Shrewsbury to join with the 5,000 foot and 400 horse raised for him in Wales and the Borders. With confidence Secretary Nicholas could report that 'the King's army is much increased within these eight days and near 2,000 arms have been hither brought in from this and adjacent counties'.[107] As he consolidated his strength in the most responsive part of his kingdom, he readied himself for the forthcoming hostilities as the head of the royalist party.

Notes

1 Conrad Russell, *The Causes of the English Civil War*, pp. 209–11.
2 *HMC De L'Isle*, v, pp. 219–20.
3 Quoted in Hibbard, *Popish Plot*, pp. 147–8.
4 *CSPV 1640–1642*, p. 35.
5 Ibid., p. 37; *Proceedings of the Short Parliament of 1640*, ed. Esther S. Cope and Willson H. Coates (Camden Fourth Series, London, 1977), pp. 118–9.
6 *CSPV 1640–1642*, p. 37.
7 *HMC De L'Isle*, v, p. 245.
8 *CSPV 1640–1642*, p. 37.
9 Samuel R. Gardiner, *History of England from the Accession of James I to the Outbreak of the Civil War, 1603–1642* (10 vols, 1883–4), ix, pp. 102–05, 115.
10 *Proceedings of the Short Parliament*, pp. 69–70.
11 Gardiner, *History of England*, ix, p. 109.
12 *CSPV 1640–42*, p. 43.
13 William Laud, *History of the Troubles and Tryal of the Most Reverend Father in God, and Blessed Martyr, William Laud, Lord Archbishop of Canterbury* (London, 1695), p. 78.
14 Kenyon, *Stuart Constitution*, pp. 433–4.
15 *CSPD 1640*, pp. 127–8.
16 Louis A. Knafla, 'Finch, John, Baron Finch of Fordwich', *ODNB*.
17 John Rushworth, *Historical Collections of Private Passages of State* (8 vols, 1721), III, pp. 1160–7.
18 *CSPD 1640*, pp. 152–4.

Royalist-in-chief (1640–42) 153

19 *CSPV 1640–1642*, p. 46.
20 *HMC De Lisle*, p. 262
21 *Letters and Memorials of State*, ed. Arthur Collins (2 vols, 1746), II, p. 652.
22 *CSPD 1640*, p. 233.
23 William Laud, *The History of the Troubles and Tryal of the Most Reverend Father in God, and Blessed Martyr, William Laud, Lord Arch-bishop of Canterbury* (1695), p. 79; Laud, *Works*, III, pp. 235–6.
24 Barry Coward and Peter Gaunt (eds), *English Historical Documents, 1603–1660* (London, 2010), p. 1200.
25 *CSPV 1640–1642*, pp. 58–9.
26 Ibid., p. 65; *CSPD 1640*, p. 155; *HMC De Lisle*, p. 267.
27 Parker, *Global Crisis*, p. 340; John Adamson, *The Noble Revolt: The Overthrow of Charles I* (London, 2007), pp. 40–2, 50–1.
28 *CSPD 1640*, p. 148.
29 Ibid., p. 196.
30 Ibid., p. 203.
31 Ibid., p. 204.
32 Ibid., pp. 205–06.
33 Ibid., p. 179.
34 Ibid., pp. 305–06.
35 *HMC De Lisle*, pp. 284–5.
36 *CSPD 1640*, p. 603.
37 *HMC De Lisle*, pp. 284–5.
38 *CSPD 1640*, pp. 639–40.
39 Laud, *Works*, III, p. 237.
40 Edward, earl of Clarendon, *The History of the Rebellion*, ed. W.D. Macray (6 vols, Oxford, 1888)., I, pp. 209–10.
41 *CSPV 1640–42*, p. 86.
42 *HMC De Lisle*, p. 325.
43 Earl of Hardwicke (ed.), *Miscellaneous State Papers, from 1501 to 1726* (2 vols, London, 1778), II, pp. 244, 256, 263, 270, 288.
44 Clarendon, *History of the Rebellion*, I, p. 220. [III. 1].
45 *HMC De Lisle*, p. 343.
46 Laud, *Works*, III, pp. 238–9.
47 Kenyon, *Stuart Constitution*, pp. 19–20.
48 *CSPV 1640–42*, pp. 126–7.
49 Clarendon, *History of the Rebellion*, I, pp. 318–9, 334.
50 *CSPV 1640–42*, pp. 147–8.
51 Gardiner, *History of England*, ix, pp. 316–7.
52 Clarendon, *History of the Rebellion*, pp. 352–3.
53 Gardiner, *History of England*, ix, pp. 348–9.
54 *CSPV 1640–42*, p. 119.
55 Petrie, *Letters of Charles I*, p. 115.
56 Laud, *Works*, III, p. 441.
57 Petrie, *Letters of Charles I*, p. 116.

154 *Royalist-in-chief (1640–42)*

58 Gardiner, *History of England*, ix, p. 368; Adamson, *Noble Revolt*, p. 301.
59 Warwick, *Memoirs*, p. 162.
60 Laud, *Works*, III, p. 443.
61 Gardiner, *History of England*, ix, p. 401.
62 Clarendon, *History of the Rebellion*, pp. 368–9 [III.25].
63 *The Nicholas Papers: Correspondence of Sir Edward Nicholas, Secretary of State, Vol1: 1641–1652*, ed. George F. Warner, Camden Society, New Series, XL (London, 1886), pp. 1, 23–4.
64 Nicholas was reported to be about to succeed Windebank in December 1641. *HMC Buccleuch & Queensberry MSS*, I, p. 288.
65 Ronald G. Asch, 'Porter, Endymion', *ODNB*; *The Nicholas Papers*, p. 45.
66 Austin Woolrych, *Britain in Revolution, 1625–1660* (Oxford, 2002), pp. 190–1; Hardwicke, *Miscellaneous State Papers, from 1501 to 1726* (2 vols, 1778), II, pp. 299–300.
67 *The Nicholas Papers*, pp. 55–8; Hardwicke, *Miscellaneous State Papers*, II, p. 303.
68 Rushworth, *Historical Collections*, IV, p. 421.
69 Clarendon, *History of the Rebellion*, I, 409–12.
70 *Letters of Queen Henrietta Maria, including her Private Correspondence with Charles the First*, ed. Mary Anne Everett Green (London, 1857), p. 45.
71 Petrie, *Letters of Charles I*, p. 117.
72 Laud, *Works*, III, p. 242; *CSPD 1641–1643*, p. 168; *CSPV 1640–1642*, p. 241.
73 *CSPD 1641–1643*, p. 181.
74 Clarendon, *History of the Rebellion*, I, p. 399; Coward and Gaunt, *English Historical Documents*, pp. 494–5.
75 *HMC Denbigh MSS*, p. 286.
76 *CSPSD 1641–1643*, p. 180.
77 Rushworth, *Historical Collections*, IV, p. 425.
78 Kenyon, *Stuart Constitution*, pp. 230–2.
79 *His Majesty's Answer to the Petition which accompanied the Declaration presented to him at Hampton-Court, 1 Decemb. 1641*. Rushworth, *Historical Collections*, IV, pp. 452–3.
80 On which phenomenon, see David L. Smith, *Constitutional Royalism and the Search for Settlement, c. 1640–1642* (Cambridge, 1994).
81 *HMC Buccleuch and Queensberry MSS*, I, p. 287.
82 *CSPD 1641–1643*, p. 214.
83 *HMC MSS Lord Montagu of Beaulieu*, pp. 139–40.
84 On Digby's influence, see Ronald Hutton, 'Digby, George, second earl of Bristol', *ODNB*; *HMC Lord Montagu of Beaulieu*, p. 141.
85 Clarendon, *History of the Rebellion*, I, pp. 442, 482–3.
86 Sir Philip Warwick, *Memoirs*, p. 204.
87 *CSPD 1641–1643*, pp. 241–3.

Royalist-in-chief (1640–42) 155

88 *HMC Lord Montagu of Beaulieu*, p. 141.
89 *CSPD 1641–1643*, p. 246.
90 A term first used by Conrad Russell. See Richard Cust, *Charles I: a Political Life* (2007), pp. 288–9, 471.
91 Clarendon, *History of the Rebellion*, I, p. 520.
92 *HMC Buccleuch and Queensberry*, I, p. 250.
93 *Letters of Queen Henrietta Maria*, pp. 55–6.
94 *HMC Buccleuch and Queensberry*, I, p. 291.
95 *CSPV, 1642–43*, pp. 27, 30, 39, 42, 51, 68–9, 71.
96 Sir Philip Warwick, *Memoir*, pp. 210–1.
97 *HMC Buccleuch and Queensberry*, I, pp. 296–7.
98 *Letters of Queen Henrietta Maria*, pp. 60–61.
99 Kenyon, *The Stuart Constitution*, pp. 242–3, 'Remonstrance of both Houses, in answer to the King's declaration concerning Hull', 26 May 1642.
100 *HMC Buccleuch and Queensberry*, I, p. 304.
101 Ibid.,pp. 305–06.
102 Coward and Gaunt, *English Historical Documents*, pp. 501–3. Charles's proclamation in support of commissions of array, issued at York, 20 June 1642.
103 *CSPV 1642–43*, pp. 71–2, 96.
104 *CSPD 1641–1643*, pp. 337–8, 353.
105 For the significance of which, see J.S.A. Adamson, 'The baronial context of the English Civil War', *Transactions of the Royal Historical Society*, vol. 40 (1990), pp. 93–120, at p. 94.
106 Kishlansky, *Charles I*, p. 84.
107 *CSPD 1641–1643*, pp. 362, 389.

5 Warlord (1642–46)

Charles's conduct of the Civil War highlighted many of his positive as well as negative attributes as king. As has been seen, he showed himself adept at raising and motivating a body of loyal supporters and, with some help from his moderate advisers, successfully presented himself as a defender of the established constitution and Church. He would continue to inspire great loyalty from many of his subjects, whether in the significant financial sacrifices of his wealthier aristocratic backers or the physical trials and risks of fighting for him on the battlefield. Despite lacking formal military training, or indeed experience (aside from observing the enemy through a telescope during the stand-off at Kelso in 1639), he showed himself to be able to inspire and enthuse his troops (notably at Edgehill), to be physically courageous, and to possess some tactical skill, as for instance when in personal command he defeated Essex's army in the Lostwithiel campaign in 1644. Yet he also displayed significant shortcomings as a commander-in-chief. His innate social conservatism frequently led him to a poor choice of commanders based on birth rather than ability, while, when faced with divided counsels and radically conflicting advice he frequently chose the wrong option (notably the disastrous decision to fight at Naseby in June 1645), and himself issued confusing or ambiguous orders, most notoriously his instructions to Prince Rupert in the run up to the battle of Marston Moor. Meanwhile on a political level his efforts to maintain his image of moderation were hampered by the influence of Henrietta Maria and her circle, who opposed efforts at negotiation and pushed military solutions and the prospect of foreign (often Catholic) assistance at every turn.

Warlord (1642–46) 157

A common analysis of the First Civil War contends that Royalist defeat was inevitable given the superiority of Parliament's resources. Some royalists, such as Sir Philip Warwick, argued this case after the war, suggesting that having

> assum'd the sword [the militia] and the purse [notably the City of London], the Navy and the Exchequer, as well as all the strong holds and sea-towns of this trading land; it is no marvell, that at last their arms were prosperous.

A pamphlet purporting to contain two speeches made at a meeting of the Privy Council in Oxford in February 1643 (but whose authenticity remains in doubt) has the Earl of Dorset making a similar case, when urging negotiation on the basis of the parliamentary peace proposals. Dorset argues that, despite having men of courage in the royalist ranks, 'yet have we infinite disadvantages on our side, the parliament having double our number' and similar bravery. Meanwhile, Parliament could replace its losses more easily than the King could, 'they having the most popular part of the kingdom at their devotion, all or most of the cities, considerable towns and ports, together with the mainest pillar of the kingdom's safety, the sea, at their command'. As well as this, 'which is most material of all, an unexhausted Indies of money to pay their soldiers'.[1] In other words, Parliament's resources were just too great, and the King's defeat, if he fought on, inevitable.[2] Yet of course it suited some of those, such as Warwick, coming to terms with defeat to suggest that blame for it lay in an overwhelming material disadvantage. Warwick also conceded that 'it was a great marvell, how the King sometimes came to those fair probabilities of overthrowing them [Parliament]' and, as will be seen, there were various contingent decisions and approaches, for many of which, as commander-in-chief Charles must take overall responsibility, that help to explain the ultimate failure of the Royalist cause.[3]

1642–43: The year of victories

In the wake of the raising of the King's standard at Nottingham, the prospects for the royalist cause did not look promising. To start with

158 *Warlord (1642–46)*

he was short of funds and adopted a tone of desperation in seeking financial assistance. For example, from Derby on 14 September he wrote to Sir Edward Leech, a local landowner and former MP, asking for a loan of £1,000 on the basis that

> though we are unwilling in the least degree to press upon our good subjects, yet we must obey that necessity which compels us in this public distraction, when our money and revenue is seized and detained from us, to lay hold of anything which, with God's blessing, may be a means to preserve this kingdom.[4]

When Prince Rupert, the King's nephew, arrived at Nottingham, he 'found there a very thin and small army and the Foot very meanly armed'. The parliamentarian forces were also larger in number and more quickly in the field to advance against the king, leaving Charles's own position extremely vulnerable and compelling him to move to Shrewsbury in an effort to raise troops from Wales and the north-west.[5] His efforts to recruit soldiers by means of commissions of array met with decidedly mixed results, and even in areas which were subsequently to be seen as 'royalist', such as Shropshire, Worcestershire, Somerset, Dorset and Devon, there was a lack of overt enthusiasm.[6] Many counties exhibited deep divisions, often between leading families vying to take control on behalf of either king or parliament. In Leicestershire the Grey and Hastings families battled for supremacy, while in Warwickshire Lord Brooke acted for Parliament and the earl of Northampton for the king. Even areas of apparent strength started to look less impressive as hostilities opened: the earl of Derby, who was to prove a conspicuously poor commander, controlled most of Lancashire and Cheshire for the king, but failed early on in an attempt to take Manchester; while the marquess of Hertford sought to raise forces for the King in the south-west and managed to hold Sherborne against the earl of Bedford, though Portsmouth was lost to Parliament and, added to Hull and Bristol, this meant that Parliament controlled all of the principal ports at the beginning of the war.[7]

Nevertheless, Charles himself was confident. On 19 September, as he moved between Stafford and Wellington in Shropshire, he issued a rallying cry to his army in which he praised them for their 'courage and resolution' and declared that it was 'Your conscience and your loyalty' which had brought them together to fight 'for your religion, your king, and the laws of the land'. Meanwhile he denounced his enemies as 'traitors, most of them Brownists, Anabaptists and Atheists; such who desire to destroy both Church and State, and who have already condemned you to ruin for being loyal to us'. He finished his preface to the more formal protestation by declaring that 'you will believe you cannot fight in a better quarrel; in which I promise to live and die with you'. Charles's ability to motivate his supporters, while invariably assisted by the public-relations skills of his closest advisers, were considerable. His manifesto then proceeded to present him as the defender of 'the true Reformed Protestant religion established in the Church of England' as well as the 'known laws of the land' and the 'just privileges and freedom of Parliament', all of which fitted with the propaganda drive begun in the previous year and embodied in his answer to Parliament's *Nineteen Propositions*.[8] Yet in some ways this was belied by the desperate need to raise adequate forces, as illustrated by a letter he sent from Shrewsbury on 23 September to his commander in the north of England, the earl of Newcastle:[9]

> This is to tell you that this rebellion is grown to that height, that I must not look what opinion men are who at the time are willing and able to serve me. Therefore I do not only permit, but command you to make use of all my loving subjects' services, without examining their consciences (more than their loyalty to me), as you will find most to conduce to the upholding of my just regal power.[10]

The implication, that Catholics be allowed to serve in the royalist ranks, reflected the urgency of raising viable forces with which to confront the earl of Essex's army as did his reliance on loans from Catholic aristocrats such as the earl of Worcester to pay and equip his troops. It could also be said that the willingness of English Catholics to serve as they did, often at great personal cost, is to their credit, though partly also surely a reflection of their greater terror of a parliamentarian victory. Yet on the very same day as the letter to Newcastle, the king's nephew, Prince Rupert,

160 *Warlord (1642–46)*

won a victory at a small engagement outside Worcester, Powick Bridge, which immediately gave the royalist side heart. Within a few weeks he would have assembled a strong force of around 14,000 men, with more experienced officers and cavalry than his enemies could muster, and be in a position to take the initiative in the early phase of the war.

The king remained at Shrewsbury for some three weeks, and from there Lord Spencer reported that 'The king's condition is much improved of late; his Force increaseth Daily', though he added that this 'increaseth the Insolency of the Papists'.[11] The motivation of those who joined the king inevitably varied. Catholics, terrified of the prospect of a victory for the virulently anti-Catholic parliamentarians, were naturally inclined to support the king, while others for whom the defence of the episcopal Church of England mattered more than political and constitutional niceties tended to be similarly drawn to the royalist side. Then there were others, such as, famously, Sir Edmund Verney, who, while feeling no great affection for the king or his religious policies, nevertheless felt 'that my conscience is only concerned in honour and in gratitude to follow my master. . .[having] eaten his bread, and served him near thirty years, and will not do so base a thing as to forsake him'.[12] Just as a sense of honour was central to Charles's own conduct as king and war-leader, so it was to many of those who followed him. It was also central to the stance taken by Henrietta Maria, whose constant stream of missives from abroad, where she was still trying to raise money and support, emphasised the need for 'Resolution and constancy'. She saw it as her role to stiffen her husband's backbone, worried as she was that Charles's civilian councillors would push him towards compromise and negotiation. She urged him that 'Neither God nor men of honour will abandon you, provided that you do not abandon yourself'.[13] In many ways this was his natural instinct. As he left Shrewsbury and proceeded, via Birmingham, to Meriden Heath, just outside Coventry, it was observed that 'the King is in so good Condition at this Time, that if the Parliament would restore all his Right [and] unless the Parliament will deliver up to a legal Trial, all those Persons named. . .he will not hearken to Peace'. Lord Spencer added that, with money coming in 'beyond Expectation', and the infantry (if not the cavalry), 'reasonably well paid', he

Warlord (1642–46) 161

'never saw the King look better, he is very chearfull, and by the baudy Discourse, I had thought I had bin in the drawing Roome', the latter a reminder that, contrary to widespread perception, Charles did have a lively sense of humour.[14]

As the second son of a father with a horror of violence and an attachment to peace, Charles lacked formal military training or experience. Despite his portrayal by Van Dyck in armour and on horseback, his active participation in warfare had been negligible, delegating military and naval affairs to Buckingham in the early years of his reign and then to Strafford and Arundel in his campaigns against the Scots, though he had faced the enemy at Kelso in the battle that never was during the First Bishops' War. Even so, Charles was expected to cultivate a martial image and to perform a leadership role in the field, hence his stirring injunctions to his troops over the preceding weeks. His overarching military objective was to try to reclaim London, the capital he had abandoned in January, and to do so he would have to confront the main parliamentarian field army led by the earl of Essex. The first major battle of the war took place at Edgehill in Warwickshire on 23 October 1642. Charles would later describe the battle as a victory, referring to 'the defeat of the rebels' in a letter to the earl of Newcastle, but in truth Edgehill was a missed opportunity.[15] The royalists did indeed have the better of the fighting and Charles himself was observed to encourage and cajole his troops, and was reported as having 'performed all his duties with prudence and also with spirit', giving 'proofs of great courage and established the devotion of his troops to his cause', while 'more than once, he placed himself, without reservation, at the head of his army'.[16] Unfortunately the royalist cavalry, who would become notorious for their indiscipline, rather spoiled the chance of total victory by charging after the enemy baggage train and failing to return in sufficient numbers to support their infantry. As a result the parliamentarians held firm and the battle ended in a draw. Charles himself might be criticised for not ensuring greater co-ordination between infantry and cavalry, and for allowing Rupert too much independence of command. Indeed the earl of Lindsey, who should have commanded in the field, refused to do so if the cavalry was exempt from his overall direction (part of a wider dispute as to whether the royalist army

162 *Warlord (1642–46)*

should deploy in the Dutch or the Swedish style) and so Charles placed Lord Ruthven, the Earl of Forth, in charge instead.[17] Whatever the qualities of personal bravery and encouragement of his men he had displayed, Charles had also shown his lack of experience as a commander-in-chief.

Nevertheless, after Edgehill the royalists enjoyed the advantage of the road open to London and, had they seized it with sufficient vigour, might have achieved a swift and outright victory. The king's enemies were chastened and 'the consternation was very great at London and in the two Houses'.[18] Instead, despite Rupert's entreaties to him at Oxford, which became his wartime capital, Charles refused to allow his nephew to attempt to storm London with his cavalry. Given their inferiority of numbers, as well as the strength of the city's fortifications, his caution was understandable. As representatives of Parliament explored peace terms, there followed a further missed opportunity, as Charles, while at Reading, attempted to negotiate the return of Windsor Castle, but Rupert's assault on Brentford on 12 November was perceived by the parliamentarians as bad faith while negotiations were ongoing. The royalist forces were then halted by the London trained bands at Turnham Green a day later and so perhaps the king's best chance to recapture his capital city was lost, though given that his forces were outnumbered by the 24,000 parliamentarians, perhaps by as much as two-to-one, his decision to turn back at this stage was surely the right one.[19] He still very much had the upper hand, however, and when Parliament requested that he return to London without troops to resume his position, his response was scathing, scorning the 'traitorous endeavours of those desperate men [who] could not snatch the crown from his head, it being defended by the providence of God and the affections and loyalty of his good subjects'.[20]

While some fighting continued during November and December in the south, notably the royalist capture of Marlborough in Wiltshire and Waller's advances in Sussex and Hampshire, the main armies of both sides retired into winter quarters and did not resume campaigning until late the following spring. The length of the pause in the fighting was mainly due to the time it took the munitions convoy supplied by Henrietta Maria's landing in Yorkshire reaching Oxford to resupply the king, while in any case

Warlord (1642–46) 163

informal truces obtained while the peace negotiations ran their desultory course.[21]

The Oxford Propositions

Parliament's peace proposals were put to the king at Oxford at the beginning of February 1643. They required Charles to disband his armies and 'return to your parliament', surrender 'delinquents' (i.e. his main supporters) to trial by Parliament, agree to the wholesale reform of the Church, including the abolition of episcopacy, ally more closely with foreign Protestant states, notably the United Provinces, and 'settle the militia' as agreed by both Houses of Parliament, which implied at least partial loss of his control of the armed forces. Charles himself, particularly given the favourable course of his war effort so far, was in no mood to surrender on one of his red lines, the government of the Church by bishops, nor indeed on the giving-up of his supporters to parliamentarian retribution. Indeed it is doubtful whether Charles ever seriously entertained the possibility of a peace at this stage, given that the military advantage so clearly lay with him. His first answer to the proposals, on 4 February, expressed doubt in his opponents' sincerity in seeking peace, while he claimed to have been 'always for peace', and signalling his dislike of the terms, suggested he would nevertheless 'take as much honey out of the gall as I can'. His second and more detailed answer, communicated via the earl of Holland to the Lords two days later, conveyed his displeasure, suggesting that the terms 'appear very derogatory from, and destructive to, his just power and prerogative, and no way beneficial to his subjects' and was unable to resist a barb: 'how unparliamentary it is, by arms to require new laws, all the world may judge'. He instead offered his own counter-propositions, which required: the immediate restoration of his revenue, towns, magazines and ships currently held by Parliament; the renunciation of published material contrary to his rights and powers; the annulment of all illegal exactions, imprisonments and confiscations; in relation to religion (perhaps unsurprisingly his most combative proposal), a bill 'for the better preserving of the Book of Common Prayer from the scorn and violence of brownists, Anabaptists, and other sectaries'; a promise that those of his followers exempt from

164 *Warlord (1642–46)*

pardon be tried by their peers; and finally that the cessation of arms precede any treaty, thereby refusing Parliament's request that he entrust himself to its protection. He ended by warning that if Parliament refused these terms, the 'the guilt of the blood which will be shed, and the desolation which must follow, will be upon the heads of the refusers'.[22] These were terms which he must have known his opponents would never countenance. His wife stiffened his resolve by letter: she told him forthrightly 'Never allow your army to be disbanded till it is ended, and never let there be a peace until that [the Parliament] be put an end to', and threatened that she herself (who had recently landed in Yorkshire with a cargo of arms) would flee back to France if he agreed to it. Little could he know it but the notion of 'blood guilt' would eventually come back to haunt the king.[23] At this stage, however, Charles was still positive, confident in his military strength and contemptuous of his adversaries.

1643–44: The search for resources and allies

When the conflict did resume, the royalist war effort enjoyed notable successes over the summer of 1643, with news reaching the king of the victory of Newcastle in Yorkshire at Adwalton Moor and in the southwest a resounding defeat of the parliamentarian forces by Wilmot at Roundway Down on 13 July, one of the most conclusive battlefield victories of the entire war. The king himself, when apprised of the threat posed by Waller to the royalist position in the West, had despatched Wilmot and then Byron to reinforce him, to take the fight to the parliamentarians and so might claim some credit for the victory.[24] The culmination of this period of royalist success, however, was the capture of Bristol, arguably England's second city and certainly its premier western port, later that month, cementing royalist control of Somerset and the south-west and prompting the king to assemble his Privy Council at Oxford 'to consider how this great blessing in war might be applied to the procuring of a happy peace'. Charles's rationale in investing so much in the seizure of England's second port is clearly understandable, though Clarendon, with the benefit of hindsight, suggested that the elation at the seizure of Bristol among some of the royalist courtiers was excessive.[25] It was

Warlord (1642–46) 165

achieved at a high price, with heavy royalist casualties, Hopton (who was still recovering from wounds received at Lansdown when a power-wagon exploded very near him) going so far as to describe it as an 'unhappy assault'. Indeed Hopton had cause to be somewhat sour as, though he had been promised the governorship of Bristol by the marquess of Hertford, Charles decided to give the post to Rupert and so found himself having to write an emollient letter to his disappointed general, assuring him that 'wee have bin so far from intending you thereby any disrespect' and emphasising how much he was valued as commander of the western army, such 'that we can thinke of noe man fitter for that command then yourself'. Charles's insecurity is perhaps revealed, however, by his asking further that Hopton 'make knowen to all your friends the true value wee sett upon you, and hinder any misinterpritations, that malitious people may sett upon this accion of ours', though perhaps this is also an indication of the propensity towards factional division within the royalist side.[26] Charles's decisions regarding appointments within the royalist armies can be called into question, and this instance, of his favouring his nephew over perhaps his competent commander, is an instance of questionable man-management.

In any case the euphoria was quickly checked as first the king's efforts to take Gloucester, which was, Spencer reported, 'in the Opinion of most very unadvised' (including the queen), and with it secure Wales and the north, were defeated by a relieving force under Essex.[27] Nevertheless, despite the disappointment at Gloucester, the king now exploited the opportunity to force a decisive encounter with the main parliamentarian army. Even the great Victorian historian, S.R. Gardiner, no defender of Charles, suggested that this ploy demonstrated that Charles was 'a strategist of no ordinary skill'.[28] As it turned out, his attempt to smash Essex's army at Newbury on 20 September (and at which Lord Spencer, by now Earl of Sunderland, as well as Lord Falkland, Secretary of State, were killed) also met with failure.[29] The battle itself was a stalemate – 'night parted them when nothing else could' – but Charles's losses, particularly of officers, were heavier, and he was unable to prevent Essex from returning to London, where he was joyously received.[30] True to his reputation for chivalry and his desire to appear scrupulous in his observance of the laws and customs of war at this

166   *Warlord (1642–46)*

stage in the conflict, Charles wrote to the mayor of Newbury on the day after the battle to instruct him to give medical attention to the wounded parliamentarian soldiers, even 'though they be rebels, and deserve the punishment of traitors'.[31] As the campaigning season of 1643 came to an end, the royalists were still in the ascendant but were beginning to count the cost of missed opportunities. Both sides sought help from outside in order to tip the balance and the king's political acumen was now to be put to the test.

The king had established an alternative government and his wartime capital at Oxford. Historians have often caricatured this as a hotbed of factional division between 'moderates' and 'ultras' or civilians and soldiers, but, as recent work by David Scott has shown, this is an oversimplification.[32] The royalist court and councils were indeed beset with 'discomposures, jealousies, and disgusts' which 'produced great inconveniences' though these were less consistent and more fluid than is often thought.[33] Nevertheless the politics of the royalist court at Oxford mattered a huge amount and had a significant impact upon the way in which the royalist war effort was conducted. Charles had established a council of war before he had left York the previous year and it comprised both civilian and military councillors, though it never entirely eclipsed the Privy Council.[34] Nor, however, did it supplant the more informal means of influencing the king found at court, and the importance of the bedchamber should not be overlooked, notably, for instance, in influencing the king's decision to discontinue negotiations over the Oxford Propositions in the spring of 1643. Prince Rupert, his nephew, as has been seen, quickly acquired huge influence over military affairs given his experience of continental warfare and his early successes in the field. His 'sharpnes of temper of body, and uncommunicableness in society or council' did, however, cause tensions with some of the king's civilian councillors, who in any case distrusted 'such downright soldiers. . .lest he should be too apt to prolong the warr' while they sought opportunities for a negotiated settlement.[35] Among the civilians, figures such as Endymion Porter and John Ashburnham, both grooms of the bedchamber, were singled out by contemporaries as particularly influential, and Ashburnham in particular was noted by Hyde (while allowing for the latter's resentment of a perceived threat to his own influence), as having 'so great an interest in the affections of his master, and

Warlord (1642–46) 167

so great an influence upon his counsels and resolutions, that he could not be ignorant of anything that moved him'.[36] As a courtier 'whom the king loved, and trusted very much', Ashburnham was also used by privy councillors such as Culpeper in order to transmit advice to the king.[37] The adviser who proved perhaps most influential at Charles's wartime court, however, was one who straddled both court and council, Lord Digby, who as Secretary of State from 1643 (replacing Falkland after the latter's death in battle at Newbury) enjoyed close formal political contact with the king but who also had significant influence within the royal bedchamber. Archbishop Williams wrote to Ormond in 1643 to the effect that the king 'out of his too much goodness and piety' was 'so obnoxious to be shaken and removed, by variety of counsels, out of any settled resolution', a clear criticism of Charles's handling of the politics of his court, but added that 'The Lord Digby is like to be the only man of affairs upon whom your Excellency can place your rule'.[38] Digby would prove a divisive figure, clashing notably with Rupert in 1644–45, and this was a rivalry which significantly damaged the royalist cause in the latter part of the war.

The role of Henrietta Maria was also hugely significant. She returned to England in February 1643, weathering storms and evading parliamentarian ships to land at Bridlington in Yorkshire, though, forced to shelter with the earl of Newcastle at York for several weeks, she did not arrive in Oxford until July.[39] Prior to her return her letters to the king from the continent had been almost constant and upon her arrival at court she proceeded to dominate the king's counsels at Oxford (until her departure a year later), suspicious that Rupert was supplanting her.[40] She made use of her trusted messengers, such as Henry Jermyn and Wat Montagu, to enhance her influence even when away from court, and this caused tensions with Charles's own preferred advisers. In 1644 it was reported that Prince Rupert and others of the king's councillors lacked 'any efficacy, but are cyphers, without Lord Jermine'.[41] The queen nevertheless appeared to be conscious of how negatively her hard-line advice was perceived in some quarters: when urging the king in May 1643 to declare the Westminster Parliament not to be a 'free parliament', she said 'Let it be done before I arrive, or else it will be said that it is I who am always for all sorts of violent measures'.[42]

168   *Warlord (1642–46)*

Managing the sometimes fractious politics of the royal court while also overseeing the war effort was a challenge and not one to which Charles always rose. When, in the wake of the run of royalist victories, the earls of Holland and Bedford defected from Parliament to the court at Oxford, Charles was lukewarm in his reception of them, such was his obsession with honour and loyalty. He could not bring himself to trust these erstwhile opponents, and, in relation to Holland, 'was always upon his guard towards him, and did not, in truth, abate any thing of his former rigour or prejudice'.[43] When Holland sought the return of his post as groom of the stool, Charles denied it him, having already promised it to the marquess of Hertford, prompting Holland to slope back to Westminster. Arguably his treatment put other potential defectors off from switching sides and so may have damaged the efforts of some of his councillors, notably Hyde, to present the King as an emollient and unifying figure.[44]

One significant source of contention within the royalist ranks from 1643 onwards was the matter of foreign alliances. The queen and those around her were anxious to exploit any opportunities for financial and military help from abroad, even if from Catholic countries, while Hyde and others of Charles's moderate councillors were more cautious of the risks to the king's reputation if he was seen to fight with the help of foreign Catholic money and arms. The first attempt to exploit assistance from overseas came from Ireland, where the Catholic insurgents had by now captured most of the kingdom. Charles was in correspondence with the marquess of Ormond, the commander of the royal forces in Ireland, from January 1643 onwards regarding a possible truce with the rebels. He refused to countenance the toleration of the Catholic religion which the latter wanted, recognising that it 'would give such an advantage to the King's enemies here, that it may not be granted without apparent danger of ruin to the King's affairs', but by April he was authorising Ormond to

> agree with them for a present cessation of arms for one year, in as advantageous and beneficial a manner as you in your wisdom and good affection to us. . .shall conceive to be for our honour. . .the particulars whereof we cannot prescribe unto you.

Warlord (1642–46) 169

While he regretted that it 'be not so formally legal as I could wish', it was urgent that Ormond then bring the Irish army to Chester to assist in his northern campaigns, and a cessation along the lines Charles had suggested was agreed in September 1643.[45] This made sense on grounds of political expediency, though Hyde commented that 'The King well foresaw to what reproaches he should object himself by entering into any treaty with those rebels', particularly given the ubiquity of the rumours that he himself had instigated, or been a party to, the rebellion of 1641, and it made for useful propaganda for Parliament, which put 'all the sharp glosses upon it to his majesty's dishonour that can be imagined'.[46] The Irish troops ultimately proved of less use than Charles had hoped, with Parliament's control of the seas ensuring that they could only reach England in dribs and drabs and, inauspiciously, a large number of the first detachment to make it across the Irish Sea to Cheshire were part of a force under Lord Byron defeated by Sir Thomas Fairfax at Nantwich, and at which 1,500 Royalist prisoners were taken. Other hopes for foreign help were mainly directed towards France: following the deaths in December 1642 of Richelieu, whose hostility to England dated back to Charles's assistance to the Huguenots in 1627–28 and who had encouraged the Scots Covenanters in their revolt in 1639–40, and of Louis XIII (Henrietta Maria's brother) in May 1643, Charles hoped the new regime of Anne of Austria and Cardinal Mazarin might prove more receptive. The early signs were positive, as Lord Goring reported from his mission to Paris that Mazarin 'gave me all assurance that words could testify, of real and speedy assistance from hence', though the caveat that this was only as far as their other military commitments (notably in Germany) would permit, proved prescient.[47] As it turned out, and despite repeated requests for aid over the next few years, which increased in urgency as the royalist war effort declined in 1645–46, the French proved reluctant to intervene directly.

The royalist war effort also underwent significant reorganisation during 1643. Previously Charles had appointed local magnates to command the various regions under royalist control, a reflection of his faith in the social prestige of the traditional aristocracy. As Sarah Poynting has highlighted from a detailed

170 *Warlord (1642–46)*

study of Charles's correspondence, this even extended to a decidedly deferential tone to particular noble commanders in his correspondence. For example he wrote to the earl of Newcastle at the end of 1642, in the context of ongoing negotiations with Parliament: 'I promise you to be weary of a treaty as you can desire. I pray you let me hear from you as oft as you may'.[48] However, other than Newcastle, who won control over most of Yorkshire and northern Lincolnshire during the spring of 1643, these aristocratic commanders generally fared poorly. Even the marquess of Hertford, who ostensibly achieved success in the south-west, began to alienate many of his soldiers and the local population, while the credit for his victories was arguably due to his subordinates, Sir Ralph Hopton and Prince Maurice, Rupert's brother. The earl of Derby had shown himself an incompetent field commander through his loss of much of the north-west and his retreat to the Isle of Man (leaving his formidable countess commanding the defence of the family seat, Lathom House); while the commanders in Wales and the Marches, Lords Herbert (son of the marquess of Worcester), Capel (chosen for his noted wealth) and Carberry all demonstrated ineptitude borne of inexperience, Capel losing much of Cheshire and Shropshire, areas of huge importance to the king. As such, he now rectified his initial error by replacing Hertford with Maurice in July and Capel with Rupert in December, before augmenting Rupert's command the following April by the addition of those formerly under Herbert and Carberry. To these changes in personnel, an eventual realisation on Charles's part of the need to appoint commanders of merit rather than merely social status, were added important administrative and financial changes.

To pay for these various regional armies, the king had to resort to more radical fiscal expedients. Parliament, driven on by Pym, had been much quicker to implement new modes of taxation coupled with significant administrative reorganisation, establishing county committees to administer the areas it controlled and committees of sequestration to seize and exploit captured royalist estates, while also devising a new direct tax, the assessment, and an excise tax on consumption, both of which proved hugely efficient. Charles was initially reluctant to risk undermining his claims to be defending traditional practices and customs but the

Warlord (1642–46) 171

pressures of paying for troops and supplies left him no choice but to emulate his enemies' innovations. In July 1643 he had begun to establish committees in each shire to exploit captured parliamentarian property and in November he authorised local gentry to conscript men for service in the various royalist armies. As a further indication of the extent to which Charles sought to replicate the traditional structures of civil government in a wartime context, towards the end of 1643 a Parliament was summoned to meet at Oxford in January 1644 and Charles used this to legitimate the new financial system, including the new excise tax on merchandise, which he then had men in the wealthier English counties collect from May 1644 onwards.[49]

1644: Marston Moor

With his newly instituted taxes and the backing of the Oxford Parliament, which he soon after prorogued until October, following its rather irritating request for guarantees that these exactions would not continue into peacetime, Charles had to respond to a more challenging military situation in 1644. The alliance signed by the Parliamentarians and the Scots the previous autumn laid his control of the north of England vulnerable to the invading Scottish troops and prompted him to listen to overtures from dissident Scots for the raising of a Scottish royalist army under the earl of Montrose. These efforts would eventually bear fruit later in the year but in the short-term the biggest threat was to the north of England where an increasingly embattled marquess of Newcastle was confronting the Scots and by the end of March was sending urgent appeals to Rupert to come to his aid.

Meanwhile in the south, the royalist war effort started to go awry and Charles's choice of military commanders was once again in question. In March Charles tried to strengthen Hopton's cause by sending him another 800 cavalry and 1,200 infantry from Oxford, but also sent his commander-in-chief, the earl of Forth (recently created earl of Brentford in the English peerage), and whether this or Hopton's earlier injury after the explosion of a powder-wagon at Lansdowne (on 5 July 1643) disrupted the campaign, the result was a decisive defeat at Cheriton on 29 March 1644.[50] Charles himself set out from Oxford early in April, for a

172 *Warlord (1642–46)*

campaign which would highlight both his defects and virtues as a commander. With Oxford increasingly vulnerable to parliamentarian attack and Henrietta Maria now with child, the queen was destined for Exeter where she might thereafter embark for France to seek more foreign assistance for her husband. Charles meanwhile, conscious of his weaker position, hoped to separate Essex's army from that of Waller and deal with it separately to give himself the best chance of success.[51] Following several weeks of shadow-boxing and intermittent returns to Oxford, Charles left his capital again early in June and headed east towards Buckingham, seemingly threatening the undefended Eastern Association. He finally encountered Waller at Cropredy Bridge on 29 June. Waller made a slight mess of his bold initial attack, and Charles had to send his own life guard to help Wilmot drive the parliamentarians back.[52] Seemingly in a strong position, however, the king mismanaged what was a fragmented engagement, declining to attack when the odds were in his favour and then losing confidence in 'the temper of his own army', allowed the opportunity to pass, before somewhat optimistically offering terms to Waller which he, despite having suffered the heavier losses, unsurprisingly explained that he had no power to accept.[53] Worse than this, however, Charles would soon after hear news of a catastrophic defeat in the north, for which, despite his being several hundred miles away, the king could take a significant amount of blame. Two weeks before he had written to Rupert, buoyed by successful assaults on Bolton and Liverpool, with his orders for a northern campaign to assist an increasingly desperate Newcastle. Yet the orders were confusing to say the least:

> If York be lost, I shall esteem my crown little less, unless supported by your sudden march to me, and a miraculous conquest in the South, before the effects of the northern power can be found here; but if York be relieved, and you beat the rebel armies of both kingdoms which are before it, then, but otherwise not, may possibly make a shift (upon the defensive) to spin out time, until you come to assist me: wherefore I command and conjure you, by the duty and affection which I know you bear me, that (all new enterprises laid aside) you immediately march (according to your first intention) with all

Warlord (1642–46) 173

> your force to the relief of York; but if that be either lost, or
> have freed themselves from the besiegers, or that for want of
> powder you cannot undertake that work, you immediately
> march with your whole strength to Worcester to assist me
> and my army; without which, or your having relieved York
> by beating the Scots, all the successes you can afterwards
> have most infallibly will be useless to me.[54]

It is possible of course that the ambiguous instruction was given
in the King's name but was authored by one of his councillors, most likely 'the unfortunate pen of the Lord Digby'. It
was unclear here precisely how much autonomy Rupert had
in making decisions about whether to engage the Scots outside
York, 'whether his directions were positive as he said; or an
intimation only, that the king could have wish'd it, as the Lord
Digby said'.[55] Rupert himself seems to have been anxious about
the politics behind the instruction, with Archbishop Williams
recounting that, following his taking of Liverpool, Rupert had
written to him from Warrington to say that he was 'gone in full
speed to relieve the Marquess of Newcastle at York; if the ill-
conduct of the Court-army do not call him thither'. Nevertheless
it seems that the prince interpreted the letter as a definite command to seek a decisive showdown with the enemy.[56] Following
an impressively rapid march across the Pennines, Rupert
reached York on 1 July and, despite Newcastle's entreaties to
the contrary, the tiredness of his troops and the fact that he
was significantly outnumbered (28,000 men to 18,000) he gave
battle the following day. While on the right the royalist forces
had the better of the fighting, the opposite was true on the left
and as night dawned it was clear that the battle had ended in
a heavy defeat, for which in many quarters the 'fault is laid
wholly upon the M. of Newcastle'. Additionally the loss of York
soon after and eventually the whole of the north of England, left
the situation of the surviving royalist garrisons there as, in the
words of one royalist soldier, 'like monitors in schools observe
faults only in the absence of the master'. While fighting a battle
against such odds and with so much at stake was certainly in
keeping with Rupert's impetuous and aggressive character, it
seems hard to doubt that the frantic tone of Charles's orders,

174 *Warlord (1642–46)*

issued without knowing the extent of the parliamentarian advantage and couched in such ambiguous fashion, contributed to an avoidable disaster. If Digby was to blame then this can only have added to the growing animus between him and Rupert, who was obliged to retreat with what little of his army remained (around 6,000 horse and dragoons) to Chester, from where it was reported that the 'disorderly retreat' of the royalist forces from Marston Moor, combined with the poor conduct of the cavalry, had caused 'some scandal and much prejudice to his Majesty's affairs here, where neutrality is epidemical', none of which augured well for the royalist war effort.[57]

And yet, hearing news of this calamity only spurred Charles on to force his own encounter with Essex's army, one that would have a much happier outcome for the king and allow him to demonstrate some skill as a field commander. Leaving Exeter on 27 July, the king moved into Cornwall with an army of 16,000 men and established a base at Lostwithiel and by the end of the following month had managed to trap Essex's forces there: '. . .his majesty himself from his new fort. . .sent a company of musketeers, who quickly beat those that were left and thereby preserved the bridge; over which the King presently marched to overtake the rear of the army'.[58] A large portion of Essex's infantry, along with plentiful muskets, pikes, canon and gunpowder were captured, though perhaps unwisely, if once again chivalrously, Charles allowed the enemy troops to depart unmolested, having left their arms and ammunition behind (and at least half of them rejoined the parliamentarian armies) while Essex himself suffered the ignominy of escaping to Plymouth in a fishing boat.[59] The king now sought to relieve Donnington Castle and Basing House before returning to Oxford, and this led to a further confrontation with the parliamentarian forces at the second battle of Newbury on 27 October. Once again the fighting was inconclusive, though while the losses were higher on Parliament's side, it was Charles who 'quitted the field, and marched away in the night' and so Parliament claimed victory. Nevertheless, Charles was able to relieve Donnington (a success which prompted a seismic row on the parliamentarian side between the earl of Manchester and Oliver Cromwell) before moving to Marlborough and then into winter quarters at Oxford, where he was able to inspect the new fortifications erected around his capital in his absence.[60]

The end of the campaigning season of 1644 left the king in a strangely ambiguous position. Despite the heavy defeat at Marston Moor, and the ensuing loss of control of the north, he himself had won a notable victory over the main parliamentarian army in the south at Lostwithiel and avoided defeat at Newbury while keeping his army intact. The consoling letter he had Nicholas write in his name to the marquess of Newcastle at the end of November, in which, despite the 'misfortune of our forces in the North', he reassured him of his gracious 'memory of your merit' and of his 'affection and courage' for one who had 'assisted us in the time of our greatest necessity and troubles' was a further sign, perhaps, of Charles's deference towards this pre-eminent aristocrat, though Newcastle's flight to the continent was probably not the response he was looking for.[61] Nevertheless news from Scotland was also giving encouragement, the earl of Antrim having landed in the Highlands in late September where Montrose's royalist activities were soon causing significant problems for Parliament's Scottish allies. In other ways Charles's position was weaker than before: having lost the north he was deprived of one of his most fertile recruiting grounds which would make it harder in future to replenish his losses. In addition, political tensions on the royalist side became more apparent at Oxford during the winter lull in the fighting. Rupert, who had rejoined the king in the south and been placed in overall command of the royalist forces, was 'so great an enemy to Digby and Culpeper, who were only present in debates of the war with the officers, that he crossed all they proposed', while the elevation of Culpeper, who was widely disliked within the army, to a barony only fed petty jealousies surrounding patronage and preferment. Though the circumstances of wartime tension and privation, combined with the temperamental characters of some of those involved, no doubt exacerbated these tensions, it is hard to argue with Hyde's verdict that Charles himself was culpable for not having 'been solicitous enough to preserve the respect due to it [the army], in which he lost his own dignity'.[62]

1645: The turn of the tide

At the beginning of 1645, and as if conscious of the increasing precariousness of his position, Charles pursued plans to recruit

176 *Warlord (1642–46)*

further troops from Ireland. The need was certainly urgent, as Charles's commander in the north, Lord Byron, had written to Ormond the previous November complaining of the delay in seeking help from the Irish, urging that 'If the King thinks to reap any benefit by the Irish peace, I wish he would conclude it quickly that we might have some timely assistance hence'.[63] The king himself wrote to Ormond on 9 January, urging that 'I must again remind you to press the Irish for their speedy assistance to me here, and their friends in Scotland', requesting specifically that 'the Irish would send as great a body as they can to land about Cumberland; which will put those northern counties into a brave condition', though he was conscious of the logistical difficulties, 'the rebels being masters of the seas'. He even told Ormond to promise on his behalf a suspension of the penal laws against Catholics in Ireland, going so far as to undertake 'that when the Irish give me that assistance, which they have promised, for the suppressing of this rebellion, and I shall be restored to my rights, then I will consent to the repeal of them by a law'. He reiterated to Ormond that he was 'to conclude a peace with the Irish, whatever it cost, so that [i.e. so long as] my Protestant subjects there may be secured, and my regal authority preserved' and again said that even if it involved a temporary suspension of Poynings' Law (the law dating to the reign of Henry VII which required all Irish legislation to be approved first by the English Privy Council) and the 'taking away of the penal laws against Papists by a law will do it', then 'I shall not think it a hard bargain'.[64] This was telling testimony of Charles's willingness to be pragmatic and flexible in the cause of political expediency, and indeed was a sign of Charles's considerable shortage of troops following his loss of the north. Nevertheless this willingness to relax the anti-Catholic legislative framework would, when it became known, play into the hands of those of his enemies who claimed the king was not to be trusted when it came to resisting the Catholic threat.

These undertakings would also suggest that Charles expected little from the new peace overtures he was making to Parliament, this time via the duke of Richmond and the earl of Southampton. Parliament was in any case unreceptive, and demonstrated as much by proceeding to execute Archbishop Laud on 10 January 1645, though not before Laud had written to Hyde and had him solicit

Warlord (1642–46) 177

from Charles a pardon under the Great Seal, an empty gesture if ever there was one given the king's powerlessness to prevent the sentence from being carried out.[65] Indeed Laud's rather pathetic request highlights the extent to which, in his case, Charles's famed loyalty to his servants was less than usually apparent. That said, that Charles did feel some indignation at the decision to execute his archbishop is suggested by his mention of it in a letter to Henrietta Maria a few days later, when, in the context of arguing that 'Straffords innocent blood hath beene one of the great causes of Gods just judgements upon this Nation by a furious civill warre', he added that 'now this last crying blood [i.e. Laud's]' would be the source of divine retribution upon his enemies.[66] The lingering and deeply felt conviction that he had been forced into the judicial murder of an innocent man when he had consented to Strafford's death would remain with him until his own execution four years later.

Nevertheless, Parliament proceeded to draw up a more detailed set of peace proposals, the Uxbridge Propositions, which were presented to the king later in the month. Their most stringent terms related to religion, and included the abolition of bishops, deans and chapters, obliged Charles to take the Covenant and sought to replace the Book of Common Prayer with a Presbyterian Directory of Public Worship. They also included a lengthy list of all of Charles's leading supporters who were to be excluded from any pardon. Of less immediate political import but more chilling in intent, the propositions also stipulated that Catholic children were to be taken away from their parents and educated by Protestants.[67] Charles's commissioners at Uxbridge were unimpressed, and suggested that Parliament 'insisted only on such particulars as were against law and the established government of the kingdom'.[68] Charles's initial answer on 21 January returned to the same six points that he had advanced in response to the Oxford Propositions two years previously, the only difference being an undertaking to summon a national synod to help resolve religious matters.[69] Charles nevertheless appreciated the need to be seen to be amenable to negotiation (even while he was scheming to bring over more Irish troops) in order to win the ongoing public-relations battle. He wrote to Secretary Nicholas two weeks later urging him 'to try if the Rebells will be content that all the treaty be layed open; I meane that the disagreeing to one or more articles (on either side)

178 *Warlord (1642–46)*

hinder not the treating upon all the rest'. His aim, he revealed, was to show that 'if the Rebelles shall not consent to this free dealing (when we desire it) it will clearly appeare to all the world, that they are ashamed to manifest theire intentions, and that we doe avow ours'.[70] Yet, in a sign that Charles had not lost his contempt for his opponents and determination to assert his authority, he also suggested, in annotations he made to a letter from Nicholas, that behind the scenes the commissioners should play hard-ball and 'put them in mynde that they were arrant Rebelles & that their end must be damnation, ruine, and infamy, except they repented'. In a further missive to Nicholas a few days later, he expressed some disquiet at the commissioners' approach to negotiations, suggesting that they had appeared willing to concede too much too soon, particularly over the militia. Above all he worried about the longer-term consequences of surrendering the Crown's control of the armed forces:

> And for the tyme, I should thinke a much shorter tyme than three years were sufficient, to secure the performance of conditions, whereas one cannot tell how any men may be tempted, being so long settled in a manner in the Regall Power, to fynde excuses & delayes for the parting with it, besides the people being once inewred to that way of gouernement may not be so willing to returne to the owld way, as believing it less subjecting than Monarchicall. . .[71]

This anxiety that any concessions regarding the royal monopoly of legitimate force would risk bequeathing an irrevocably weakened Crown to his successor would become a lingering preoccupation and reflected Charles's persistent concern to uphold what he could of those prerogatives he regarded as essential to the discharge of his functions as king. At the same time, Charles was becoming frustrated with his Oxford Parliament, thinking it too keen on negotiations. In a letter to Henrietta Maria he lamented the 'base and mutinous motions' of 'our Mongrell Parliament here', an indication of a further continuity in Charles's political thinking, suggesting as it does the kind of contempt for parliamentary interference in the formation of royal policy that is reminiscent of his attitude towards the parliaments of the later 1620s.[72]

Warlord (1642–46) 179

Again the peace negotiations delayed the resumption of the fighting, and while there was positive news from Scotland, as Montrose had won a run of victories at Inverlochy and Auldearn, the king's military position in England did not appear to improve in the early months of 1645 after a surprise attack by local parliamentarian forces seized Shrewsbury towards the end of February. Nor indeed did the factional squabbles abate at court: it was reported in April that 'At Oxon we are at great faction' with 'the Marquess of Hertford and all the rest against Lord Digby and Cottington'. Rupert, who was described as 'in with the Marquess of Hertford', was regarded as increasingly influential, such that it was being said that 'All is governed by P. Rupert who grows a great courtier'. The same correspondent added ominously that 'Certainly the Lord Digby loves him not'. The fault line was over whether to seek accommodation with Parliament, as Hertford and now Rupert advocated, or to pursue foreign alliances with the Irish and on the continent, the position taken by Digby and Cottington (who, having resigned and retired to his property in Wiltshire in 1641, had joined the king at Oxford in 1643 and now served as Lord Treasurer).[73] This would be the basis of the political machinations at Oxford for the next few months. Amidst all this, Charles perhaps then welcomed the renewal of campaigning, which began in earnest in the spring, and would finally produce a decisive engagement. Charles moved north to assist his forces in and around Chester, though he wrote en route from Staffordshire that he was 'not yet resolued whether to goe afterward'.[74] This changed when he heard that Oxford was under siege by Fairfax's parliamentarian forces from 22 May and he decided to try to lure them away from his capital by an offensive in the midlands. At the very end of the month, on the night of 30–31 May, he stormed and sacked Leicester with some brutality, causing 'a wonderful impression of terror upon the hearts of those at Westminster'.[75] It was at this point that Charles made a fateful decision. Angry at the council of war's attempt to advise on military strategy from afar, when he himself was at the head of his army in the field, Charles took the advice of Digby, who urged him to go on the front foot against the only recently formed 'New Noddle' (as he derisively called Parliament's New Model Army), rather than that of Rupert, who urged caution and preferred a northward advance

180 *Warlord (1642–46)*

to attack the Scots in Yorkshire. As a parliamentarian officer wrote later, had Charles gone north from Leicester, or towards Wales, and delayed facing the parliamentarian army, he might have consolidated this success, but seeking battle with the New Model so soon was to prove an error.

When he faced the parliamentarians at Naseby in Northamptonshire on 14 June, Charles was outnumbered by perhaps 14,000 to 10,000 and, while the royalist cavalry on the right under Rupert had the better of the contest with the parliamentarian horse under Ireton, on the left the outcome was reversed, with Cromwell's disciplined cavalry beating the royalists under Langdale. While Rupert's men charged on in search of plunder, Cromwell regrouped his horsemen to rejoin the fight, helping tip the balance of the infantry contest in favour of Parliament. Charles himself, watching the battle with the royalist reserve, 'was even upon the point of charging the enemy, in the head of his guards', a death or glory charge which would have imperilled his life and with it the entire royalist cause. As such one of his attendants, the earl of Cornewarth, with some boldness, asked him in astonishment 'will you go upon your death in an instant?', put his hand on the bridle of the king's horse and turned it around, preventing Charles from carrying out a foolish, if brave, cavalry charge, but also serving as an unwitting signal for the rest of the royalist army to give up the fight and retreat.[76] Charles's baggage train was also captured by the parliamentarians and so they gained possession of his correspondence, which they gleefully published later in the year in order to reveal the King's dealings with foreign powers and his willingness to make concessions to Roman Catholics. The very title, *The King's Cabinet Opened*, conveyed the sense that the world was now given access to the sovereign's secretive and, by implication, underhand schemes. Some of it was indeed damning: for instance, a letter to Henrietta Maria from March 1645 which authorised her 'to promise in my name. . .that I will take away all the penal laws against the Roman Catholicks in England as soon as God shall inable me to do it', as well as his correspondence with Ormond empowering him to promise the same for the Catholics in Ireland as an incentive to a military alliance with the Confederates. The 'Annotations' or commentary supplied by the parliamentary editors (Henry Parker among them) sought to present Charles as submissive to his Catholic queen's

Warlord (1642–46) 181

wishes ('It is plaine, here, first, that the Kings Counsels are wholly managed by the Queen') as well as soft on Catholicism ('he prostitutes his pardon and grace to the Irish Rebels') and insincere in his participation in treaty negotiations ('He in shew seekes Treaties, and wins upon the People by that shew, yet chooses such Commissioners, and bindes them up with such instructions, that all accommodation is impossible').[77] The damaging nature of these revelations served to further discredit Charles in the eyes of those of his subjects for whom Catholicism and deceit were two sides of the same coin and marked a distinct triumph for Parliament in the public-relations battle.

Following his defeat Charles was determined nevertheless not to yield, and indeed his apparent optimism in the face of this adversity is striking. He accelerated his efforts to bring further Irish forces over to England, writing again to Ormond four days after Naseby to urge that 'The late misfortune which I have had makes the Irish assistance more necessary than before' but expressing the hope that if such help could arrive within the next two months,

> my last loss would be soon forgotten, and likewise it may (by the grace of God) put such a turn to my affairs, as to make me in a far better condition before winter than I have been at any time since this rebellion began.[78]

Incredible as it may seem, early the following month he was writing to Secretary Nicholas to play up the 'so good hopes of my Welsh levies that I doubt not but (by the grace of God) to be in the head of a greater Army within this two monthes, than any I haue seene this yeare'.[79] Though that this was more propaganda for the consumption of the royalist court than a true reflection of the situation in Wales is suggested by Hyde's later recollection that having reached Raglan Castle Charles found 'there was little probability of raising an army in those parts, where all men grew less affected or more frightened'.[80] Yet this optimism was not to last long. On 10 July came news of the decisive defeat of the western royalist army at Langport. Charles's subsequent correspondence with Ormond assumed a more desperate tone, lamenting that 'It hath pleased God, by many successive misfortunes, to reduce my affairs, of late, from a very prosperous condition to so low an

182 *Warlord (1642–46)*

ebb as to be a perfect trial of all men's integrity to me'. One man who retained Charles's trust was Digby, who was commended to Ormond as the key intermediary in the negotiations for the projected alliance with the Irish, Charles using him to communicate the details to Ormond, but himself restating his willingness to allow the Irish Catholics some freedom of worship 'if there be no other impediment for obtaining a peace' with the Confederates. He was still, however, unwilling to make it a general toleration, and invoked, as he would time and again in his extremity, his conscience as reason no 'ever to abandon my religion and particularly either to English or Irish rebels', a subtle and increasingly strained position which was to make life extremely difficult for Ormond.[81]

Charles's more realistic appraisal of the military situation led him to fall back upon defiance. Having reached Cardiff early in late July, he issued a more indignant statement of his stubborn refusal to give in, asking Nicholas to let his other councillors know of his determination 'that no distresse of fortune whatsoeuer shall euer make me (by the grace of God) in any thing receade from those grounds I laid downe to you [the Uxbridge commissioners]'.[82] When he reached Doncaster in mid-August he was positive about 'my present condition, wch considering what it was at the beginning of this monthe, is now (I thanke God) miraculously good', particularly thanks to the response of the Yorkshire gentry, and asked Nicholas to recruit and amass supplies and men at Oxford for the campaigning the following year.[83] It obviously behoved the king to seek to sustain morale by denying that all was lost, but at the same time he was still boosted by news of Montrose's continued successes in Scotland (at Alford, near Aberdeen, in July and at Kilsyth in August) and possessed reserves of fortitude which might call into question the inevitability of royalist defeat, in the king's mind at least, even after Naseby.

Yet at the same time, Charles held fast to his 'grounds', those principles he had articulated during the abortive Uxbridge negotiations and which would remain his red lines during the coming years. In a striking letter to Rupert, who was increasingly urging accommodation, he wrote of his continued 'defence of my religion, crown, and friends' and acknowledged that while 'speaking either as a mere soldier, or statesman, I must say that there is no probability but of my ruin', nevertheless 'as a Christian, I must tell you, that God will not

Warlord (1642–46) **183**

suffer rebels to prosper, or this cause to be overthrown'.[84] Charles's confidence in divine favour for his cause rivalled that of any puritan on the other side.[85] Three weeks later (and in a sign of how much this was a war of rapid movement), he wrote from Huntingdon to Secretary Nicholas on 25 August in a similar vein, insisting on his refusal to compromise his central precepts:

> . . .let my condition be neuer so low, my successes neuer so ill, I resolue. . .neuer to yeald up this Church to the gouernement of Papists, Presbiterians, or Independents, nor to injure my successors, by lessening the Crowen of that ecclesiasticall & military power wch my predecessors left me, nor forsake my frends, much lesse to let them suffer when I doe not.[86]

His equation of the Presbyterians and Independents with 'Papists' is indicative of his long-held view that these opponents of episcopacy were as dangerous, if not more so, to royal power and right religion as the Catholics were, and reflects the anti-Puritanism which he and Laud had enunciated so trenchantly in the 1620s. Charles's optimism and defiance were to take a crushing blow, however, with news of the fall of Bristol on 10 September. This was a huge disappointment to Charles, who had asked Rupert to hold the city (and vital port) at all costs. Culpeper reported that the 'unexpected loss' had 'plunged these parts into such a desperate gulf of despair', while Charles branded the surrender 'strange and most inexcusable' and claimed that it had 'given me more grief than any misfortune since this damnable rebellion'.[87] His letter to Rupert suggested that he saw it as a kind of betrayal by one 'so near to me as you are both in blood and friendship', a typically Caroline trope, and he reminded his nephew of his undertaking in August to hold the city for four months, when he had now not managed to hold it for four days.[88] Charles instructed Nicholas to arrange the dismissal of his nephew from his commission on pain of imprisonment if he refused to surrender it. Perhaps the most damning line, though surely written in burning anger so soon after receiving the bad news from Bristol, was found in the postscript, where he asked Nicholas to tell Prince Charles that he would 'less grieve to hear that he is knocked on the head than that he should do so mean an action

184   *Warlord (1642–46)*

as is the rendering of Bristol castle and fort upon the terms it was'.[89] All of this, of course, was a gift to Digby, who lost no time in milking this misfortune to blacken the name and reputation of his adversary. He wrote to Nicholas soon afterwards and laid the doom on thick: 'Never was there soe sadd a relapse into a desperate condicion from soe happy a recovery as the prodigious surrender of Bristoll'.[90] Indeed Digby was later described as being 'generally believed to be the sole cause of revoking the prince his commission'.[91] While Naseby has so often been seen as the decisive engagement of the war which finally doomed the royalist cause, it was the loss of Bristol two months later which really set the seal upon the king's defeat. The symbolism of the loss of England's second major port, and with it the gateway to the south-west as well as its proximity to traditionally royalist Wales, combined with the acrimonious dismissal of Rupert, the king's nephew and erstwhile commander of the royalist armies, left Charles with few realistic hopes of victory. True to form, believing in the justice of his cause and refusing to contemplate surrender until all else was lost, he now placed all of his hopes in the Irish alliance, while some of his courtiers advocated equally radical overtures to the Scottish Covenanters.

1645–46: Endgame

It was at this point that Digby, who increasingly favoured more radical expedients to try to turn the war back in the king's favour, began to push the case even more strenuously for the use of Irish Catholic forces. Indeed in a striking demonstration of the multiple uses to which the three-kingdoms paradigm could be put, he sought to stiffen Ormond's resolve by suggesting that 'no man can think England divided (though the major part against the King) able to resist Scotland and Ireland entire for him, with any considerable party here'.[92] Digby, who wrote to Nicholas two days later of Charles's plan to break through to Newark and then to move north to join up with Montrose, was clearly unaware that the Scottish royalist forces had suffered a crushing defeat at the battle of Philiphaugh on 13 September.[93] Nevertheless, he was already proposing an alliance with the Covenanters themselves, under which at the very least Charles would pledge not to alter

Warlord (1642–46) 185

the Presbyterian system of Church government in Scotland and that when the time came to settle the government of the English Church by means of a 'neutral synod', there would be nothing prejudicial to the Scots.[94]

This more radical initiative, which Charles openly admitted was 'first proposed to him by the Queen his dear Consort', would likely have involved the King making more extensive concessions to Presbyterianism, and as a consequence was hugely divisive at the royalist court.[95] Digby and Culpeper, supported by Henrietta Maria from afar and by her courtiers such as Henry Jermyn, championed it as a justifiable expedient for Charles to reclaim the throne at all costs, a concession that could always be revoked once he had been restored to the plenitude of his regal power; but Hyde, Richmond and the other more moderate councillors, saw such a compromise as likely to damage Charles's consistent efforts to present himself as the defender of the Elizabethan Church settlement. This fed into the broader competing visions of monarchy held by the two camps: the one, possibly influenced by the neo-Tacitean ideas associated with Justus Lipsius which had also heavily influenced Stafford, and which justified the use of force to uphold royal authority at all costs; the other prioritising the maintenance of the love of the King's subjects as the bedrock of his power.[96] Culpeper wrote to Ashburnham, whose closeness to the king as a gentleman of the bedchamber made him a vital intermediary, urging him 'again most earnestly to intreat you to bend all your wits to advance the Scottish treaty', which he labelled 'the only way left to save the Crown and three kingdoms'. The rationale was straightforward desperation, the realisation now among many of the king's party being stark that 'the King's condition is such that less than a miracle cannot save him without a treaty'. In a blunt statement of the position taken by the advocates of the Covenanter alliance, Culpeper finished by saying: 'All that they [the Covenanters] can ask, or the King part with, is a trifle in respect of the price of a Crown'.

The French also urged a deal with the Scots through their envoy Montreuil, including that Charles should promise to introduce Presbyterianism in England. Charles was clearly uneasy with doing deals with Scottish Presbyterians, and, given his long-standing antipathy to those he regarded as enemies

186 *Warlord (1642–46)*

of monarchy and whose rebellion had begun the sequence of events leading to Civil War, it is perhaps not surprising. His principled attachment to the institution of episcopacy, seen in his responses to parliament's peace proposals at Oxford and Uxbridge, was also central to this reluctance to treat. He therefore maintained that the introduction of Presbyterianism into England was 'that which he cannot with the safety of his conscience condescend unto', the most he was prepared to concede being the freedom of Scots resident in England to worship as Presbyterians. This was despite an increasing sense that military help from France might be his 'best security'. Nevertheless, he continued to tell the French that 'no necessity shall compel me to do that which I have refused to do at the desire of two Queens [Henrietta Maria and the French Queen Regent, Anne of Austria]'.[97] Indeed Charles was frustrated with the French, perceiving that Cardinal Mazarin, to whom Anne of Austria entrusted the running of her regency government, was not serious about offering genuine help. He suggested to his wife that 'if Cardinal Mazarin were but half so kind to us as he professes to be, it would be not great difficulty for him to secure our weekly intelligence'. In heartfelt correspondence with the queen, who continued to urge the abandonment of his bishops as the price for an alliance with the Covenanters, Charles outlined his conscientious determination to hold fast to his view of the English Church, stating that he 'I am of thy opinion to a tittle in everything else', but that 'if I should give way as is desired, here would be no Church, and by no human probability ever to be recovered; so that besides the obligation of mine oath, I know nothing to be an higher point of conscience'.[98] More than this, he expressed the belief that 'my yielding this is a sin of the highest nature'. Meanwhile, his attempts during January to arrange to visit Westminster to negotiate a personal treaty with his opponents were rebuffed by Parliament.[99]

Yet his Irish schemes were fraught with problems, many of which reflect flaws in Charles's approach to these diplomatic initiatives. He managed to alienate his chief Irish royalist representative, Ormond, by issuing a rival commission to the earl of Glamorgan, son of the Catholic marquess of Worcester, to negotiate a treaty with the Confederates and empowered him to make

Warlord (1642–46) 187

significant religious concessions. Charles was forced to seek to placate Ormond in January 1646, pleading that 'upon the word of a Christian, I never intended that Glamorgan should treat anything without your approbation, much less without your knowledge', insisting that 'besides the injury to you, I was always diffident of his judgement', which was hardly an endorsement of his earlier strategy, and blamed Glamorgan for exceeding his instructions.[100] This was disingenuous of Charles. Digby, who had control of the king's Irish policy, had told Hyde earlier in the month of his hopes for Glamorgan's expedition, leading 'great forces. . .already in readiness for England'.[101] Now that revelations of the scheme had offended Ormond, Charles was distancing himself from the young aristocrat. Glamorgan might, therefore, have reflected, along with Rupert and, to an extent Laud, that there were limits to Charles's much-vaunted obsession with personal loyalty.

As the royalist cause suffered further reverses in the early months of 1646, Charles sought to ensure that the Prince of Wales did not fall into parliamentarian hands. He had already, in September of the previous year, instructed Culpeper to make arrangements for the prince's removal to his mother's charge in France, though he specified very clearly that he was to be subject to the queen in everything except religion, aware as he no doubt was of Henrietta Maria's desire to see their children converted to the Catholic faith.[102] In February 1646 Charles was still saying that his son was not to be sent overseas until there was an 'evident necessity', that is, an imminent likelihood of his falling into rebel hands. By the spring, however, he was instructing Henrietta Maria to invite their son to join her in France, an action which ran contrary to Hyde's advice, who, mindful as ever of the need for the king to appear conscious of his subjects' anti-Catholic sensitivities, thought it better for the prince to remain on English soil, in Jersey, rather than risk the opprobrium resulting from seeking shelter with the acme of Catholic absolutism.[103] In this, and not for the first time, Charles had sided with his wife and her advisers, notably Jermyn, rather than his moderate councillors.

Meanwhile the king's position was ever more desperate. Attempts to broker a peace treaty on his own terms came to nothing when Parliament refused his request to allow Richmond,

188 *Warlord (1642–46)*

Southampton and Ashburnham safe conduct to London to begin negotiations. Similarly his hopes for exploiting the divisions on the parliamentarian side between the Independents and the Presbyterians were hampered by his own refusal to make meaningful concessions on religion to his English enemies.

Charles's decision to surrender to the Scots army at Newark was heavily influenced by the French envoy, Montreuil. Though the king continued to be frustrated by Cardinal Mazarin's self-interested reluctance to intervene with French troops, since it suited him to see a diplomatic rival weakened by internal strife, Montreuil was pushing hard to broker a deal for the Digby-Culpeper scheme of an alliance with the Covenanters, with whom, he assured Charles, he would be 'safe both in person, honour, and conscience' (language reflecting his experience of Charles's perennial preoccupations).[104] Charles was by now showing a little more willingness to appear flexible in relation to his 'grounds'. While he was adamant that any such arrangement with the Scots must guarantee that his friends would be protected from parliamentarian vengeance, he was less stringent in his religious conditions, promising that he would be 'very willing to be instructed concerning the presbiterial gouernement', provided that he was not obliged to agree to anything 'against my conscience'.[105] Obviously this gave him plenty of scope to continue to insist that he had conscientious objections to the total abolition of episcopacy, but as a bargaining ploy it made the Scots more likely to agree to a deal and so suggested that Charles was now adopting a more pragmatic approach to negotiations. As the remaining royalist armies met with defeat, the last significant force under Lord Astley having been caught and beaten outside Stow-on-the-Wold on 21 March, Charles ultimately accepted the suggestion that his best hopes lay with the Scots. He fled from Oxford in disguise with one Mr Hudson and John Ashburnham on the night of 27 April to surrender to the Covenanter forces who were besieging one of the last royalist garrisons, at Newark, which he did early in May. He then ordered both Newark and Oxford to surrender, which they did over the following weeks, with only a few isolated garrisons (for instance Raglan in Wales) continuing to hold out. From Newark, Charles was subsequently transferred to Newcastle as the Scots' prisoner.[106]

Warlord (1642–46) 189

Assessment: How far was Charles to blame for the royalist defeat?

The king has to bear significant responsibility for the royalist defeat. Though it is undeniable that Parliament possessed superior resources through its control of London and the wealth of the south-east, its administrative structures and access to the major ports, it is not clear that these contributed directly to any of the significant royalist defeats in set-piece battles, though certainly superior parliamentarian numbers were probably important in the defeats at Marston Moor and Naseby.[107] Rather, operational decisions and contingencies, such as the failure of the royalists to take London after Edgehill late in 1642, the decision to mount the successful, but costly, storming of Bristol in summer 1643, the king's insistence on besieging Gloucester in autumn 1643, his subsequent failure to follow up a potentially winning position at Newbury, and his confused and ambiguous instructions to Rupert ahead of Marston Moor, all proved highly damaging, while his fateful choice to fight at Naseby in June 1645, against Rupert's advice, proved terminal to his cause. More than this, his approach to running the royalist war effort, particularly early on his belief in aristocratic blood as the main qualification for command, his failure to address the factional divisions within the royalist council of war at Oxford and, increasingly from 1644 onwards, his trust in and the influence allowed to Digby, can be criticised. His harsh treatment of Rupert after the surrender of Bristol, likely encouraged by Digby, does not reflect well on him as a leader, given all that Rupert had done before, the hopelessness of the position at Bristol, and the fact that he was clearly the most competent of the royalist generals.

His deference to his wife's advice, often given from afar with little knowledge of the real circumstances of the campaigns in question, and reinforced by her courtiers and agents, made it harder for his other councillors to persuade him of more moderate courses, notably the Richmond-Southampton group and their efforts to engineer a negotiated settlement from a position of relative strength. Other characteristics of Charles, which his enemies had long suspected or hinted at since the late 1630s, and the hysteria surrounding the alleged Popish Plot, were also

190 *Warlord (1642–46)*

borne out by his conduct of the war, notably his conviction that Catholicism was less of a threat to the institutions of monarchy and episcopacy than were Presbyterians and Independents, and his consequent willingness (amply demonstrated by his captured correspondence after Naseby) to make concessions to the Irish and even to the English Catholics, if it would help win support either from the Confederates or the French Crown. That this would potentially have involved foreign, Catholic troops being used to fight against his English and Scottish subjects appeared similarly indicative of a ruthless desire to resurrect the plenitude of his regal powers and failed to take account of the anxieties this caused both to many of his supporters and to the wider political nation.

And yet, Charles's performance as warlord during the First Civil War had its positive side. He had shown that he was able to motivate and recruit support across his kingdom, demonstrating immense energy and mobility to keep returning to the royalist heartlands in Wales and Cheshire as well as parts of the midlands in order to show himself to his subjects and maximise the power of the presence of his royal person. He had recognised the weaknesses in the aristocratic-dominated command of the first two years of the war and reconfigured it, placing Rupert in overall charge and allowing him the space and autonomy to run the war. His disappointment with Rupert's disobedience to his orders regarding the surrender of Bristol reflects the trust he had reposed in him accentuated by their close familial relationship. Charles's operational decisions were sometimes astute, and his pursuit and defeat of Essex in the south-west in 1644, and victorious encounter at Lostwithiel while in personal command, show that he was not devoid of qualities of military leadership and even generalship on the field. Further, his personal bravery cannot be questioned, notably in his rallying of his troops at Edgehill and his willingness to throw himself into the fray at Naseby in the hope that it might turn the tide of a losing battle whose importance he well understood. Nor can his magnanimity following stalemates, as at Newbury when he ordered the mayor to treat enemy prisoners generously, or after Lostwithiel where he allowed Essex's troops to leave the field unmolested, be doubted.

Warlord (1642–46) 191

Though criticised for a lack of sincerity in peace negotiations, it might be observed that his parliamentarian enemies seemed willing to give little ground, with the Oxford Propositions bearing remarkable similarity to the original Nineteen Propositions they had presented back in 1642 as the basis for a settlement that would avoid war. Given the largely successful showing of the royalist armies in the first year and a half of the war, refusing to agree to terms that would have so markedly diminished his royal prerogative seems entirely understandable. While by the time of the negotiations at Uxbridge early in 1645, the king's position had been weakened by the loss of the north, he still had enough troops in the field, the heartening news of Montrose's early successes in Scotland, and wider diplomatic options for foreign help, for him to see the stringent parliamentarian terms as unworthy of serious consideration. Although he is often criticised for intransigence, the same charge might be levelled at his parliamentarian enemies. In relation to the substance of his objections, his principled and consistent refusal to countenance the abolition of episcopacy, as well as his reluctance to give up the control of the armed forces in such a way that his royal successors may never regain it, while baffling to his wife (who regarded all Protestant churches as equally heretical) and those of her (usually Catholic or crypto-Catholic) advisers who sought a restoration of royal authority at any price, illustrates a conscientious determination not to abrogate his coronation oath or give up an institution he had sworn to uphold and defend from the start of the conflict. Though by 1646 he was indicating that he might make concessions to Presbyterianism, as will be seen, he continued to include a reservation regarding his own conscience when making such undertakings and he would continue, during the search for settlement in the years 1646–8, to attach huge importance to this principle. Above all, his absolute conviction and certainty that his cause was a just one, and his deep-seated faith in divine providence (something his puritan opponents were unable to understand) ensured that, even when his military position looked hopeless, as he told Rupert, he was sure that 'God will not suffer rebels to prosper'. Behind this lay his ultimate and abiding faith in the institution of monarchy as a divinely ordained institution, closely linked to his powerful sense of personal honour and reputation, all of which had been clear throughout his reign.

192 *Warlord (1642–46)*

Notes

1 Sir Philip Warwick, *Memoirs* (London, 1701), p. 220.
2 Quoted in Peter Gaunt, *The English Civil War: A Military History* (London, 2014), p. 204; on the doubts about the pamphlet's authenticity, see David L. Smith, '"The More Posed and Wise Advice": The Fourth Earl of Dorset and the English Civil Wars', *The Historical Journal*, 34 (1991), pp. 797–829, at p. 815n.
3 Warwick, *Memoirs*, pp. 219–20.
4 *HMC MSS Lord Montagu of Beaulieu*, pp. 158–9.
5 Warwick, *Memoirs*, p. 226.
6 Ronald Hutton, 'The Royalist War Effort', in John Morrill (ed.), *Reactions to the English Civil War, 1642–1649* (Basingstoke, 1982), pp. 51–66, at p. 53.
7 Peter Gaunt, *The English Civil War: A Military History* (London, 2014), pp. 55–60, 62–3, 64–5.
8 Barry Coward and Peter Gaunt (eds), *English Historical Documents, 1603–1660* (London, 2010), p. 516.
9 Newcastle would be raised to Marquess in October 1643.
10 Petrie, *Letters of King Charles I*, p. 128.
11 *Letters and Memorials of State in the Reigns of Queen Mary, Queen Elizabeth, King James, King Charles the First and Part of the Reign of King Charles the Second*, ed. Arthur Collins (2 vols, London, 1746), II, p. 667.
12 Quoted in Gardiner, *History of the Great Civil War*, I, p. 4.
13 *Letters of Queen Henrietta Maria, including her private correspondence with Charles I*, ed. M.A.E. Green (London, 1857), pp. 108–09.
14 *Letters and Memorials of State*, II, 668.
15 *Letters of King Charles I*, p. 129
16 *CSPV 1642–1643*, p. 191.
17 Gardiner, *History of the Great Civil War*, I, p. 43.
18 Clarendon, *History of the Rebellion*, II, p. 376.
19 Gaunt, *English Civil War*, pp. 80–2.
20 Clarendon, *History of the Rebellion*, II, pp. 394–7, 401.
21 Gaunt, *English Civil War*, p. 125.
22 Coward and Gaunt (ed.), *English Historical Documents*, pp. 690–5.
23 *Letters of Henrietta Maria*, pp. 177, 182.
24 J.P. Kenyon, *The Civil Wars of England* (London, 1988), pp. 71–3.
25 Clarendon, *History of the Rebellion*, III, pp. 115, 149.
26 *Bellum Civile: Hopton's Narrative of His Campaign in the West (1642–1644) and Other Papers*, ed. Charles E.H. Chadwyck-Healey (Somerset Record Society, XVIII, 1902), p. 59.
27 *Letters and Memorials of State*, II, pp. 668–9.
28 Gardiner, *History of the Great Civil War*, I, p. 207.
29 *Letters and Memorials of State*, II, p. 671.
30 Clarendon, *History of the Rebellion*, III, pp. 175–6.

Warlord (1642–46) 193

31 *Letters of King Charles the First*, p. 136.
32 David Scott, 'Counsel and Cabal in the King's party, 1642–1646', in Jason McElligott and David L. Smith (eds.), *Royalists and Royalism during the English Civil Wars* (Cambridge, 2007), pp. 112–135.
33 Clarendon, *History of the Rebellion*, III, p. 222.
34 Cust, *Charles I*, pp. 368–9.
35 Warwick, *Memoirs*, p. 228.
36 Clarendon, *History of the Rebellion*, IV, p. 267.
37 Scott, 'Counsel and Cabal', pp. 118–21.
38 *Collection of Letters and Papers Concerning the Affairs of England from the Year 1641 to 1660*, ed. Thomas Carte (2 vols, London, 1739), I, pp. 44–6.
39 *Letters of Henrietta Maria*, pp. 166–7; Cust, *Charles I*, p. 369.
40 Clarendon, *History of the Rebellion*, III, pp. 148–9.
41 Scott, 'Counsel and cabal', p. 121.
42 *Letters of Henrietta Maria*, p. 206.
43 Clarendon, *History of the Rebellion*, III, p. 194.
44 Ibid., pp. 198–9.
45 *Letters of King Charles I*, pp. 132–6.
46 Clarendon, *History of the Rebellion*, III, pp. 266, 268.
47 *Clarendon State Papers* (3 vols, Oxford, 1767–86), II, p. 163, Lord Goring to the Queen, 15 Jan. 1644.
48 For the letter, dated 29 December 1642, see Petrie, *Letters of King Charles the First*, pp. 130–1; Sarah Poynting, '"I do desire to be rightly vnderstood": rhetorical strategies in the letters of Charles I', in McElligott and Smith (eds.), *Royalists and Royalism*, pp. 136–54, at p. 140.
49 Gaunt, *English Civil War*, pp. 133–4; Hutton, 'Royalist War Effort', pp. 55–6, 59.
50 Kenyon, *Civil Wars of England*, p. 94.
51 Gardiner, *History of the Great Civil War*, I, pp. 318, 330, 351.
52 Kenyon, pp. 99–100.
53 Clarendon, *History of the Rebellion*, III, pp. 370–1.
54 *Letters of King Charles I*, pp. 144 –5.
55 Warwick, *Memoirs*, pp. 274–5, 279.
56 *Collection of Original Letters and Papers*, I, p. 51.
57 *Collection of Original Letters and Papers*, I, pp. 57–8, 61–2.
58 Clarendon, *History of the Rebellion*, III, pp. 385, 403–04.
59 Gaunt, *English Civil War*, pp. 194–5; *Collection of Original Letters and Papers*, I, pp. 63–4.
60 Clarendon, *History of the Rebellion*, III, pp. 437–8, 441.
61 Petrie, *Letters of King Charles I*, p. 148.
62 Clarendon, *History of the Rebellion*, III, pp. 443–5.
63 *Collection of Original Letters and Papers*, I, pp. 71–2.
64 Petrie, *Letters of King Charles I*, pp. 150–3.
65 Clarendon, *History of the Rebellion*, III, pp. 466–7.

194 *Warlord (1642–46)*

66 *The King's Cabinet Opened: or, Certain Packets of Secret Letters & Papers Written with the Kings own Hand* (London, 1645), pp. 23–4.
67 For the Uxbridge Propositions in full, see Coward and Gaunt, *English Historical Documents*, pp. 696–702.
68 Clarendon, *History of the Rebellion*, III, 500.
69 Coward and Gaunt, *English Historical Documents*, p. 703; Petrie, *Letters of King Charles I*, p. 149.
70 *Clarendon State Papers*, II, pp. 186–7 [Charles to Secretary Nicholas, 5 Feb. 1644/5].
71 *Diary and Correspondence of John Evelyn. . .To which is subjoined the Private Correspondence between King Charles I and Sir Edward Nicholas. . .*, ed. William Bray (London, 1906), pp. 796–7.
72 *The King's Cabinet Opened*, pp. 12–13.
73 *Collection of Original Letters and Papers*, I, pp. 79–80, 90; see also Scott, 'Counsel and Cabal', pp. 125–6; Fiona Pogson, 'Cottington, Francis, First Baron', *ODNB*.
74 *Diary and Correspondence of John Evelyn*, p. 800.
75 Clarendon, *History of the Rebellion*, IV, p. 40.
76 Ibid., pp. 42–3, 45.
77 *The Kings Cabinet Opened: or, Certain Packets of Secret Letters & Papers written with the Kings own Hand and taken in his Cabinet at Nasby-Field, June 14. 1645* (London, 1645), pp. 7, 18–19, 43, 45–6.
78 Petrie, *Letters of King Charles the First*, p. 153.
79 *Diary and Correspondence of John Evelyn*, p. 803.
80 Petrie, *Letters of King Charles I*, p. 153; Clarendon, *History of the Rebellion*, IV, pp. 71–2.
81 Petrie, *Letters of King Charles I*, pp. 154–5.
82 *Diary and Correspondence of John Evelyn*, p. 804.
83 Ibid., p. 805.
84 Clarendon, *History of the Rebellion*, IV, pp. 74–5.
85 For Charles's providentialism, see Richard Cust, 'Charles I and Providence' in Kenneth Fincham and Peter Lake (eds.), *Religious Politics in Post-Reformation England: Essays in Honour of Nicholas Tyacke* (Woodbridge, 2006), pp. 193–208.
86 *Diary and Correspondence of John Evelyn*, pp. 803–06.
87 *Clarendon State Papers*, II, pp. 188–9.
88 Clarendon, *History of the Rebellion*, IV, p. 93.
89 Petrie, *Letters of King Charles I*, pp. 156–7.
90 *Nicholas Papers*, pp. 64–5.
91 Clarendon, *History of the Rebellion*, IV, p. 117.
92 *Collection of Original Letters and Papers*, I, p. 95.
93 *Nicholas Papers*, p. 66.
94 *Clarendon State Papers*, II, pp. 189–90.
95 Ibid., p. 209.
96 See Scott, 'Counsel and Cabal', pp. 126, 127–35.

Warlord (1642–46) 195

97 *Clarendon State Papers*, II, pp. 207, 209–11.
98 Petrie, *Letters of King Charles I*, pp. 165–7.
99 Ibid., pp. 165–7.
100 Ibid., pp. 160–1.
101 *Clarendon State Papers*, II, p. 201.
102 Clarendon, *History of the Rebellion*, IV, p. 97.
103 *Clarendon State Papers*, II, pp. 235–6.
104 Warwick, *Memoirs*, p. 292.
105 *Diary and Correspondence of John Evelyn*, p. 812.
106 Warwick, *Memoirs*, p. 293; Gaunt, *English Civil War*, pp. 222–3.
107 Gaunt, *English Civil War*, pp. 227–8.

6 Conscientious objector (1646–49)

Charles's decision to surrender to the Scots was a strategic one: he hoped he might obtain better terms from them than from his English enemies. It was a decision made against the advice of Sir Edward Hyde, however, who later reflected that Charles would have been better off fighting on at Oxford 'until the last biscuit' and then surrendering with his 'honest retinue' rather than hazarding his cause with his Scottish enemies.[1] The Scots themselves were aware of the potential advantages of possessing the king's person, and so transported him to Newcastle where they thought he would be more securely in their power. It was here, the city whose capture by the Scots in August 1640 had signalled his decisive defeat and compelled him to summon the Long Parliament, that Charles was to spend the next ten months (from 13 May 1646 until 3 February 1647) as their prisoner.

Charles as negotiator

The chief debate surrounding Charles's performance in negotiations with his erstwhile enemies in the years 1646–48 is over his sincerity: did he seriously intend to honour the concessions he made, or was he, all along, playing for time and plotting to recover the plenitude of his full powers through military means? Mark Kishlansky, who as noted previously argues strongly for Charles's sincerity and flexibility in his negotiations with the Scots Covenanters in 1638–39, has tended to view his dealings with Parliament in a similar light. He suggests that, while the king was undoubtedly keeping his options open by pursuing

Conscientious objector (1646–49)   197

opportunities for foreign assistance from Ireland and France at the same time as negotiating with Parliament and then the Army in the period 1646–48, this does not mean that he was not honestly seeking a negotiated settlement. When he himself came up with counter-proposals to those he was offered, they might reasonably (or as Kishlansky puts it, 'charitably') be considered as 'opening gambits in a process of negotiation'.[2] Equally, Charles's determination to hold fast to those things he referred to as his 'grounds', chiefly the preservation of episcopacy and the prayer book, can at least be seen as consistent, even if he was eventually prepared to entertain their temporary or partial suspension. The fact that he instigated a Second Civil War, however, by his Engagement with the Scots in December 1647, does rather militate against the image of the king as an entirely ingenuous negotiator. As so often in Charles's life, he was pursuing a dual strategy while hoping for some kind of deliverance, sometimes characterised as a kind of early Stuart 'Micawberism'. While it is tempting to suggest that actions that ended in failure implies that the decisions behind them were themselves misguided, as ever, contingency and historical accident played a significant role in the king's ultimate demise.

The Newcastle Propositions

Soon after his arrival at Newcastle, Charles wrote letters dealing with practical matters: he issued commands that the remaining royalist forces should surrender, and instructed the Prince of Wales, who was by now in France, to obey his mother in everything, 'except in religion', while commending to him John Ashburnham, his trusted courtier who had also departed for France.[3] These two things, a preoccupation with religion, and the counsel of Ashburnham, would play a significant part in the ensuing negotiations.

Despite Charles's apparent concession to political reality, however, the sense that he was already contemplating how he might build another royalist party with which to reclaim his position by force was already apparent. He expressed a negative view of his Scottish captors ('no honest man can prosper in these people's company'), and thought 'it is more than apparent that the Scots

198   *Conscientious objector (1646–49)*

will absolutely hinder my being any more king in England than they have made me in Scotland', where, of course, he felt that they had reduced him to the status of a 'Duke of Venice'.[4] At the same time he identified four principal factions among the Scots, suggesting that 'these divisions will either serve to make them all join with me, or else God hath prepared this way to punish them for their many rebellions and perfidies'.[5] Here were blended Charles's propensity to divide the world into friends and enemies and his habitual tendency to seek to exploit divisions among his opponents. Expecting peace proposals from Parliament in July, he confided to his wife that he would 'make no concessions but such as (I do not say all that) the French ambassadour shall advise me to', an indication that he continued to hope for and rely upon help and advice from abroad.[6]

When he was finally presented with Parliament's terms, the so-called 'Newcastle Propositions' (though to him they were always the 'London Propositions' given whence they originated), the main demands were: his surrender of his control of the militia to Parliament for a period of twenty years (binding himself and his successor if he died within that time); the abolition of episcopacy and the introduction of Presbyterianism into England; and parliamentary nomination of all major officers of state in future, along with the punishment of a significant number of named royalists by their exclusion from pardon. While objectively this represented a significant reduction in his royal power, for Charles his main concern was clearly the religious terms. As Anthony Milton has recently demonstrated, throughout the 1640s, Charles was hugely influenced by the advice of royalist clergy such as Juxon (who would later attend him on the scaffold), Duppa and Wren (the latter in writing from the Tower), who, far from having just a 'meek pastoral role', were important in hardening his aversion to giving up episcopacy or consenting to the sale of episcopal lands, invoking his coronation oath as a particularly persuasive tactic.[7] Charles was therefore the more dismayed that so many of his followers (including his wife and, perhaps under her influence, his followers Jermyn, Culpeper and Ashburnham) were advising him to agree to the surrender of episcopacy. As Charles wrote:

Conscientious objector (1646–49)   199

> Now, as for your advice to me, you speak my very soul in everything but one; that is, the Church. Remember your own rule, not to expect to redeem that which is given away by Act of Parliament. Shall I then give away the Church?. . .It is not the change of Church government which is chiefly aimed at (though that were too much); it is by that pretext to take away the dependency of the Church from the Crown, which, let me tell you, I hold to be of equal consequence to that of the Militia for people are governed by the pulpit more than the sword in times of peace.

His analysis of the power of the Pulpit no doubt reflected in part his experience of the 1640s, but in his linkage of Church government with the power of the Crown, he showed himself very much his father's son ('No bishop, no king'). In a further sign that Charles neither forgave nor forgot, agreeing to the introduction of Presbyterianism would vindicate the Covenanter rebellion 'which does not only make good all their former rebellions, but likewise lays a firm and fruitful foundation for such pastimes in all times to come'. His objections were mainly political. Even when he proceeded to discuss his 'theological' reservations, they were not only the loss of lawful priests and sacraments ('worse than if Popery were brought in') but also 'we should have the doctrine against kings fiercer set up than amongst the Jesuits'.[8] The establishing of the Covenant 'in all my kingdoms', he averred, 'will ruin this monarchy'.[9] He would rather, he insisted, agree to the surrender of the militia than to the abolition of episcopacy, so far was his 'conscience' against it. So much of Charles's religious world-view was structured around the Church and Crown as interdependent and mutually reinforcing, a theme traceable back the horror expressed by him and by Laud in the Parliament of 1626 at the growth of Puritanism. Yet had he been hard-headed enough to surrender episcopacy at this early stage in the negotiations with the intention of restoring it once he was back on this throne, he might, as his wife continually urged him, have confounded his enemies more completely than by his stubborn adherence to the institution of bishops on grounds of 'conscience', only to finally show himself willing to bend on it when it was too late. Whatever else, Charles was seemingly ingenuous in this: he

200 *Conscientious objector (1646–49)*

sincerely believed that an episcopal Church and a monarchical state were mutually interdependent.

Charles's approach was in any case to play for time: his first answer to the Newcastle Propositions (on 1 August) was in many ways emollient, merely arguing that 'so great alterations in government both in the Church and kingdom' required weighty consideration, asking that therefore he be allowed to come to London to discuss them at greater length. His true feelings were made manifest in his other correspondence, however. He once again, in a letter to Jermyn, Culpeper and Ashburnham, wrote scornfully of the Scots, suggesting that the establishment of Presbyterianism would vindicate their rebellion, and that they had 'resolved to destroy the essence of monarchy'. He also reiterated his conviction that episcopacy was integral to the maintenance of his royal power:

> Believe it, religion is the only firm foundation of all power; that cast loose, or depraved, no government can be stable. For where was there ever obedience where religion did not teach it? . . .And I am most confident that religion will much sooner regain the Militia than the Militia will religion.

This was a position that he also sought to transmit to his son and heir. In a letter to the Prince of Wales dated 26 August, he reminded him that the 'chiefest particular duty of a King is to maintain the true religion' and explicitly emphasised the interdependence of Church and Crown, for just 'as the Church can never flourish without the protection of the Crown, so the dependency of the Church upon the Crown is the chiefest support of regal authority'. He therefore urged his son to 'be constant in the maintenance of the Episcopacy' not only for the reason aforesaid but also 'to hinder the growth of the Presbyterian doctrine, which cannot but bring anarchy into any country, wherever it shall come for any time'. While Charles would later modify his position, such that he subsequently offered a temporary suspension of episcopacy and introduction of Presbyterianism, that would be from a position of much greater political weakness, and the strident tone of his condemnation of it to his son would suggest that he had no serious intention to honour any commitment to modify government of the Church by bishops. While prioritising

Conscientious objector (1646–49) 201

episcopacy, he also appeared to be much more reluctant than in other correspondence to give up the Crown's control of the militia, and in some ways even assigned it equivalent importance:

> Next to religion, the power of the sword is the truest judge and greatest support of sovereignty which is unknown to none (as it may be that of religion is to some). Wherefore, concerning this, I will only say that whosoever will persuade you to part with it, does but in a civil way desire you to be no King; reward and punishment (which are the inseparable effects of regal power) necessarily depending upon it, and without which a King can neither be loved nor feared of his subjects.[10]

With that apparent evocation of Machiavelli (and indeed of the Lipsian ideas that influenced him as well as several of his councillors), Charles revealed his conviction that royal power was nothing without control of the armed forces and this is again reminiscent of his earlier, trenchant opposition to the Militia Ordinance in 1642. It would prove a consistent theme in his dealings with his opponents and, ultimately, the Engagement he reached with the Scots in December 1647 would be notable for its explicit preservation of his military power.

Hopes and fears

Charles began to fear that some of his supporters, notably the queen and those gathered around her, might undermine his position by venturing to offer the surrender of episcopacy. At the same time, feeling cut off from news and events going on in London, he feared that Parliament might 'do their work without any more taking notice of me'. Again, therefore, he hoped to play for time and obtain assistance from abroad, trusting that 'if we can make use of this delay of time, to persuade France and others of my friends, to resolve, and realy to prepare, with speed, for my restitution, then, and not before, there will be life in my business'. This might include, he thought, the French government demanding his release from his Scottish captivity.[11]

His hopes of the French appeared to be misplaced, however. Cardinal Mazarin, with France still at war with Spain, was anxious

202 *Conscientious objector (1646–49)*

to avoid souring his relationship with the parliamentary leadership in London, and insisted that the French role was to be one of mediation rather than intervention. Charles was annoyed that the French ambassador, Bellièvre, who consulted parliamentary representatives before journeying to see the king, tried to persuade him to accept Presbyterianism, as the only way to recover his throne. He pointed out that the French had persuaded him to surrender to the Scots in the first place on the basis that they would give him the most favourable terms, and that this was now far from the case. When the ambassador returned disappointed, the queen sent Sir William Davenant as someone known to Charles and more likely to persuade him, but once again, Charles was furious at this lack of regard for his 'scruples of conscience'. When Davenant went so far as to suggest that the religious concessions he was asked to make were unimportant relative to the advantages he would gain by them, Charles was reported to have flown into a rage, being 'transported with so much passion and indignation that he gave him more reproachful terms, and a sharper reprehension, than he did ever towards any other man; and forbad him to presume to come again into his presence'.[12] He in turn upbraided the queen that she 'would break my heart if she any more undertake to obtain my consent for Presbyterian government'. It seems so many of those around Charles underestimated the depth of his commitment to an episcopal Church.

Other voices continued to urge the king to compromise his episcopalian principles. Jermyn and Culpeper wrote to him urging their plan 'to unite you with the Scots nation and the presbiterians of England against the anti-monarchical Party, the Independants'. They sought to persuade him that his conscience need not be infringed by surrendering episcopacy as it was not the only legitimate form of Protestant Church government (not an argument likely to cut much ice with Charles), while they rejected his view that 'monarchy ought to fall, because Episcopacy cannot stand'. Charles replied angrily to these missives, insisting that the survival of monarchy was absolutely endangered by any compromise over episcopal Church government.[13]

And yet, within a short while Charles was proposing a compromise where before he had been apparently intransigent. At the end of September, using his favoured courtier Will Murray

Conscientious objector (1646–49) 203

(who was with him at Newcastle) as an intermediary, he presented his own counter-propositions under which he pledged to allow the establishment of Presbyterianism for a period of three years, providing that he and his household were permitted to worship according to the Book of Common Prayer. In the intervening period, he suggested that a committee of divines meet to debate the future character of the English Church, a group that would comprise twenty Independents, twenty Presbyterians, and twenty of the king's own choosing. Such a dramatic change in Charles's mind may seem improbable, and indeed his decision to consult the Bishop of London as to whether or not this would infringe his coronation oath, reflects the enormity of his about-turn. The likelihood of his honouring these undertakings is in any case questionable, given that he also told the bishop that 'my regal authority once settled, I make no question of recovering Episcopal Government, and God is my witness, my chief end in regaining my power is to do the Church service'.[14] He also wrote afterwards to Murray telling him that if he could secure a promise from the Presbyterian peers that after five years he could have a 'regulated Episcopacy', then he was prepared to tolerate the establishment of Presbyterianism for that time and to drop the planned assembly containing twenty of his chosen divines. He continued to insist, to the queen, that the permanent establishment of Presbyterianism would render him but a 'titulary king'.[15] He was also now increasingly showing a preoccupation with divine providence, which, as has been pointed out, links closely to his concern to be true to his conscience.[16] His solitude seems to have produced a level of self-reflection which prompted feelings of regret for some of his past actions. On 21 November he wrote to his wife referring to the 'basse unworthy concession concerning Straford; for which, and lykewais for that great wronge and unjustice to the Church, of taking away the Bishops' votes in Parlament, I have been most justly punished'. Remorse for these actions back in 1641–42, combined with a fear of 'God's further wrath upon me' should he concede anything else, impelled him to an even firmer attachment to his conscience, despite the queen's entreaties to adopt a more pragmatic approach by abandoning episcopacy in order to reclaim his throne.[17] In any case, Charles made clear that he expected

204 *Conscientious objector (1646–49)*

his offer to be rejected in London and contemplated alternative strategies, including fleeing abroad as a way of ensuring that

> if I were in secure freedom anywhere else, I believe the two nations [the English and Scots] must needs fall out, and so give me an opportunity, either to join with the weaker party, or frame one of my own; for then men will begin to perceive that, without my establishing, there can be no peace.

This remained Charles's strongest card: that his adversaries would tire of their inability to reach a settlement and ultimately conclude that the king's restoration on his own terms was the only way to avoid continued political instability. In December he also once again petitioned Parliament that he be allowed to come to London to negotiate in person in an effort to break the impasse, arguing that 'tis your King who desires to be heard, the which if refused to a subject by a King, he would be thought a tyrant for it'.[18] Once again, however, his pleas fell on deaf ears. He continued to face the choice of two main approaches to the negotiations: the queen and those around her (Ashburnham, Jermyn and Culpeper principally), as well as Lord Digby, advocated pragmatism, doing whatever necessary to regain his regal power even at the price of surrendering episcopacy while prioritising the retention of his control of the militia, and thereby his coercive power to undo his concessions; contrastingly, Hyde, Nicholas, and the more moderate royalists argued that Charles's best hopes lay in a willingness to 'preserve his good principles' and that he should remember his own injunction, that 'if he could not live a King, he would die a gentleman', for 'if he recedes from his kingly resolutions, of honour and conscience, he must be most miserable'.[19] These differing policies reflected the principal divisions within the royalist cause, which, as David Scott has recently argued, were more nuanced (and more fluid) than the traditional 'constitutional royalist' vs 'ultra-royalist' or 'swordsmen' split and were instead polarised by their attitudes to foreign intervention that reflected deeper differences over the basis of royal power, the Crown's relationship with its people and differing conceptions of English nationhood.[20] The 'foreign-alliance' faction, comprising chiefly the queen, Digby, Jermyn, Ashburnham and Culpeper regarded involving the Irish

Confederates and the Scottish Covenanters as legitimate ways of restoring the king's authority across his three kingdoms, and saw control of the militia as integral to the primacy of 'force' as the ultimate basis of the Crown's relationship to its people. Meanwhile the opponents of foreign intervention, principally Hyde and Nicholas, together with the aristocratic circle grouped around the marquess of Hertford and the duke of Richmond, opposed any foreign intervention that would risk compromising, if not betraying, the integrity of Charles's cause as well as alienating many of his English supporters, and saw upholding episcopacy as about more than Church government but rather as central to the bonds of love between ruler and nation. They instead thought Charles's best hopes lay in fomenting divisions among his English opponents and accordingly cultivated links with the Independent peers. Any alliance with Presbyterian Scots or Catholic Irish risked undermining their strategy.[21] The king was torn between both of these approaches and, characteristically, attempted to blend them together in a way that was neither politically consistent nor ultimately successful. The whole-hearted pursuit of either one might have proved more fruitful than oscillating between the two.

Return to England

Charles was aware by early in the new year that he was likely to be moved back to England. Indeed this was a development he welcomed, on the basis that

> I think to be better used in Eng. though I have more frends in Scotland (I mean of Parl. men). So that I am no wais yet resolved what to doe, but only to gaine tyme as much as I may.[22]

Once the Scots had agreed to ransom the king back to the English Parliament, towards the end of January 1647, a delegation from the Lords and Commons went to meet him and, though they treated him with formality and respect, were careful to ensure that only servants named by Parliament were allowed to attend on his person. This apparent suspicion of Charles's intentions was not to prove unfounded.[23] The king began the journey to England on 3 February 1647, accompanied by the parliamentary

206   *Conscientious objector (1646–49)*

commissioners. En-route he received a warm reception, and exploited the opportunity to tap into continuing awe of the mystique of monarchy by touching for the King's Evil at Ripon.

Charles's negotiating strategy now appeared to be bearing fruit: encouraged by his counter-offer made in September, a group of leading Presbyterian peers (including Warwick, Holland, and Manchester) as well the moderate Independents represented by Northumberland, put together a modified version of the Newcastle Propositions which would have placed a three-year time-limit upon the concession of Presbyterianism, involved a surrender of the king's control of the militia for ten years rather than twenty, and, crucially, removed the requirement for Charles to sign the Covenant and therefore offered a salve for his conscience. Yet some observers had already begun to perceive that the king was merely using such developments as a tactic to divide his opponents: Bellièvre heard of a report in which the king was alleged to have said that if he could merely be patient for six months, there would be such political confusion as to enable him to attain all of his objectives.[24]

By now the king was confined at Holdenby House, in Northamptonshire, at which he would remain until November, and a more congenial location which allowed him to hunt and to play bowls at the earl of Sunderland's nearby Althorp estate. He was also allowed access to his library, and the offices of his own servants. Much less congenial, however, was the fact that he was denied the ministrations of his own chaplains, being instead forced to accept the attendance of Presbyterian ministers (as had also been the case at Newcastle). Charles wrote to the House of Lords twice to request that he be permitted access to his own clergy, arguing that without their advice he was unable to further consider their proposals for reform of the Church. Continually denied this by both Houses, where Presbyterian majorities were now entrenched, he was unable to attend worship or receive the sacrament, an indignity which can hardly have improved his view of his adversaries.[25]

Prisoner of the New Model Army

It was at this point that the divisions between Parliament and the New Model Army began to manifest themselves in a way that potentially offered Charles an advantage. Alarmed by the plans

Conscientious objector (1646–49) 207

of the Presbyterian leaders in Parliament to send part of the Army to Ireland to assist in crushing the still ongoing rebellion and to disband the remainder, and resentful of arrears of pay, some regiments, such as those stationed in East Anglia, began to contemplate direct overtures to the king over the head of Parliament. Indeed in April he received a message apparently from the Army inviting him to take refuge in their ranks, to which Charles gave a positive reply, anxious to 'let the army know that we highly respect their expressions' and promising that 'when restored to our throne in peace, we shall auspiciously look upon their loyal affections towards us', a sign that he was not going to miss the chance to appeal to the Army's dissatisfaction with Parliament.[26] It was in this context that Parliament sent the Newcastle Propositions to the king for a third time to seek his answer, which he finally gave on 12 May. He once again offered to confirm Presbyterianism for a period of three years until an assembly of divines, including twenty of his own nominees, had decided upon a permanent Church settlement, while maintaining some of his earlier evasiveness in declaring himself 'not therein yet satisfied' concerning his swearing of the Covenant, particularly not until he could consult his chaplains (thus far a right denied him). In response to the proposed surrender of royal control of the militia to Parliament, he again offered ten years instead of twenty.[27] This answer was favourably received by both the Scottish commissioners and the Presbyterian majority in the English Parliament as a basis for a settlement, even if Charles's earlier epistolary confidences suggest that he had no intention of doing anything other than restoring full-blown episcopacy when he had the chance. The Lords invited Charles to move to his palace of Oatlands on 20 May, so that he would be nearer London, with the assumption that he would be able to participate more fully in political discussion, though a few days later the Lords may have regretted this gesture when they heard read an intercepted letter from Ashburnham to the King expressing hopes for foreign intervention on his behalf at the behest of the Dutch.[28]

Yet the prospects for at least an initial settlement based on a coalition of Scots, English Presbyterians and royalists were quickly undermined by the dramatic escalation of the tensions between Parliament and the Army. Pre-empting the planned disbandment

208   *Conscientious objector (1646–49)*

of regiments, on 3 June a cavalry force under Cornet Joyce went to Holdenby to seize the king and take him into the custody of the Army. A good deal of mystery surrounds this episode, not least because it is unlikely that a soldier of such junior rank would take such a drastic step without at least conditional orders from his superiors. The suspicion that Cromwell at least ordered Joyce to go with force to Holdenby to deter any Presbyterian attempt to move him further away, and if necessary bring him to a more secure place (from the Army's point of view) is a strong one, though difficult to prove definitively.[29] The king's reaction, was, perhaps unsurprisingly, one of surprise and no little apprehension. Having been at Althorp playing bowls and then awoken from his rest, he might have imagined that some harm was intended to his person. He was naturally anxious to ascertain by what authority Joyce was acting, and the Cornet's evasions eventually resulted in a crude pointing to the soldiers behind him as his 'commission', to which Charles could only answer with wry humour: 'A very handsome commission'.[30] He was eventually taken, via Hinchingbrooke and Childerley, to Newmarket, where he found the Army's hospitality much more comfortable than that of the Scots or Parliament: he was allowed to receive an assortment of visitors including 'every day the faces of many who were grateful to him', and, crucially, his chaplains were now permitted to attend him, all of which led Charles to begin 'to believe that the army was not so much his enemy as it was reported to be'. In some ways it felt like one of the royal progresses of old, meeting with local gentry and catching up with familiar friends in the surrounding area, while being able to practise his religion was a great boon to him.[31] He had also been encouraged by the visible expressions of royalist sentiment that he had encountered on his journey to Newmarket, and may have heard news of an increased outpouring of royalist pamphlets being published in London, engendering sympathy for the plight of a captive king.[32] Yet the king's political situation was still finely balanced. While he might feel buoyed by the apparent contest between Army and Parliament for control of his person, and the further opportunities which it presented for him to divide his enemies, 'that both sides would in the end be willing to make the King the umpire'[33] (in Clarendon's words), it was not clear that all was as it seemed: could the Army, and

Conscientious objector (1646–49) 209

any alternative proposals for settlement they presented to him, be considered a lawful authority of equivalent status to that of Parliament? Could such men whose religious, political and social views were, in light of recent declarations, more radical than those of the Presbyterians, really be more reliable allies?

The Heads of the Proposals, Hampton Court and the royal escape

During July, and as the quarrel between Army and Parliament escalated, Charles was moved on progress, with Hampton Court the ultimate destination. On the way, he stopped at the earl of Craven's house near Reading, and it was while staying there that he was finally allowed to see his children, 'to his infinite content and joy'.[34] By now, James, Duke of York (aged 14), Henry, Duke of Gloucester (aged 7), and the two princesses, Elizabeth (aged 11) and Henrietta Anne (aged only 3) were in the custody of the earl of Northumberland. Charles expressed gratitude to Sir Thomas Fairfax, commander-in-chief of the Army, that he was able to enjoy the free exercise of his religion as well as the company of his children and of those who wished to see him.[35] And yet, as Sir Philip Warwick, who saw him at Reading, observed, the king was 'very apprehensive, in what hands he was' and feared 'that the army would not be able to stemm the tide, both of their old Masters, the Presbyterians, and of his own party', but he was forced to accept the political reality that they now had him in their possession.[36]

Charles was soon faced with an alternative set of terms put forward by the Army, the Heads of the Proposals, which were finalised that month at the meeting of the Army Council at Reading. Also there to represent the king's interests was Sir John Berkeley, who had commanded the royalist garrison at Exeter until its surrender in 1646, had then fled to join the queen in France but who had remained on good terms with many of the parliamentarian generals and who was therefore sent back to England by Henrietta Maria to gauge the army's stance towards her husband. Berkeley met with Cromwell on 12 July and was hugely encouraged by his remarks concerning the king: Cromwell said that as far as the Army was concerned, they merely wanted

210 *Conscientious objector (1646–49)*

'leave to live as subjects ought to do', and 'no men could enjoy their Lives and Estates quietly, without the King had his Rights'. He relayed this to Charles, expecting him to be pleased with such warm words, but he was to be sadly disappointed. He found that the king 'discovered not only to me, but to every one he was pleased to converse with, a total diffidence of all the Army', on the grounds that they had been slow 'to treat of receiving any favour, or advantage from his Majesty'. The explanation appeared to be the king's refusal to believe that men who had recently fought against and killed his followers on the battle-field could be trusted, and that instead, therefore, they 'ought absolutely to be well dissembled-with, whilst his Majesty was in their hands, at least, that he might the better get out of them'.[37] Charles's view of Cromwell was also far from positive. Berkeley relayed to him that Cromwell had wept at the sight of the king playing with his children at Caversham, 'the tenderest sight that ever his eyes beheld', regarding Charles as the 'uprightest and most conscientious man of his three Kingdoms' and professed the indebtedness of the Independents to the King for not reaching agreement with 'the Scots Propositions at Newcastle, which would have totally ruined them'. Charles, however, 'seemed not well edified with it [this account], and did believe, that all proceeded out of the use Cromwell and the Army had of his Majesty, without whom, he thought, they could do nothing'. Berkeley concluded that Charles's attitude was influenced by the Scots and Presbyterians through Lord Lauderdale, who had had frequent access to the king, and who feared a conjunction between the king and the Army. As such Charles remained cynical and if he could not get a 'speedy' agreement with the Army then he would seek to make his escape.[38] Once again, therefore, Charles's default position appeared to be mistrust and scheming, as well as susceptibility to the suspicions of some of his courtiers, even when he was to be offered the most favourable terms he would ever receive. The *Heads of the Proposals*, the terms of which Charles was given an indication even before they were formally presented, were more generous than the Newcastle Propositions, particularly in relation to the Church settlement. Charles was to be allowed to retain a national Church governed by bishops and using the prayer book, though the bishops were

Conscientious objector (1646–49) 211

to be deprived of coercive power and those who wished could 'opt-out' and worship freely according to their consciences. In relation to the civil power, he was to be deprived of his control of the militia for ten years rather than twenty, and to have royal officials appointed by Parliament for the same period of time. There was also a more comprehensive pardon offered to his supporters and much less in the way of vindictive punishment. In relation to the wider constitutional settlement, the Proposals contained provision for biennial parliaments and redistribution of seats 'to render the House of Commons (as near as may be) an equal representative of the whole [kingdom]'.[39]

Charles's aversion to compromise remained. When he moved to Oatlands on 12 August, he was said to be 'very merry', and his reported remark that he took particular pleasure in his son being out of the rebels' hands, indicated that he intended any immediate concessions to be non-binding upon his successor.[40] Charles's reply to the Proposals on 9 September acknowledged that the terms now offered were better than those contained within the Newcastle Propositions, which, aware of the need to cultivate his audience, he described as 'destructive to the main principal interests of the Army, and of all those whose affections concur with them'. And still, he stopped short of indicating his acceptance. While he conceded that the Proposals 'much more conduce to the satisfaction of all interests, and may be a fitter foundation for a lasting peace, than the Propositions', he merely averred that he saw them as the basis for negotiations, 'upon which there may be a personal treaty with His Majesty' of which the Proposals would form a part but along with 'such other Propositions as His Majesty shall make, hoping that the said Proposals may be so moderated in the said treaty as to render them the more capable of His Majesty's full concessions'.[41] Again balancing this evasion with a sop to opinion within the Army, he articulated a desire that any settlement would "give full satisfaction unto his people for whatsoever shall concern the settling of the Protestant profession, with liberty to tender consciences' as well as 'the laws, liberties and properties of all his subjects, and the just privileges of Parliament for the future".[42]

And so Charles's game went on: he clearly hoped to buy yet more time in which to assess the range of options available to him, both at home and abroad.

212   *Conscientious objector (1646–49)*

Charles is often criticised for having failed to respond favourably to these proposals, particularly given that they appeared to satisfy the demands of his conscience concerning episcopacy. Yet one might reasonably point out that, given the vague hopes he had been encouraged to entertain since coming into the Army's custody, they were a disappointment. They still involved his being deprived of the militia, the 'power of the sword' which, as has been seen, he referred to repeatedly in his correspondence the previous year as being central to his status as king, and which he might hope to retain should others of his schemes come to fruition. He may also have wondered whether these proposals reflected the will of the Army as a whole or merely a few of its ambitious leaders, and, whether the Army as a political entity could actually deliver on these terms given the continued rupture with Parliament, which had formally rejected the Proposals. Likewise, he may have baulked at the more radical suggestions for reforming Parliament and the franchise. As such, Charles's actions, while with hindsight open to question, are understandable within the context of the time.

At Hampton Court, where he arrived on 24 August, the king was gratified to now be attended by loyal noblemen such as the duke of Richmond, the duke of Ormond (over from Ireland), the marquis of Hertford and the earl of Southampton, as well as his chaplains, Drs Sheldon and Hammond. More in touch with events, he was now able to engage more fully with the political situation, and continued to be served by Ashburnham and Berkley as intermediaries in his dealings with the Army.[43] He 'enjoyed himself at Hampton Court much to his content, the respects of the chief officers of the army seeming much greater than they had been', while he was once again able to be visited by his children (who were nearby at Northumberland's residence of Syon House), as well as lords and ladies from London.[44] He was given cause for hope by news of developments in Scotland, where the Hamiltons, who were less inclined to push Charles towards Presbyterianism, began to gain the ascendancy. Yet he became increasingly uneasy with the growing rancour between his guards and the Scots Commissioners who were in continued attendance in the hope of a settlement based on the Propositions, and began to fear that one or other party might be planning to remove him

Conscientious objector (1646–49) **213**

once again. While Hyde urged that his best hopes lay with the Army, who could not hope to rule by the sword for any length of time, and who were more inclined to uphold Charles's interests because they lacked popularity in the country at large, Charles had growing hopes that the Scots Commissioners might now be his best support and requested Parliament that he be moved to London to negotiate a treaty in person.[45]

Equally news of the debates taking place at the General Council of the Army at Putney only added to his anxiety, with an apparent growth in republican sentiment and calls for the king to be held accountable for the 'innocent blood' that he was alleged to have shed.[46] Ashburnham began to encourage the king's suspicions of the Army leadership, with Charles confiding that he had long imagined 'they had never design'd anie reall service to Him, but made use of His Interest to advance their owne, which lay some other way than by His Restauration'. Ashburnham's discussions with Cromwell and Ireton reinforced his sense that Charles had little to hope for from the Army, and as a result the king began to entertain plans for escape, enjoining Ashburnham to withdraw his parole, justifying this with reference to the increasingly irksome behaviour of his guards in disturbing his rest as well as fears for his personal safety.[47] Rival plans emerged. Charles appeared to favour a flight abroad, suggesting Jersey, to which Ashburnham pointed out the danger of leaving the kingdom in the control of his enemies. Soon he suggested (by his own account at least) fleeing to the Isle of Wight, whose governor, Colonel Robert Hammond, he had met and who was regarded as friendly and potentially willing to defy his commanders. From there Charles could assess the situation, enjoying greater freedom of action, and, potentially, take ship more easily to the continent should he so desire.[48]

It seems unlikely that the Isle of Wight was intended to be the ultimate destination, however, and Ashburnham's self-serving account lends the venture an organisation and purpose that it clearly lacked. Leaving Hampton Court by dead of night, Charles rode with Berkeley, Ashburnham, and Will Legge (former governor of Oxford and who had been attending the king at Hampton Court) towards the New Forest, but when they neared the coast and Charles asked where the expected

214 *Conscientious objector (1646–49)*

ship was to be found, he was dismayed when Ashburnham went to look and 'returned without any news of the ship'. He then ordered a detour to Titchfield, an estate belonging to the earl of Southampton, and it was here, as the king and his three servants reassessed the situation, that the Isle of Wight was suggested (or again suggested) as a plausible destination given the governor, Colonel Robert Hammond's, favourable disposition. The trust in Hammond, however, proved misplaced and when Ashburnham, on his own initiative, brought him to Titchfield to see the king, Charles became distressed at the hostage to fortune involved in the willing surrender of his freedom of action. Recriminations by royalists later on tended to suggest, as in Sir Philip Warwick's assessment, that the whole affair was a bungle: 'the choosing of this place did not arise from a beleife either of the King or Mr Ashburnham in the Governour, but from the failing of some ship there expected'.[49] As Clarendon wrote, 'The not having a ship ready, if it were intended, was in-excusable; and the putting the King into Hammond's hands without his leave could never be wiped out'. The blame, he suggested, lay squarely with Ashburnham (given the extent of his influence with the King) for such an ill-conceived plan, having the Isle of Wight in mind from the start and perhaps reposing too much trust in his ability to read the intentions of the Army leadership.[50] This of course also reflected the divisions among the royalists, divisions which Charles was persistently unable to settle or override. Either way, Charles exchanged one captivity for another, being taken to Carisbrooke Castle on the Isle of Wight, though given the lightness of the guard he imagined that he would be able to leave the island with ease in due course. It was from here that he would mount his boldest attempt to recover his full royal authority.

Isle of Wight (Nov 1647–Dec 1648)

Lodged at Carisbrooke from 14 November, Charles enjoyed the positive reception he was given by the islanders, even if his material comfort was somewhat less than at Hampton Court. Shortly after his arrival, he heard the news of the Army mutiny at Ware in Hertfordshire and the evidence of political radicalism among the

Conscientious objector (1646–49) 215

rank and file. As well as support for the Leveller cause reflected in the copies of the *Agreement of the People* that the mutineers wore in their hats, there were further indications of hostile sentiment towards the king as a 'man of blood', all of which inclined him to think he ought to focus his energies on negotiating with the Army high command.[51] On 16 November he wrote to Parliament offering a compromise between the Proposals and the terms he had suggested in return, arguing for the retention of episcopacy but in modified form, the by now standard three-year trial for Presbyterianism prior to a more permanent settlement, and with guarantees for himself and other believers in episcopalianism that they could worship according to their consciences in this period, with a full liberty of conscience (excluding Catholics and atheists) to be enacted as part of the final settlement.[52] In a further significant move, he also offered to give up his control of the militia to Parliament for the duration of his life, provided that it was guaranteed that his successors would once again enjoy this power. He was also prepared to entertain consideration of some of the Army's demands relating to parliaments and elections. Overall he hoped that these proposals of his would serve as the basis for a personal treaty which he might be able to negotiate directly with Parliament by coming to London.

Doubts about Charles's sincerity were, however, too deep-rooted to proceed on this basis. By now the leaders of the Army, principally Cromwell and Ireton, were suspicious that Charles might be negotiating with the Scots behind their backs, particularly now that he was further away from their oversight. As a consequence, the Independent majority in the House of Lords took the initiative by putting forward four propositions, subsequently sent to the Commons to become the Four Bills, to which Charles was asked to assent before being allowed to come to London to negotiate further. These required him to concede the surrender of the control of the militia for twenty years while additionally revoking his declarations against the Houses and voiding honours he had recently granted, at the same time as allowing the existing Parliament the right to adjourn to any place of their choosing (thereby preserving their freedom of action should the king try to move against them). Charles's efforts in response, sending Berkeley to the Army Council at Windsor to try to stir

216 Conscientious objector (1646–49)

the commanders to oppose Parliament and instead place him back on his throne, unsurprisingly came to nothing, and instead Berkeley came away with the firm impression that Cromwell was now much more hostile towards Charles and his interests.[53]

It was in this context that Charles decided to roll the dice. He was faced with two delegations of commissioners eager for a settlement on their terms: the Scottish Commissioners who continued to seek a treaty which would include concessions to Presbyterianism, and English Commissioners possessed of written copies of the Four Bills. Charles had so far failed to satisfy the Scots Commissioners regarding their religious demands, and while considering how to break the impasse he was formally presented with the Four Bills on 24 December, and given four days to answer. During this time he reached agreement with the Scots for an 'Engagement' whereby he accepted the introduction of Presbyterianism and the Directory of Public Worship for three years (though with him and his household allowed to continue using the Prayer Book) until a more permanent religious settlement could be reached by an assembly of divines, and he now also agreed to confirm the Covenant by Act of Parliament. He at the same time agreed to suppress heresy and schism, which fulfilled the Scots' hopes for the final defeat of the radical religious sects. In return the Scots would support his demand for a personal treaty in London, and, if necessary, back this up with military intervention. As a manifesto, it criticised the conduct of the Army, referring to Charles as having been 'carried away from Holmby against his will . . . and detained in their power until he was forced to fly from amongst them to the Isle of Wight' while denying his subsequent requests to be allowed to come to London to negotiate a personal treaty. Crucially, Charles upheld his other powers and prerogatives, the Scots pledging to assist him in asserting his control of the militia, the appointment of his councillors and servants, and the preservation of his negative voice (veto) over parliamentary legislation. If necessary the Scots would send an army into England:

> . . .for [the] preservation and establishment of religion, for defence of His Majesty's person and authority, and restoring him to his government, to the just rights of the Crown and his

Conscientious objector (1646–49) 217

full revenues, for defence of the privileges of Parliament and liberties of the subject, for making a firm union between the kingdoms, under His Majesty and his posterity, and settling a lasting peace.[54]

There is perhaps an irony here that, given his trenchant rejection of any concessions over Church government back in 1646, he was now willing to accept the introduction (albeit temporary) of Presbyterianism for a period, whereas the militia he insisted on retaining. This was the approach that Henrietta Maria had recommended all along, and might be seen to reflect Charles finally choosing prudence over conscience. The other about-face the King appeared to be making was over religious toleration: having promised the Army that he would promote liberty of conscience, he now undertook to the Scots to repress the sects rigorously, grist to the mill of those who accuse the king of wilful dishonesty.[55] Obviously this reflects the particular priorities of the Scots with whom he was negotiating, and it will be remembered that even back in 1646 he had been arguing in his correspondence that his control of the kingdom's armed forces was as essential to the maintenance of his royal power as was the preservation of episcopacy in the Church. Church and State remained interdependent. He was now staking his throne on a Scottish alliance which envisaged a firm union between the kingdoms. Perhaps his father would have been proud. Accordingly on 28 December he rejected the Four Bills, giving his answer in writing and sealed to the earl of Denbigh.[56] Suddenly Charles succeeded in creating a greater sense of unity between the Army and Parliament, which promptly responded to news of the king's rejection of the Four Bills and his dealings with the Scots by a Vote of No Addresses, stating that no more terms be put to the king and no more messages be received from him. The Army was prepared, it said, to now seek a settlement without the king, and the Commons were now seeming to be coming round to this view too. Even in the Lords, where there remained unease with the idea of overturning the established government, the Vote was eventually accepted. Suddenly the deposition of the king was a genuine possibility.[57] To emphasise this, on 11 February, after a week-long debate, the Commons passed a *Declaration of the Commons of England,*

218 *Conscientious objector (1646–49)*

which outlined how Charles's actions had eroded confidence in him as king. It even dredged up the allegation made in 1626 that he had been a party to his father's supposed murder as well as the claims of the Irish rebels of 1641 to have been acting in his name and under his commission. His attempts to introduce foreign armies into England during the Civil War were, however, the paramount charge, and made use of the correspondence captured after Naseby by way of evidence. As such, a government ought to be settled that would 'best stand with the peace and happiness of this kingdom', an ominous opening of the door to a settlement without the king.[58]

Royalist hopes

Given that the Second Civil War was to end in ignominious failure and ultimately in the King's trial and execution, it might be surmised that the whole enterprise was misguided and foolish. Yet, there was evidence of considerable support within the nation beyond Westminster for the King's cause. Petitions flooded in to Parliament urging that a settlement be reached with the King, while London apprentices appeared in the streets shouting 'For God and King Charles'.[59] Emotional support was not the same as active military backing, however. The king's own presence was surely essential for any serious revival of his cause and so plans were hatched to spring him from his captivity in Carisbrooke Castle. The scheme was in the hands of one of Charles's former pages, Henry Firebrace, who planned to have the king squeeze through the casement window of his bedroom on the courtyard side of the castle and then be lowered from the outer castle wall with a rope. A waiting escort would then take him to the coast to take ship for wherever he wished, presumably Scotland to join with the Engagers and rally his supporters there. As with so many of the conspiratorial schemes with which Charles was involved throughout his reign, however, it ended in failure: on the appointed night, 20 March, and despite Charles's earlier insistence to the contrary, he found himself unable to get through the gap in the window, having declined Firebrace's suggestion to cut though a plate at the bottom to widen it. As a result, the king was never able to test how far the popular sympathy for him

Conscientious objector (1646–49)   219

across his kingdoms would translate into active support were his presence to be felt.[60]

Some encouragement was to be found for the king from outside of England. Since July 1647, when Ormond had surrendered to parliamentary forces in Ireland, and returned to England to attend the king at Hampton Court, the king's cause there had looked bleak. By April of 1648, however, his prospects improved as Lord Inchiquin defected to his side and urged an alliance with both the Irish Catholic Confederates and the Scots in defence of Charles's rights. At the same time, the Scottish Parliament, which Cromwell hoped would assist against the Engagers by remaining loyal to the original alliance of 1643, declared the alliance at an end on the basis that their key demand (which they now reiterated) for the establishment of Presbyterianism in England, had not been honoured. Meanwhile in Wales, disaffected parliamentarian garrisons in the south mutinied, taking control of Pembrokeshire, and joined with Welsh royalists to declare for the king and the Book of Common Prayer.[61] This uprising, particularly given the defection of troops formerly loyal to Parliament, was deemed the most serious and Cromwell was dispatched to Pembrokeshire to face it down.

In Charles's absence, royalist uprisings did materialise in England. There were petitions from Surrey and from Essex demanding the return of the king, with some petitioners marching to London to make their demands in person. There was a revolt in Kent in late May, which led to plans for a rendezvous of 20,000 men on Blackheath and which hoped to receive support from parts of the navy stationed in the Downs that had mutinied over arrears of pay. Reinforcements from Essex were also expected, while the Prince of Wales, who given his father's captivity was trying to coordinate the risings, appointed the earl of Holland to command such forces as could be raised in England (though he soon delegated active field command to the earl of Norwich).

The Second Civil War

All of this, however, was fairly small-scale and poorly supported, and ultimately crushed with relative ease by the experienced forces

220　*Conscientious objector (1646–49)*

of the New Model. In Wales, the royalist forces were defeated at St Fagans on 8 May even before Cromwell, who had then reached as far as Gloucester, had arrived. He was therefore able to concentrate on besieging Pembroke Castle. In Kent, Fairfax demonstrated his supreme abilities of military organisation and dispersed the bulk of the royalist forces, most of whom quietly returned to their homes upon receipt of promises that they would not be harmed. Norwich attempted to march on the City but found the gates closed against him and was forced to turn east to Essex to try again but parliamentary forces under Whalley quickly mobilised to block his efforts by early June. As a result, what royalist forces remained in the eastern counties concentrated in Essex and eventually took refuge at Colchester, which was soon subject to a lengthy siege by Fairfax's troops.[62]

The tragedy for Charles, in addition to his own failure to escape to the mainland, was that the Scots invasion, so central to his scheme, did not occur until after these uprisings were already petering out.[63] He continued to explore opportunities for escape during the summer, and these reveal a further dimension of his character. One royalist supporter who tried to assist him was a woman, Jane Whorwood, who it appears may have been Charles's mistress. Two letters from the King addressed to her survive among Firebrace's papers, and these include his expressions of longing for an assignation with her in his chamber as 'the one way possible you may get a swyuing from me'. This plain speaking about sexual matters and the clear intention towards an adulterous liaison has been seen as jarring rather with Charles's known reputation for marital and familial devotion, but, as has been pointed out, having been separated from his wife by distance for several years it is not improbable that he may have sought solace with another woman, particularly as she was clearly assisting him with his efforts to escape. It does certainly convey the human side of the King's captivity.[64]

By the time the Scottish invasion finally did take place, on 8 July under the marquess of Hamilton, the earl of Holland's efforts in Surrey had already come to naught and he himself was captured having fled to St Neots. Hamilton occupied Carlisle but his army was only 10,500 strong and mainly consisted of inexperienced recruits, and hopes for reinforcements from English royalists proved misplaced. In the end he was roundly defeated

Conscientious objector (1646–49) 221

by Cromwell at the battle of Preston over the course of 17–18 August. Some royalists blamed Hamilton for failing to coordinate his invasion with the English royalist uprisings, when had he timed it to coincide with Holland's actions in the south, a more formidable royalist army might have materialised. Mutual suspicion between the disparate elements of the king's cause undoubtedly played a part, and English royalists' fears that Hamilton himself was pursuing a narrow Scots, Presbyterian interest may have contributed to their rushed and ill-prepared pre-emptive uprisings in the south.[65] The English royalist troops under Sir Marmaduke Langdale fought bravely against overwhelming odds. Though Lord Byron observed of Hamilton's forces that 'I had the sad assurance of his overthrow, by the disordered troops that in great confusion, came running through those countries, pursued by none but their own fears', he noted that 'Langdale had so well despatched the business with Cromwell, that he was in no case to follow the execution'.[66] Hamilton, 'a brave man though a bad general', was forced to surrender at Uttoxeter a few days later, and the news of the defeat at Preston prompted the final surrender of the royalist garrison at Colchester.[67] The price of the king's service was revealed by the fate of the senior officers there, three of whom were condemned to die and two of those, Sir Charles Lucas and Sir George Lisle, shot on the spot on Fairfax's orders, on the basis that taking up arms for the king a second time equated to treason and rebellion.[68] Though he was far away on the Isle of Wight, Charles's actions in repeatedly rejecting terms of peace and then in re-starting the Civil War by means of his Engagement with the Scots, undoubtedly contributed to this harsher treatment of the defeated royalists compared with the First Civil War.

The Treaty of Newport

The catastrophic defeat of the king's armies in the Second Civil War, leaving him without 'earthly hope', and the less forgiving climate which pervaded the conflict, did not, however, prevent renewed attempts to reach a settlement which retained him as king.[69] The Vote of No Addresses, passed by Parliament following news of Charles's duplicitous dealings with the Scots, was repealed on 24 August, leaving the way open for parliamentary commissioners

222 Conscientious objector (1646–49)

to be appointed to treat with Charles at Newport on the Isle of Wight from 18 September, though in an effort to avoid further temporising by the king, it was stipulated that negotiations were not to last for longer than forty days. In the end, they continued intermittently until 28 November. The basis for the discussion was the old Hampton Court Propositions (a re-hash of the Newcastle Propositions) of 1647, beginning with a demand that Charles abrogate all of his declarations against Parliament. This soon led to a dispute as to which party was the more responsible for the outbreak of the Civil War in the first place, and of the bloodshed that had ensued. Charles unsurprisingly baulked at the inclusion of any statement of his culpability, notably the suggestion (as he told his son) that the two Houses of Parliament had been 'necessitated to undertake a war in their just and lawful defence'.[70] He told one of the parliamentary commissioners, using the analogy of a comedy in which it is claimed that an 'affray' took place despite all the blows falling upon one man, that he had made the concessions demanded of him while his opponents had made none.[71] To the continued wrangling over the religious settlement, which had now once again become a proposal that Charles consent to abolish bishops and the prayer book, establish Presbyterianism, and take the Covenant himself, the king once again sought to compromise with a three-year trial of Presbyterianism but refused to take the Covenant, while in response to the demand that he abandon the militia for twenty years he again sought to limit this to ten years, anxious to avoid the hostage to fortune entailed by the prospect of his successor being denuded of it permanently.[72]

These negotiations, of all of those to which he had been a party, affected Charles the most deeply. Sir Philip Warwick, in attendance upon him at Newport, recounted the King saying that he wished he had consulted nobody but 'my owne self, for then, where in honour or conscience I could not have complied, I could have early bin positive' and then shedding tears in the corner of his room, 'the biggest drops, that I ever saw fall from an eye', according to Warwick.[73] Gradually Charles felt himself backed into a corner. Seeing no prospect of a satisfactory settlement, early in October he told the commissioners that he would agree to surrender his control of the militia for twenty years, and allow Parliament to settle Ireland as they saw fit, as well as

Conscientious objector (1646–49)   223

conceding a modified episcopacy after three years of Presbyterian Church government, in which bishops would govern alongside presbyters. He even agreed to abolish all of the rest of the Church hierarchy apart from bishops.[74] All this, however, seems to have been merely a smokescreen for renewed plans to leave the island, the King telling the owner of the house in which he was staying at Newport, William Hopkins, that he made these concessions 'merely in order to my escape, of which if I had not hope, I would not have done. . .for my only hope is that now they believe I dare deny them nothing, and so be less careful of their guards'.[75] He still, however, refused to agree to exclude his principal followers (thirty-seven of whom the commissioners named as delinquents, as well as all recusants) from pardon. He continued to prize loyalty to those who had shown him devotion and service, even if he had felt it necessary to make strategic concessions elsewhere. Crucially also, he managed to secure acceptance at Westminster of a condition whereby nothing agreed during these negotiations would be binding on either side until everything had been agreed.

While it is a commonplace to criticise Charles for intransigence and duplicity, and as already shown he clearly had no intention of honouring many of the concessions he had made, but rather to use them to delay ahead of an escape or to secure an invitation to Westminster to treat in person, the impact of his appearing to give in to so much was nevertheless considerable. There was evident surprise and concern among some of his supporters. Royalist newsletter writers such as Marchamont Nedham lamented that the king had 'in a manner resigned up his Sword, Scepter and Crowne' and Sir Edward Nicholas expressed concern at 'how deare a rate the king is content to purchase a peace for his subjects in England'.[76] Even Hyde, writing to Digby, said that while he would not 'censure nor rebel against no conclusion the King shall make' he would not 'contribute towards, nor have any hand in any, which in my judgment promises nothing but vexation and misery to himself, and all honest men'.[77]

While an air of despondency had appeared to descend on the king and many of his followers, he had still not given up on hopes for an armed intervention in his favour. Though only English royalist garrisons at Scarborough and Pontefract continued to hold out in Charles's favour, and by mid-October Cromwell had

224   *Conscientious objector (1646–49)*

been to Edinburgh, done a deal with Hamilton's enemy Argyll and thereby ensured at least a temporary end of royalist action from Scotland, Charles still had expectations of support from outside. News of the end of the Thirty Years War by the Treaty of Westphalia in October prompted hopes of intervention from France, where Henrietta Maria was attempting to orchestrate what help she could, though she found herself having to report that the outbreak of the Fronde and the disturbances spreading beyond Paris 'hath quite obstructed the design of his majesty's friends'.[78] The greatest hopes therefore remained from Ireland. Despite his concessions at Newport in that regard, he was in correspondence with the marquess of Ormond, who had returned to Ireland and by late October was, with Charles's knowledge and approval, preparing to join with the Catholic Confederates against the parliamentarian forces in Ireland, while he resisted Parliament's efforts to compel him to disavow Ormond's actions. He consulted Hopkins about tides and obstacles to his escape, hoping to leave the Isle of Wight to join up with Ormond, while the appointment of Prince Rupert to command loyal naval forces in Holland presaged a concerted effort to unite royalist forces for an assault on the mainland.[79] The Army leadership became aware of these schemes, however, and instructed Colonel Hammond to take steps to prevent Charles's escape. Soon they would lose confidence in Hammond, and send a delegation to remove Charles to closer captivity at Hurst Castle in early December. This was a sign of the Army's growing control of events even as Parliament attempted to continue negotiating with the king.

The Army takes the initiative

On 16 November the Army made a final offer to the king, by which he would be required to agree to a permanent constitutional settlement including provision for biennial parliaments with a redistribution of seats, the control of the militia by a Council of State, and the appointment of royal councillors to be in the hands of parliament for ten years and subsequently the King would appoint them from a parliamentary shortlist, while the Army was to remain in being. As Gardiner commented in the Victorian era, if accepted this would have substituted a 'monarchy of influence

Conscientious objector (1646–49) 225

for a monarchy of authority. . .the system which prevails in the reign of Victoria'.[80] In any case, a day later, as surely the Army leaders had expected, Charles rejected the propositions, asking instead that he be allowed to come to London to negotiate terms in person. The King's reluctance to issue a declaration against Ormond in order to forestall a possible royalist invasion from Ireland, also proved a sticking point with the parliamentary commissioners who still hoped that the Newport treaty would form the basis of a settlement, while he steadfastly refused any advance on his willingness to suspend episcopacy for only three years.[81] At the behest of Henry Ireton, Cromwell's son-in-law, the Army now presented to the House of Commons on 20 November *The Remonstrance of the Army*, which denounced Charles as a 'man of blood' and demanded that he be put on trial. While the notion of calling the king to account for the bloodshed of the Civil War was not new (it had been articulated by the Levellers at the Putney Debates in autumn 1647 and had then been adopted by the Army at its Windsor Castle Prayer Meeting following the outbreak of the Second Civil War in April 1648) a formal demand for justice from the Army, written by one of its leaders, was of huge significance. Cromwell, whose role became pivotal over the following weeks, also hardened his position, describing Charles as 'this man against whom the Lord hath witnessed'.[82]

Awareness of the Army's increasing direction of events may have crystallised thoughts in Charles's mind regarding his likely fate. Though continuing to hope for a deliverance, the depth of Charles's concern for the future of his Crown is shown by the steady stream of correspondence he maintained with the Prince of Wales. On 29 November he wrote to his son to urge him not to be critical of him 'for having parted with too much of our own right' as it was done in pursuit of 'security to us, [and] peace to our people', while he expressed himself 'confident [that] another Parliament would remember how useful a King's power is to a people's liberty'. There was a reflective quality about this letter, containing instruction derived from bitter experience. He urged Prince Charles to 'give belief to our experience, never to affect more greatness or prerogative than what is really and intrinsically for the good of our subjects (not satisfaction of favourites)'. Whether he had specifically in mind his ill-starred attachment to the duke of Buckingham in the 1620s

226 *Conscientious objector (1646–49)*

or a more general reflection upon the vicissitudes of kingship and the shifting sands of his various alliances and negotiations, it suggests a greater self-awareness than he had displayed formerly. His reflections on the broader political situation were that 'The English nation are a sober people; however at present under some infatuation' and, perhaps betraying a degree of foreboding, speculated that 'We know not but this may be the last time we may speak to you or the world publicly' and counselled him against vengefulness should he attain power in his turn, 'that you may in due time govern, and they be governed, as in the fear of the Lord'.[83]

Charles's air of resignation appeared more apparent when, as he learned that he was to be removed from Carisbrooke Castle by the Army, his followers Richmond and Lindsey urged him to seize what might be his last chance to escape. To their frustration, the king now hesitated and suggested that his conscience would not allow him to break his promises. He once again demonstrated the lack of his resolve that his wife so frequently lamented. Accordingly on 1 December he was moved to Hurst Castle. It was from there that a declaration purporting to be from the king began to circulate in London, which even if not from his hand very much reflects the conviction he would display in the face of the growing movement towards a trial. In an echo of his *Answer to the Nineteen Propositions* seven years previously, he denounced the 'illegal proceedings of them that presume from servants to become masters and labour to bring in democracy, and to abolish Monarchy', and while insisting that he himself had 'earnestly laboured for peace', asserted that 'they that endeavour to Rule by the Sword shall at last fall by it'. He appeared to condemn the Army's seizure of political control, asking 'whether it be expedient for an Army to contradict the Votes of a Kingdome'. He finished with a further evocation of his providentialism:

> I thank my God I have armed myself against their fury: and now let the arrows of their envie flee at me, I have a breast to receive them, and a heart possest with patience to sustaine them: for God is my Rock and my Shield; therefore I will not fear what man can do unto me. I will expect the worst, and if any thing happen beyond my expectation, I will give God the glory: for vain is the help of man.[84]

Preparations for the trial of the king

It was at this point that the divisions between Parliament and the Army reared their head. Having rejected the *Remonstrance* and angered by the Army's presumption in moving the king, on 5 December the Presbyterians in the House engineered a vote declaring the king's answers to the propositions to be a basis for settlement. It was this that precipitated the decisive intervention of the Army when, a day later, Colonel Pride marched into the chamber and purged the Commons of the Presbyterian majority which had defied them. Though Cromwell was still ostensibly away besieging Pontefract when Pride's Purge took place, his arrival in Westminster later that night lent suspicion to the idea that he himself was behind it, or had at least been consulted about the steps taken. Superficially the significance for the king's position was clear: now the Commons had been distilled down to a 'Rump' of those who desired to bring him to justice, the likelihood of his being brought to trial increased considerably, and he was brought first to Farnham and then to Windsor in anticipation of the commencement of proceedings.[85] As Sir Edward Nicholas, who had, like Hyde, opposed the Engagement on the basis that it compromised his religious and political integrity, warned Sir Philip Warwick on 10 December (and urged him to relay to the king) Charles's:

> still adhering so much to the Presbyterian faction and his late interchanging some dispatches with some Scots is too well known and hath, as I am advised, irritated those against him who have now the power of the sword in England, and I tremble to think what may be the consequence thereof to his person.[86]

A different interpretation may be placed upon these events, however. Rejecting the notion of the inevitability of regicide from November 1648 based on the Army's determination to kill him and the king's embrace of martyrdom, the work of Sean Kelsey in particular, has argued that regicide was in fact the least likely outcome of proceedings.[87] Not only did the notion of 'blood-guilt' widely articulated in 1648, most notably in the *Remonstrance of the Army* not necessarily presage the King's death (on which

228   *Conscientious objector (1646–49)*

the text of the *Remonstrance* was albeit for good reason, in any case ambiguous), removing the king was in any case fraught with difficulties for the Army leadership. Civilian politicians were anxious to avoid the 'rule of the sword' and discussions were held that mooted the possibility either of 'having no king at all', or of deposing Charles and replacing him with one of his sons. Fears surrounded the instability almost certain to result from his deposition (even if replaced with his youngest son, the duke of Gloucester, as some were now suggesting, whom they could 'educate after their own fashion, and in other words train up to be a constitutional King') and the likely international outrage against any judicial killing of an anointed sovereign, the corollary of which would be strong military and naval backing for his son, the Prince of Wales, who was out of the country and therefore beyond the Army's power.[88] As such, there was a feeling that a chastened and constitutionally weakened Charles, deprived of his negative voice over legislation and forced to call off Ormond's royalist resistance from Ireland, was a safer prospect for a settlement than his death and the storm likely to ensue.

Indeed it might be said that Charles was the only figure who could stop Ormond's enterprise and the Prince of Wales's naval plans being formed over in Holland, while it may even have been confidence in such indispensability as this that lay behind Charles's refusal to countenance escape from the Isle of Wight on 30 November.[89] Further evidence in support of this would appear to be found in continuing attempts to negotiate with him in person, notably the supposed 'Denbigh mission', the visit of the earl of Denbigh to the king at Windsor Castle at Christmas 1648, an event emphasised in Gardiner's much earlier account. After several peers had been to see Fairfax, one of them, the earl of Denbigh, who had close family ties to Hamilton (his brother-in-law) was deputed to journey to Windsor in secret to make a last appeal to the king, probably on the basis of his surrender of his negative voice and thereby his reduction to the status of a figurehead-king, but perhaps also a promise to call off any prospect of renewed war.[90] It has even been suggested that he was to offer the king the option of abdicating in favour of his youngest son, Henry.[91] The enterprise may even have been supported by Cromwell, who, while Denbigh was journeying to Windsor, made

Conscientious objector (1646–49)   229

an appeal for the king's life to the Council of Officers provided he accept the final conditions being put to him. Charles in the end refused to see Denbigh, a sign that he was unwilling to entertain any such proposals, the content of which he was likely already to have known, and that he still harboured hopes of military intervention from Scotland or Ireland. He had already, according to Montreuil's report to Mazarin of 4 December, rejected pleas from the moderate royalist peers, Dorset, Southampton, Hertford and Lindsey, that he resume negotiations, insisting that he would defend his crown 'with his sword if those of his friends failed him'.[92] Indeed Charles's response to the latest initiative appears to have been contained in a pamphlet amounting to his 'Last Proposals' for peace, aimed at 'divers Officers of the Army', and issued on 28 December, insisting that 'no Law can judge a King', while further statements purporting to represent the king's views expressed his confidence that 'yet his Irish subjects will come in their time and rescue Him'.[93]

Moreover the debates surrounding the establishment of a High Court of Justice to try the king in early January can be seen as being part of a 'constitutional revolution' by which the House of Commons sought to assert its supremacy over the Lords with a view to fundamentally altering the parliamentary balance thereafter.[94] Seen in this light, far from aiming at his death, the trial of the King which began on 20 January becomes merely a part of this extended negotiation and political machination, a strategy designed to force the king effectively to surrender his negative voice by entering a plea before the High Court of Parliament, thereby implicitly recognising before all the world its constitutional superiority. Even the charges were framed in such a way as to limit the likelihood of his conviction. The flaw in this scheme proved to be Charles himself, who 'pushed his luck', bringing himself into contempt of the court appointed to try him by refusing to enter a plea, thereby sabotaging the whole strategy and forcing his reluctant judges to convict him of treason and sentence him to death.

While Kelsey's arguments are impressively constructed, and have found themselves incorporated into numerous subsequent works upon the period, they have not met with universal acceptance.[95] Clive Holmes has pointed to serious problems with perceiving

230 Conscientious objector (1646–49)

the lead up to the king's trial in this way.[96] To begin with, and as Gardiner himself appeared to concede, the evidence both for the Army Council's resolve on 25 December, at Cromwell's behest, to continue negotiations, and for the Denbigh mission itself, is tenuous. As Mark Kishlansky's rigorous examination of the basis for belief in the Denbigh mission shows, the evidence for it relies on questionable royalist newspaper accounts and two dispatches of the French ambassador, Grignon.[97] Other usually very well-informed sources, such as Sir Thomas Herbert, who attended the king in his final weeks, or the Venetian Ambassador, who kept his government appraised of developments in some detail, fail to mention it, while the practicalities of engineering such a visit were fraught with difficulties.[98] Furthermore, Kelsey's argument for the Army's willingness to continue to negotiate with Charles appears to rest on a questionable reading of the *Remonstrance of the Army* which, in its tone and content, appears unequivocal both in its refusal to entertain a settlement with 'the authour of that unjust warre' who was 'guilty of all the innocent blood spilt thereby' and in its demand for a 'judgment [to be] executed against him'.[99] While the *Remonstrance* does not state explicitly that the sentence should be death as opposed to deposition or forced abdication (which might reflect genuine fear that under the law as it then stood, calling explicitly for the king's death was treason), the tone of the language used leaves little room for doubt that the Army intended the death of the king, particularly given the prominence of the powerful and Biblically underpinned notion of blood-guilt. As such, the debate surrounding the purpose of Charles's trial, while interesting, may have generated more heat than light. The weight of evidence appears to suggest that the traditional view, that the Army leadership had resolved upon Charles's death by means of a public trial, impelled both by a political realisation that no settlement was possible with Charles I, and a religious fervour to cleanse the realm of blood-guilt, is the more persuasive.

The trial

If indeed these late attempts to barter for a settlement which saved the king's life if not any real vestige of his royal power did take place, once they had come to nothing, the Commons

Conscientious objector (1646–49)   231

passed an Ordinance making provision for the establishment of a special court for the king's trial on 1 January. In order to bring the king to trial, however, an entirely novel definition of treason had to be evolved. Previous instances of English monarchs being deposed (such as Richard II in 1399) were very different as they had involved no attempt to employ formal judicial proceedings to achieve it.[100] Under the law as it stood, namely the treason statute of 1351, treason was defined as a crime against the king himself. To plausibly charge the king with treason, the crime had to be redefined as an offence against the people or the kingdom as distinct from its ruler, and so the Ordinance declared that 'by the fundamental laws of this kingdom, it is treason in the King of England for the time being to levy war against the Parliament and kingdom of England'. Furthermore three judges and a panel of 150 commissioners (in place of a jury) were appointed to oversee the trial. The House of Lords were not prepared to endorse this, however. When the Ordinance went before the Upper House, the earl of Manchester, former commander of the army of the Eastern Association, argued that the claim that the king was a traitor flagrantly contradicted the basic principles of English law, while the earl of Northumberland pointed out that the question as to whether or not the king or Parliament had started the conflict was still a matter of dispute, but that even if the king had levied war against his own people, this was not treason by the law as it stood. Meanwhile the earl of Denbigh, leader of the supposed mission to see the king at Windsor the previous month, demonstrated his horror at the prospect of countenancing the king's death by suggesting that he would rather be "torn in pieces" than sit as a commissioner at the trial.[101] As ever, the Lords were the chamber more sympathetic to the king's predicament and more sensitive to the wider legal and constitutional implications of acting outside of established custom and practice.

Given the opposition within the House of Lords to bringing the king to trial, the Commons were forced into a revolutionary statement of their constitutional position. In a striking articulation of their claims to be the supreme power in the land, on 4 January 1649 (exactly seven years to the day since Charles I had tried to assert the Crown's authority over the Commons by his attempt to arrest the five members), the Commons resolved:

232 Conscientious objector (1646–49)

That the Commons of England, in Parliament assembled, do declare, That the people are, under God, the original of all just power: And do also declare, That the Commons of England, in Parliament assembled, being chosen by, and representing the people, have the supreme power in this nation: And do also declare, That whatever is enacted, or declared for law, by the Commons, in Parliament assembled, hath the force of law; and all the people of this nation are concluded thereby, although the consent and concurrence of King, or House of Peers, be not had thereunto.[102]

With this, the King's sovereignty was declared dead even while he himself still lived.

The King, meanwhile, was moved from Windsor to reside at St James's Palace on 19 January, where he found that he was 'treated with much more rudeness and barbarity than he ever had been before' and he was required to be in the presence of soldiers even when praying or attending to calls of nature.[103] The trial began the next day, and for the duration of it he was obliged to stay at the former house of Sir Robert Cotton (who had died in 1631), adjacent to Parliament, to avoid a daily risk of demonstrations in his support. Upon being brought into Westminster Hall, wearing his garter star, he was ushered to a crimson-velvet chair, and 'after a stern looking upon the court', declined to remove his hat (a first gesture of defiance against the proceedings, for which he was upbraided by the President of the Court, John Bradshaw), and then sat impassively while the indictment against him was read by the clerk of the court.[104] The gravamen of the charge was chiefly that he had been entrusted with a 'limited' power to govern and that he had sought to establish an 'unlimited and tyrannical power' and had levied war against his own people. There followed an account of the instances in which he had clearly taken up arms, whether in raising his standard at Nottingham, being on the battle at Edgehill, or encouraged his son, the Prince of Wales, to renew the conflict after he had been defeated. The indictment concluded by denouncing 'Charles Stuart' (un-kinged by the denial of his title, a neat illustration of the attempt to separate his person from his office), as a 'Tyrant, Traitor and Murderer, and a public and implacable Enemy to the Commonwealth of England'.[105] Even

Conscientious objector (1646–49) 233

while the clerk was still speaking, Charles, who appears to have tried to interrupt him by tapping him with his cane, suffered the indignity of the silver head of the cane breaking off and having to stoop to pick it up himself when no-one else moved to do so.[106]

One of the central planks of Kelsey's argument that the trial was essentially an exercise in extended negotiation is that the charges were 'minimalist', framed in such a way as to understate Charles's offences and give him every opportunity to refute them. For instance, some of the more lurid charges contained within the Commons' *Declaration* of February 1648, including that Charles was complicit in his father's supposed murder and had instigated the Catholic rebellion in Ireland in 1641, did not feature. Yet in many ways this is unconvincing: if, as Clive Holmes urges, we look at the charges in the context of the Commons' Ordinance establishing the court, it seems clear that, having accused the King of a 'wicked designe totally to subvert the antient and fundamentall lawes and liberties of this nation' as well as to 'introduce an arbitrary and tirannicall government' in their place, it was unlikely this could result in merely a 'slap on the wrist' for the king. Likewise the redefinition of treason discussed above was done with some care: the principal charge of levying war against the people of England was a neat inversion of the traditional offence of levying war against the king or assisting his enemies. This principal charge was also well-chosen as it could be amply substantiated: an array of eyewitness accounts would be able to attest to Charles's presence in armour, sword in hand, on various battlefields in the act of encouraging his followers to fight against those of Parliament. It was also a charge to which Charles was more vulnerable having finally agreed, as part of his negotiations with parliament in September 1648, to a bill which conceded that Parliament had acted in its own defence. As such, the suggestion that the charges against him were light or insubstantial appears misplaced.[107] In addition, while the charges themselves contained no reference to the still widely believed murder of James I at the hands of Buckingham and Charles, Sir John Cook, the Solicitor-General, acting as prosecutor, had apparently intended to make passing reference to it in the prosecution case, the case he was prevented from outlining in full by the king's refusal to plead, but which was printed after the trial as *King Charls his Case*. Its

234 Conscientious objector (1646–49)

absence from the formal charges may have been more a consequence of the difficulty in proving such a charge than an attempt to minimise the chances of a conviction.[108]

Nevertheless, the king's response to the charges may not have been what the judges were expecting. Charles was reported to have smiled or even laughed at the use of the words 'traitor' and 'tyrant' to describe him in the indictment, and his response to the charges was a total refusal to recognise the authority of the court. He was described (admittedly by a royalist account) as 'very majestic' in his deportment and, 'though his tongue usually hesitated, yet he was very free at this time, for he was never discomposed in mind', as his stutter appeared to desert him.[109] The King replied strongly:

> I would know by what power I am called hither. . . I would know by what authority. I mean lawful; there are many unlawful authorities in the world, thieves and robbers by the highways; but I would know by what authority I was brought from thence [the Isle of Wight], carried from place to place and I know not what: and when I know what lawful authority, I shall answer. Remember I am your King, your lawful King, and what sins you bring upon your heads, and the judgment of God upon this land; think well upon it, I say, think well upon it, before you go from one sin to a greater. . .I have a trust committed to me by God, by old and lawful descent; I will not betray it to answer a new, unlawful authority; therefore resolve me that and you shall hear more of me.[110]

According to the Kelsey argument, it was Charles's refusal to enter a plea that doomed him: had he pleaded, he would have implicitly recognised the legal and constitutional supremacy of Parliament and thereby given his opponents the political victory they sought. They would therefore have been in a position to find him 'not-guilty' and restore him to his throne as little more than a figurehead. In addition, as John Adamson has stressed, the news that arrived from Ireland on 24 January, that Ormond had concluded his military alliance with the Catholic Confederates at Kilkenny a week previously, appeared to demonstrate Charles's determination to start another war. This would give an additional reason for regicide, namely the disruption of the coalition united only by loyalty to his

Conscientious objector (1646–49)   235

person, and also explains the prominence of the 'renewal' of war and the agency of Ormond within both the charges and the eventual sentence.[111] While Charles's arguments were powerful, given that he had the weight of history on his side, this intransigence (a refusal to plead would be taken as a guilty plea), combined with the knowledge of events in Ireland, made it difficult to see how Charles could emerge from the trial with his life.

He must also surely have annoyed his opponents: his refusal to plead removed the necessity to prove his guilt and therefore deprived Cook of the pleasure of examining the witnesses he had carefully amassed. Furthermore, the king's response clearly irritated the court, as shown when Bradshaw demanded that Charles answer the charges 'in the name of the people of England, of which you are elected King' and the latter was able to reply with great conviction that 'England was never an elective Kingdom, but a hereditary Kingdom for near these thousand years'. In a tactic that in some ways echoed the language of 1642, he appealed over the head of the court and Parliament and embraced the mantle of protector of his subjects' freedoms, claiming that 'I do stand more for the Liberty of my people than any here that come to be my pretended judges'. He also claimed to stand for the privileges of the Commons, 'rightly understood', but challenged Bradshaw's claim that he was being tried by the Parliament of England. After all, said Charles, he could 'see no House of Lords here that may constitute a parliament', and, referring to himself as part of the parliamentary trinity, 'the king too should have been [here]'.[112] This play for constitutional orthodoxy caused Bradshaw to snap that it was not for the prisoner to interrogate the court, but Charles appeared to be enjoying himself. Once again he invoked 'Trust', this time the responsibility with which he was entrusted by God to 'keep the peace'. If he acknowledged the authority of the court without receiving proof of it, he would 'betray my Trust, and the Liberties of the people'. After some further back-and-forth with Bradshaw, Charles was led from the chamber, with some in the galleries crying 'God Save the King', though others (more in some reports) crying for 'Justice', which might be interpreted in more than one way.[113]

When the court reconvened two days later, Cook, prosecuting, petitioned the court that should the prisoner refuse to plead once

236   *Conscientious objector (1646–49)*

again, it should be taken *pro confesso* (i.e. as a guilty plea) and the court proceed 'according to justice' (i.e. to sentence). Bradshaw then invited Charles to enter a plea, but the king resumed his stout refusal, insisting that if it was only for himself, he would limit his response that 'a king cannot be tried by any superior jurisdiction on earth; but it is not my case alone, it is the Freedom and the Liberty of the people of England', once again combining his acute sense of rule by divine right with a claim to be defending his subjects' rights and liberties. If 'power without law may make laws' then no-one in the country could be sure of his person or property. Admitting that he 'was no lawyer professed', he nevertheless asserted that 'I know as much law as any gentleman in England' and therefore 'I do plead for the Liberties of the People of England more than you do'. When Bradshaw referred to him as a 'Delinquent', the label Parliament had arrived at in the 1640s for an incorrigible royalist, he replied that he did not see 'how a king can be a Delinquent'. He pointed out that 'the Commons of England was never a court of Judicature; I would know how they came to be so', again highlighting the leaps of legality his judges were taking, since as parliamentary judicature had evolved, and been revived in the 1620s, it had always been the case that the Commons acted as prosecutors while the Lords were the judges and the king had to assent to any sentence. When Bradshaw again snapped that it was not for prisoners to 'require' anything of the court, Charles stood on his dignity as king, insisting that 'Sir, I am not an ordinary prisoner'.[114] With Charles's persistent refusal to engage with the proceedings, the court was once again adjourned, until the next day (Tuesday 23 January).

By now, Charles's antagonists had run out of patience. Cook opened the next session of the trial by lamenting the king's refusal to plead and urging that the court now proceed to judgement, while Bradshaw reiterated the same point. Charles insisted on his right to be heard, once again claimed to stand for the liberties of the people of England, and reminded the court that at the point at which he was brought to trial, he believed that he was negotiating with parliament in good faith on the terms of the Newport treaty.[115] After a further adjournment, it was expected that the court would resume the next day, but in the event it was not until Saturday 27 January that the trial recommenced, this time for the

Conscientious objector (1646–49) 237

passage of sentence. Charles repeatedly demanded to be heard, and managed to interject a short speech in which he once again invoked the liberties of his people but claimed, above all, that, while he had been deprived of many things of late, it was his loss of 'conscience' and 'honour' that most troubled him, a familiar theme and a sign that he was at least being consistent. After the judges had retired for half an hour, they returned to give sentence, at which point Charles, while conceding that he had delayed proceedings, asked for a further delay. Whether this was borne of a growing realisation of the impending verdict, or a genuine sense that some sort of deal by which his life might be saved was in the offing, Charles now appeared more agitated. Bradshaw gave a lengthy preamble to his pronouncement of the sentence, and then Charles tried to interrupt him before it was given. More strikingly, after the sentence of death was pronounced, he demanded to be allowed to speak, 'I may speak after the Sentence. . .By your favour, Sir, I may speak after the Sentence ever. . .I am not suffered for to speak: Expect what Justice other People will have'.[116] With that, he was led from court, not this time to Cotton House but to Whitehall, and then to St James's, where he would spend the night before his execution.

Charles's apparent distress at not being allowed to speak after sentence is sometimes taken as evidence for the idea that the trial was merely a game in the ongoing process of negotiation: Charles never really expected enemies to proceed to the ultimate sanction, and the realisation that the court intended to put him to death caused him to panic. Indeed Kelsey suggests that Charles may have believed he was to be invited to abdicate in favour of his son and his desire to speak, which he articulated by means of an adapted quotation from Shakespeare's *Richard II* (not a play of which English monarchs were generally fond) condemning haste in rushing to judgement.[117] Perhaps more likely, having declined to plead to the charge, he had missed the chance to defend himself and his record, and now, faced with the reality of a death sentence, he sought a last opportunity to put his case before the court of public opinion. Charles's agitated state also jars somewhat with the notion that many of Charles's supporters, and indeed the king himself in his posthumously published memoir, *Eikon Basilike*, sought to present him as a patient martyr, willingly embracing

238 *Conscientious objector (1646–49)*

death as the ultimate means to confound his enemies. It is, however, perfectly possible that, while stubborn in his refusal to accept the authority of the court and determined in his desire to uphold his vision of monarchy, as well as, with an eye on the judgment of posterity, present himself throughout as the champion of his subjects' liberties, a man suddenly confronted with the reality of his impending violent death by beheading was genuinely horrified and not a little frightened. He would recover his composure soon enough and his speech from the scaffold at his execution presented him with the opportunity to defend his record in the way that he had not been allowed to do at the close of his trial. He also left behind him a written defence, the substance of a speech he had hoped to make during the session of the trial on Monday 22 January, but which he had been denied the right to make on the basis that he had not recognised the court's authority.

In this statement he expanded upon the arguments he had already made as to the court's lack of legitimacy, insisting that 'no earthly power can justly call me (who am your King) in question as a delinquent'. He based his arguments on Scripture, Law, and constitutional precedent. Having heard his opponents attempt to buttress their arguments with Biblical justifications of regicide, he cited the obedience to kings enjoined in both Old and New Testaments (including 'where the word of a King is, there is power, and who may say unto him, "what dost thou"' from Ecclesiastes VIII:4). He returned to his legal justification for not recognising the court on the basis that nowhere in statute or common law was there allowance made for the impeachment of a king: 'Besides, the law upon which you ground your proceedings, must either be old or new; if old, show it, if new, tell what authority, warranted by the fundamental laws of the land, hath made it and when'. He again attacked the 'pretended commission' by which the Commons had claimed itself to be a Court of Judicature and assumed the power to make law without either the House of Lords or the king. His final claim was that the Commons had broken faith with him and with the people of the country by bringing him to trial while he was still negotiating on the basis of the Newport Treaty and, by proceeding in such a 'lawless, unjust' way, threatening the whole constitutional basis by which the kingdom was governed. It was a strident and

Conscientious objector (1646–49) 239

in many ways cogent defence of his position (though given his continued attempts to renew the Civil War with the help of forces from Ireland the claim of good faith was disingenuous at best), and the fact of his leaving it behind him again speaks of his desire to justify himself to posterity.[118]

Execution

Charles's final days have been much mythologised. On Sunday 28 January, the day after the close of the trial, he was offered the ministrations of Presbyterian clergy, which, unsurprisingly, he spurned in favour of the good offices of Bishop Juxon of London, whose appointment as Lord Treasurer in 1636 had stoked Puritan fears of the revival of the 'clerical estate' in politics. Late in the afternoon he was moved from Whitehall to St James's Palace, where he would spend the time until his execution, appointed for the following Tuesday. He there spent much of his time in prayer and meditation with Juxon. Though generally we lack insight into Charles's innermost spiritual beliefs, his immersion in his devotions at the last, as well as his prayerful reflections, some of which are recorded in *Eikon Basilike*, suggest a genuine piety. His mind also turned to his children: while both Charles and James were out of the country, his youngest children, Elizabeth and Henry, Duke of Gloucester, were brought to see him on the day before his execution. Imagining possible constitutional scenarios after his death, he was at particular pains to ensure that Henry would not succumb to any attempt by parliament to make him king, which would of course infringe the principle of primogeniture as well as entailing the likely emasculation of the Crown with an eight year old on the throne as a puppet-king. There were last-ditch attempts to save the king's life, notably from the Dutch ambassadors, who petitioned Fairfax to intervene, but they were left in no doubt that only Parliament could undo what the High Court had done, and this was surely never a realistic proposition.[119]

On the morning of his execution, and throughout his time at St James's, he was attended by Thomas Herbert, a cousin of the earl of Pembroke and a man trusted by Parliament. Herbert slept on a pallet bed in the king's room, and was struck by how calmly his master behaved, and how soundly he slept the night

240   *Conscientious objector (1646–49)*

before his death. Upon awaking, Charles spent around an hour in prayer and received the sacrament, then dressed ready to be taken across St James's Park to Whitehall by around half past ten, where he was afforded more time with Juxon in the Green-chamber, between his closet and bedchamber, to prepare himself for death. He was particularly heartened by the fact that the appointed lesson for the day in the Prayer Book was the twenty-seventh chapter of St Matthew's Gospel, the passion of the Lord, an auspicious sign. He initially declined the offer of nourishment, but, persuaded by Juxon of the coldness of the day and the length of time since his last meal, he was prevailed upon to eat a small portion of bread and drink a glass of wine.[120] The scaffold had been erected in front of the Banqueting House, constructed by Charles's father, James, but embellished by Charles with the Rubens ceiling to become a monument to the Stuart vision of monarchy. While it is tempting to assume that the choice was a deliberate irony relished by the King's enemies, in fact the reason for holding the execution there was much more mundane: it was a more easily policed and defended space than the much bigger, traditional execution grounds at Tower Hill or at Tyburn.[121]

At just before two o'clock in the afternoon, a knock came at the door and Charles was to be escorted to the scaffold. Momentarily horrified by the sight of the metal staples which had been placed there in case there was a need to restrain him, Charles nevertheless recovered his composure and gave a final speech, even though, as he prefaced his remarks by saying, it was unlikely that many beyond those immediately in front of him would actually be able to hear what he said. Nevertheless he was not going to miss this crucial opportunity to shape judgements about his reign by defending his conduct and picking up on the charges he had declined to respond to at the trial. He once again rejected the accusation that he had started the Civil War against Parliament, and he reiterated his regret at Strafford's death, suggesting that he was being unjustly punished because he once allowed an unjust sentence to pass upon one of his servants: 'An unjust sentence that I suffered to take effect, is punished now by an unjust sentence on me'. Perhaps his most poignant reflection, if a disingenuous one, however, was that, had he really been all that his enemies had alleged, an arbitrary tyrant who ruled by

Conscientious objector (1646–49) 241

the sword, then 'I needed not to have come here', a somewhat unconvincing claim in view of his renewal of the Civil War and his continuing attempts to begin it again from Ireland. He also stood fast to his view of monarchy and of government, refuting suggestions that the people ought to have a share in government, for 'a subject and a sovereign are clear different things'. He left a statement of his religious beliefs, that he died 'a Christian according to the profession of the Church of England', and a refutation of the charge that he was a closet Papist, to the end. Meanwhile his most famous line was that he goes 'now from a corruptible to an incorruptible Crown, where no disturbance can be, no disturbance in the world'. He then took off his George, symbol of the chivalric order he had done so much to revive in the 1630s, and handed it to Juxon with the one word: 'Remember', before readying himself for the execution.[122] Having, by prior arrangement, given a sign that he was ready for the blow to be struck by stretching out his arms in front of him, the executioner severed his head from his body with one blow (a notably smoother passing than that enjoyed by his grandmother over half a century before). Even this did not appease the Army's anger entirely: on 6 March, the leading royalist commanders from the Second Civil War, the duke of Hamilton, the earls of Norwich and Holland, and Lord Capel, were tried for treason by the High Court of Justice and all were convicted. Norwich was reprieved by Speaker Lenthall's casting vote, but the others followed their royal master to the scaffold. Such was the price of service to the king, whose effort to shape his posthumous reputation had begun. In some ways, nothing became the king in his life like the leaving of it, and in death he proved to be a more powerful symbol of the royalist cause than he had been in captivity.

Notes

1 *State Papers Collected by Edward Earl of Clarendon* (2 vols, Oxford, 1767), II, pp. 338–9.
2 Mark Kishlansky, *Charles I: An Abbreviated Life* (2014), pp. 93–4.
3 Petrie, *Letters of Charles I*, p. 180.
4 *Charles I in 1646*, ed. John Bruce, (Camden Society, 1856), p. 40.
5 Petrie, *Letters of Charles I*, pp. 179–80, 182–3.
6 *Charles I in 1646*, p. 54.

242 *Conscientious objector (1646–49)*

7 Anthony Milton, 'Sacrilege and Compromise Court divines and the King's Conscience, 1642–1649' in M.J. Braddick and David L. Smith (eds.), *The Experience of Revolution in Britain and Ireland: Essays for John Morrill* (Cambridge, 2011), pp. 135–53.

8 Petrie, *Letters of Charles I*, pp. 199–201.

9 *Charles I in 1646*, p. 58.

10 Petrie, *Letters of Charles I*, pp. 202–206.

11 *Charles I in 1646*, pp. 62, 64.

12 Clarendon, *History of the Rebellion*, IV, pp. 205–06, 207.

13 *Clarendon State Papers*, II, pp. 262–5.

14 Petrie, *Letters of Charles I*, pp. 208–10.

15 *Clarendon State Papers*, II, pp. 275–7.

16 On this see Richard Cust, 'Charles I and Providence', in Kenneth Fincham and Peter Lake (eds), *Religious Politics in Post-Reformation England: Essays in Honour of Nicholas Tyacke* (Woodbridge, 2006), pp. 193–208.

17 *Clarendon State Papers*, II, p. 296.

18 Petrie, *Letters of Charles I*, pp. 210–2.

19 *Clarendon State Papers*, II, pp. 326, 333, 341.

20 David Scott, 'Rethinking royalist politics, 1642–1649', in John Adamson, ed., *The English Civil War: conflict and contexts, 1640–1649* (Basingstoke, 2009), pp. 36–60.

21 David Scott, 'Rethinking Royalist Politics', pp. 52–4, 59–60.

22 *Clarendon State Papers*, II, p. 330.

23 Clarendon, *History of the Rebellion*, IV, p. 213.

24 S.R. Gardiner, *History of the Great Civil War, 1642–1649* (3 vols, London, 1886–91), III, pp. 24, 26–7.

25 Petrie, *Letters of King Charles I*, pp. 212–4; Gardiner, *History of the Great Civil War*, III, p. 28.

26 Gardiner, *History of the Great Civil War*, III, pp. 54–5.

27 Petrie, *Letters of King Charles I*, pp. 216–7.

28 Gardiner, *History of the Great Civil War*, III, pp. 75, 77.

29 Ibid., pp. 92–93n.

30 Clarendon, *History of the Rebellion*, IV, p. 226.

31 Ibid., pp. 228–9.

32 Gardiner, *History of the Great Civil War*, III, pp. 134–5.

33 Clarendon, *History of the Rebellion*, IV, p. 234.

34 Ibid., p. 237.

35 *Clarendon State Papers*, II, pp. 373–4.

36 Warwick, *Memoirs*, p. 301.

37 Sir John Berkeley, *Memoirs of Sir John Berkley, containing an account of his negotiation with Lieutenant General Cromwel, Commissary General Treton, and other officers of the army, for restoring King Charles the First to the exercise of the government of England*, in Francis Maseres, *Select Tracts relating to the Civil Wars in England, etc* (London, 1815), pp. 360–1.

Conscientious objector (1646–49)   243

38 Berkeley, *Memoirs*, pp. 365–6.
39 Petrie, *Letters of King Charles I*, pp. 220–1.
40 Gardiner, *History of the Great Civil War*, III, p. 186.
41 Petrie, *Letters of King Charles I*, pp. 229–30.
42 Ibid., pp. 229–30.
43 Sir Philip Warwick, *Memoires of the reigne of King Charles the First with a continuation to the happy restauration of King Charles II* (London, 1703), pp. 301–03.
44 Clarendon, *History of the Rebellion*, IV, pp. 249–50
45 *Clarendon State Papers*, II, p. 379; Gardiner, *History of the Great Civil War*, III, pp. 239–40.
46 John Ashburnham, *A Narrative by John Ashburnham of his attendance on King Charles the First. . .* (2 vols, 1830), II, pp. 97, 99.
47 Ibid., pp. 99–101.
48 Ibid., pp. 108–10, 114–5.
49 Warwick, *Memoirs*, p. 307
50 Clarendon, *History of the Rebellion*, IV, pp. 266–8.
51 Ibid., p. 309.
52 Gardiner, *History of the Great Civil War*, III, pp. 256–7.
53 Gardiner, *History of the Great Civil War*, III, pp. 264, 266–8; Berkeley, *Memoirs*, p. 385.
54 Petrie, *Letters of King Charles I*, pp. 233–5.
55 Gardiner, *History of the Great Civil War*, III, pp. 277–8.
56 Ibid., pp. 270–5.
57 Warwick, *Memoirs*, p. 311.
58 Gardiner, *History of the Great Civil War*, III, pp. 298–9.
59 Ibid., pp. 336, 340.
60 Ibid., pp. 333–6.
61 Ibid., pp. 348–9, 355–8.
62 Ibid., pp. 382–90, 397–400.
63 Warwick, *Memoirs*, pp. 312, 314–16.
64 Sarah Poynting, 'Deciphering the King: Charles I's Letters to Jane Whorwood', *The Seventeenth Century*, 21:1 (2006), pp. 128–40.
65 Warwick, *Memoirs*, pp. 315–16.
66 *Clarendon State Papers*, II, p. 418.
67 Gardiner, *History of the Great Civil War*, III, p. 440.
68 Ibid., pp. 457, 459–60; Kenyon, *Civil Wars of England*, p. 192. The third officer, Sir Bernard Gascoigne, escaped death when it was discovered that he was a Florentine citizen.
69 Warwick, *Memoirs*, p. 321.
70 *Clarendon State Papers*, II, p. 428.
71 Warwick, *Memoirs*, pp. 323–4.
72 Gardiner, *History of the Great Civil War*, III, pp. 476–7.
73 Warwick, *Memoirs*, p. 326.
74 *Clarendon State Papers*, II, p. 443.
75 Quoted in Gardiner, *History of the Great Civil War*, III, pp. 479–80.

244 *Conscientious objector (1646–49)*

76 Quoted in Sean Kelsey, 'Royalists and the Succession, 1648–1649', in Jason McElligott and David L. Smith (eds.), *Royalists and Royalism during the English Civil Wars* (Cambridge, 2007), pp. 192–213, at pp. 199–201.

77 *Clarendon State Papers*, II, p. 459.

78 *Letters of Henrietta Maria*, p. 345.

79 Gardiner, *History of the Great Civil War*, III, pp. 484–5, 505–06.

80 Ibid., pp. 504–05.

81 Clarendon, *History of the Rebellion*, IV, pp. 446–7.

82 Gardiner, *History of the Great Civil War*, III, pp. 504–05, 508–09, 517.

83 Petrie, *Letters of King Charles I*, pp. 239–40.

84 *His Majesties Declaration Concerning the Treaty and his Dislike of the Armies Proceedings, Delivered by His Majesty to One of His Servants at His Departure from the Isle of Wight* (1648), pp. 5–6, 7–8.

85 Warwick, *Memoirs*, p. 335.

86 *The Nicholas Papers: Correspondence of Sir Edward Nicholas, Secretary of State, Vol1: 1641–1652*, ed. George F. Warner, Camden Society, New Series, XL (1886), p. 107.

87 Sean Kelsey, 'The Death of Charles I', *The Historical Journal*, 45 (2002), pp. 727–754; Kelsey, 'The Trial of Charles I', *The English Historical Review*, 118 (2003), pp. 583–616; for the Irish context, see John Adamson, 'The Frighted Junto: Perceptions of Ireland, and the Last Attempts at Settlement with Charles I, in Jason Peacey (ed.), *The Regicides* (2001), pp. 36–70.

88 R.H. Whitelocke, *Memoirs, Biographical and Historical of Bulstrode Whitelocke, Lord Commissioner of the Great Seal, and Ambassador to Sweden, at the period of the Commonwealth* (1860), pp. 253–4.

89 Kelsey, 'Death of Charles I', pp. 731–2.

90 Adamson, 'Frighted Junto', p.56.

91 John Morrill and Philip Baker, 'Oliver Cromwell, the Regicide and the Sons of Zeruiah', in David L. Smith (ed.), *Cromwell and the Interregnum* (Oxford, 2003), pp. 15–36, at p. 35. Morrill and Baker date the mission to 27 December, rather than 25th.

92 J. G. Fotheringham, ed., *The diplomatic correspondence of Jean de Montereul and the brothers de Bellièvre: French ambassadors in England and Scotland, 1645–1648*, 2 vols., Scottish History Society, 29–30 (1898–9), I, pp. 69–70.

93 Quoted in Adamson, 'The Frighted Junto', pp. 56–7.

94 Kelsey, 'Trial of Charles I', at pp. 588–9.

95 For an example of a scholar who does accept Kelsey's case, see Cust, *Charles I*, pp. 448–9.

96 Clive Holmes, 'The Trial and Execution of Charles I', *The Historical Journal*, 53 (2010), pp. 289–316, at pp. 296–7.

97 Mark Kishlansky, 'Mission Impossible: Charles I, Oliver Cromwell and the Regicide', *English Historical Review*, CXXV (2010), pp. 844–74.

Conscientious objector (1646–49) 245

98 Gardiner, *History of the Great Civil War*, III, pp. 555–6.
99 Holmes, 'Trial and Execution of Charles I', pp. 305–06.
100 Clarendon, *History of the Rebellion*, IV, p. 473.
101 Gardiner, *History of the Great Civil War*, III, pp. 559–60.
102 Kenyon, *The Stuart Constitution*, p. 324.
103 Clarendon, *History of the Rebellion*, IV, p. 4.
104 *State Trials*, IV, pp. 994–6. It was not read, as Wedgwood has it, by the Solicitor-General, John Cooke, who was acting as prosecutor at the trial.
105 C.V. Wedgwood, *The Trial of Charles I* (London, 1964), p. 130.
106 *State Trials*, IV, p. 997; Gardiner, *History of the Great Civil War*, III, p. 572.
107 Holmes, 'Trial and Execution', pp. 300–302.
108 Bellany and Cogswell, *The Murder of King James I*, pp. 448–51.
109 Warwick, *Memoirs*, pp. 378–9.
110 *State Trials*, IV, pp. 995–6.
111 Adamson, 'The Frighted Junto', pp. 60–2.
112 Wedgwood, *Trial*, p. 132.
113 *State Trials*, IV, 997.
114 Ibid., pp. 998–1000.
115 Ibid., pp. 1001–03.
116 Ibid., pp. 1011–8.
117 Kelsey, 'Death of Charles I', pp. 748–9.
118 Roger Lockyer (ed.), *The Trial of Charles I: A Contemporary Account Taken from the Memoirs of Sir Thomas Herbert and John Rushworth* (Folio Society, 1959), pp. 150–1.
119 Wedgwood, *Trial of Charles I*, pp. 171–2.
120 Warwick, *Memoirs*, pp. 382–4.
121 Wedgwood, *Trial of Charles I*, p. 172.
122 Ibid., pp. 190–2; Warwick, *Memoirs*, pp. 385–6.

Epilogue
The legacy of a royal martyr

Following his execution, Charles's body lay in its coffin at Whitehall to await embalming prior to burial. An apocryphal story has it that, while the earl of Southampton (who had attended the king at Hampton Court and Carisbrooke) and an unnamed royalist kept vigil by the body through the night, a heavily muffled figure, his face concealed by his cloak, appeared before the corpse, beheld it, and, shaking his head, uttered the words 'Cruel necessity!' before disappearing back into the night. Southampton recognised the voice and gait of the mysterious figure to be that of Oliver Cromwell.[1] Whether true or not, the story conveys the recognition, even by one of the leading regicides, of the enormity of what had just been done by the Commons (at the behest of the Army) in putting a reigning English king to death by means of judicial process and public execution, this after concluding that the king's refusal to compromise his principles combined with his persistence in seeking foreign military intervention, made a settlement with him impossible. In some ways, however, Charles would prove more of a threat to England's new rulers in death than he had been latterly in life.

Burial at Windsor

It does not appear that Charles himself made any provision for where he should be buried, as neither Herbert, who attended him in his final days, nor Juxon, who was with him on the scaffold, declared any such decision to have already been taken. Instead, Herbert applied for permission to bury him in the Henry VII chapel

Epilogue 247

in Westminster Abbey, where, in addition to most of the members of the Tudor dynasty (with the exception of Henry VIII), both his father and his brother (as well as his grandmother, Mary, Queen of Scots, and his former favourite, the 1st duke of Buckingham) were interred. The Commons, however, feared that this would make the late king's grave a place of pilgrimage for his former supporters and a potential shrine to royalist resistance, and so refused to allow it. As a result, Herbert and Juxon together decided to request of Parliament to be allowed to bury the king at Windsor, in St George's Chapel, a fitting resting-place given Charles's revival of the Order of the Garter (whose chapel it was) and his fondness for the building, along with the fact that it already contained the graves of Kings Henry VI (noted for his personal piety), Edward IV, and Henry VIII (architect of the royal supremacy over an episcopal English Church). On 6 February, after some debate, Herbert, was given authority to bury the king at Windsor, under the supervision of Colonel Whitchcott, the governor of the castle. The burial took place two days later, the body having been carried by water to Windsor and accompanied by some of those who had attended the king in captivity, including Richmond, Hertford, Southampton, Lindsey, and Juxon, who, while the body lay in the king's bedchamber, decided upon where in the chapel to inter the king. Ultimately they chose to place him in the same vault as Henry VIII in the centre of the quire, which was on one level fitting, given the seriousness with which Charles had taken his inherited title as 'Defender of the Faith'. After a short stay in St George's Hall, the body was carried to the chapel to be laid to rest, and, as Herbert records in his account, with more than a hint of the romantic, as they did so it began to snow, such that the black velvet was all white, just as 'the white King' was carried to his final resting-place.[2] Use of the Book of Common Prayer having been banned by Parliament, Juxon was prevented by Whitchott from using it, and, rather than suffer the use of the Presbyterian Directory of Public Worship, the king was instead buried in silence.[3]

Charles and posterity

Shortly before his execution, Charles entrusted to Juxon a letter to his eldest son, the Prince of Wales (by now Charles II to

248 *Epilogue*

his followers) which served as a kind of testament as well as an instruction-manual as to how to rule. He emphasised his desire that his son be 'well grounded and settled in your religion, the best profession of which I have ever esteemed that of the Church of England' and, in a clear reference back to the designs of the Scottish Covenanters, suggested that rebels whose 'consciences accuse them for sedition and faction, they stop its mouth with the name and noise of religion', a reflection of his consistent belief that his enemies used religious language as a fig-leaf for more material and political objectives. Reflecting on his own government of the Church he advised his son to 'take heed of abetting any factions' as 'your partial adhering as head to any one side gains you not so great advantage in some men's hearts (who are prone to be of their King's religion) as it loseth in others', perhaps an acknowledgement of the discord caused by his backing of Laud and those clergy associated with the 'Arminian' project. His injunction never to 'repose so much upon any man's single counsel, fidelity, and discretion, in managing affairs of the first magnitude (that is, matters of religion and justice), as to create in yourself or others a diffidence of your own judgement', might also have betrayed a recognition of the problems caused by the unpopularity of Buckingham, and then latterly of Strafford and Laud. Yet, again with an eye to how best to win the good opinion of posterity, he sought to present himself as the moderate king that Hyde had always attempted to make him become, with himself as the defender of tradition and his opponents as the innovators:

> In these two points of preservation of established religion and laws, I may (without vanity) turn the reproach of my sufferings, as to the world's censure, into the honour of a kind of martyrdom, as to the testimony of my own conscience; the troubles of my kingdoms, having nothing else to object against me but this, that I prefer religion and laws established before those alterations they propounded.

Charles then, saw himself as a victim of circumstances, a 'martyr' to his own, moderate understanding of the English Church and constitution and his undoing was the result of 'factions' and 'private men's covetous and ambitious designs. . .which were at first

Epilogue 249

wrapt up and hidden under the soft an smooth pretentions of religion, reformation, and liberty', his opponents little better than 'a wolf under sheep's clothing'. His advice regarding parliaments is also suggestive of studied moderation:

> Nor would I have you to entertain any aversion or dislike of Parliaments, which, in their right constitution with freedom and honour, will never hinder or diminish your greatness, but will rather be an interchanging of love, loyalty, and confidence, between a prince and his people.

How then had his relations with his parliaments been so fractious? Once again, they had been perverted by factions and 'popularity'. The Long Parliament, which Charles referred to as 'this black Parliament', had been wrecked by 'the insolencies of popular dictates, and tumultuary impressions', and parliaments would never be successful again until 'they have fully shaken off this yoke of vulgar encroachment'. His recurring suspicion of 'popularity', which, as Richard Cust has emphasised, was central to his (as well as to Laud's) mistrust of parliaments, was inextricably linked to his failure to work effectively with the institution. Perhaps his most wistful reflection was that he was 'once a King of three flourishing kingdoms' and that, along with the Church, the laws, and the privilege of parliaments (rightly understood) he had tried to preserve 'the honour of my crown' and 'my own conscience', the two things which, as he approached his likely execution, had proved both his most persistent concern and, arguably, the biggest obstacle to any settlement with his opponents.[4]

A more public and therefore more significant statement of Charles's case was, however, his *Eikon Basilike*. The king had likely approved the text while at Newport during the final stages of his captivity, and advance copies were already being sold on the morning of the execution. It quickly became a best-seller, with thirty-five editions in 1649 alone and translations into several European languages over the following decade.[5] Within days of the regicide, this book was selling rapidly in London purporting to be a memoir of the king, complete with frontispiece depicting him as a Christ-like martyr, kneeling before an altar, and ready with his crown of thorns. The work does indeed contain

250 *Epilogue*

thoughts, prayers, and reflections of the king, though it was substantially ghost-written by a royalist cleric, John Gauden.[6] One of the most interesting aspects of the work is that it displays a keen sense of the need to shape his posthumous reputation and justify his actions to posterity. He began by discussing the calling of the Long Parliament, regretting that he had allowed his 'own Judgment to be overborne in some things', perhaps a reference to the concessions he made in 1641 and against which some of his advisers, not least his wife, had warned.[7] More than that, however, he expressed contrition for allowing the death of Strafford, lamenting his 'complyance on my part. . .to his destruction, whom in my Judgment I thought not, by any clear Law, guilty of death' and 'I never bare any touch of Conscience with greater regret'. Having given in to fear (for his family's safety), he now reflected that he would have been better to have refused to sign the death warrant, given that no benefit thereafter ensued. Indeed, more than that, Charles attributed all of his subsequent misfortunes, as he had suggested on the scaffold, to the death sentence passed against Strafford. He also picked out the attempted arrest of the five members, justifying what had been an attempt proceed in 'a fair and legall way' against his opponents and denied that he had intended to violate the privileges of the House of Commons.[8] Moreover, his subsequent departure from London, which, he acknowledged some thought evidence of cowardice or indeed of a design to begin a war, he insisted was an attempt to defuse the tumults of the capital by a strategic withdrawal as well as an effort to ensure his own safety and that of his wife and children. With some sense of wistful reflection, he even suggested that he might have summoned Parliament to meet outside of London ('to any other place in England') where it would have been more insulated from the febrile atmosphere of the capital, a lesson learned by his son, Charles II, who later used this tactic to great effect to overcome the Exclusion Crisis. Some of Charles's claims sound disingenuous, such as his suggestion that he was happy to assent to the Triennial Bill on the basis that a 'continuall Parliament (I thought) would but keep the Common-weal in tune' and that 'I still counted My self undiminished by My largest concessions', it being only his enemies' 'insatiablenesse', in seeking to exhaust or obstruct his royal bounty, that had caused a rupture. Yet he

Epilogue 251

kept coming back to his most consistent theme: the importance of following his conscience, which had eventually baulked at concessions demanded from him against his will and without full and lawful debate. Making explicit the parallel drawn by the frontispiece of the book, he averred that he would 'rather choose to wear a Crown of Thorns with my Saviour, then to exchange that of Gold (which is due to Me) for one of Lead, whose embased flexiblenesse shall be forced to bend' and that, in the last analysis, there was nothing 'more worthy of a Christian King then to preferre His Conscience before his Kingdomes'.[9] The success of the book in creating and perpetuating this image of Charles as a royal martyr was staggering, and represents his most effective attempt, after so many during his reign, to justify his actions, excuse his mistakes, and shape public opinion in his favour.

Conclusions

In many ways, that preference for 'Conscience before his Kingdomes' gets to the heart of Charles's performance as king. His obsession with acting according to his conscientious convictions and refusal to bend when he thought them under threat, proved a political hindrance but, in death, a public-relations triumph. Another important dimension to his kingship, however, was that he was in many ways his father's son. While more decorous in his personal habits and presiding over a much more orderly and carefully choreographed court culture, he was in many other ways conditioned and confronted by his father's legacy. He inherited and maintained a steadfast belief in the need to uphold the royal prerogatives passed to him from his father, and which, they both believed, kings held by divine-right; he demonstrated a consistent attachment to episcopal government of the Church ('no bishop, no King', as James had famously put it), even if, at the last, he was prepared to temporarily sacrifice it (though not completely surrender it) on the altar of political expediency in 1648. He also inherited a royal favourite, in the duke of Buckingham, in whom, like his father, he displayed an inordinate (perhaps even greater) level of trust, and whose violent death so profoundly affected him and contributed so markedly to his loss of trust in Parliament. There were problems he inherited too, which his father had failed to solve and in some cases made

252 *Epilogue*

worse: the inadequate royal finances, and of an early modern monarchy that could only sustain itself financially if it did not pursue an active foreign policy; the direction of the Church of England, and whether its theology of grace and its episcopal bench should be Calvinist or Arminian; ruling multiple kingdoms, and of attempting to bring both Scotland and Ireland into greater uniformity with England in religion, politics and administration; and the British polity's relationship to a divided European continent during the Thirty Years War, British interest in which was largely created by James's marriage of his daughter, Elizabeth, to the Elector Palatine. While Charles's pursuit of solutions to these problems cannot be said to have met with much success, an appreciation of the challenging Jacobean legacy is a vital context for appreciating the difficulties with which Charles was faced and to some extent mitigates his failure.

It is also important to appreciate that Charles's approach to kingship displayed changes as well as continuities. One clear continuity is his keen sense of personal and dynastic honour, and for this the impact of his first five years as king was crucial. As a young monarch in the years 1625–29, he continued the patriotic stance he had adopted latterly as Prince of Wales and sought to fulfil his keenly felt familial obligations to his sister and (foolish) brother-in-law, to recover the lost Palatine territory by force of arms, taking on the might of Catholic Europe in the process. The military campaigns ended in ignominious failure, and while many of his subjects blamed Buckingham for mis-management of the war-effort (unfairly in the Spanish case, perhaps with more justification in the French case), the young king who felt sincerely that he was fighting the war that Parliament had wanted yet had refused to pay for it, perceived this lack of support as a slight upon his honour and a humiliation of his dynasty, hence the harshness with which he treated Sir John Eliot, who received the full force of royal anger at the actions of a Commons chamber seemingly happy to place obstacle after obstacle in the young king's path. The violent murder of Buckingham, meanwhile, gave Charles a deeply felt personal reason to resent the MPs who had appeared to provide the motivation for it. His decision to dissolve Parliament and rule without it for the next decade was, as his declarations to that effect attest, in large part motivated by a sense

Epilogue   253

of wounded honour and reputation. Central to this was a mutual breakdown of trust: Charles could not understand, nor easily forgive, the refusal of the Commons to grant him either the by now traditional lifetime authority to collect tonnage and poundage, nor sufficient parliamentary subsidies to fund the foreign war to which they had 'engaged' him; the Commons, meanwhile, were deeply suspicious of the king's resort to a Forced Loan and his punishment of those who refused to pay, as well as his ambiguous response to the Petition of Right which was designed to address these perceived wrongs. In addition, Charles, given the Commons' vigorous and persistent attacks on his favourite, blamed them for the murder of Buckingham and resented their interference in Church matters represented by their attack on Montagu and wider critique of 'Arminian' influences within the Church, while many in Parliament perceived the malign influence of an over-mighty subject and a dilution of the Church of England's Calvinist credo. To blame Charles entirely for this, for simply not 'getting' how the politics and religion of the kingdom he had recently inherited worked, is reductive and simplistic: a combination of the invidious Jacobean inheritance, parliamentary obstreperousness, as well as his own naivety, produced a fatal breakdown of trust which toxified the relationship between Crown and Parliament for the rest of the reign. When examining the politics of 1640, it is essential to remember the legacy of 1625–29.

A further theme which it is important to stress is Europe. Though he withdrew from the European wars by 1630, Charles never lost his appreciation of the importance of the European context of his reign. Having personally visited Madrid in 1623 as Prince of Wales, a rare experience for a future English monarch, he rejected the reflex anti-Catholicism of many of his contemporaries at home and in the 1630s constructed a court culture and an aesthetic which were heavily influenced by his visit to Madrid and his admiration for the art of the (largely Catholic) European Renaissance, while his purchase of the Gonzaga art collection made him one of the most significant players in the contemporary European art market. His project for a more co-ordinated fiscal-military establishment across his three kingdoms in the 1630s owed much to the model being pursued by Olivares in the Iberian peninsula, while he was happy to employ Hispanophile councillors (such as 'Don' Francis Cottington) and to turn to Spain in

254 *Epilogue*

1640 for aid against the threat of the Scottish Covenanters. Likewise in the 1640s, he sent his wife to France (more amenable to assist him after Richelieu's death) to raise funds while in extremis he sought military help from the continent (including from France, the Dutch, Lorraine, and the Papal envoy in Ireland, Rinuccini) to his flagging war-effort and then diplomatic support in his negotiations with his Scottish and parliamentary opponents. While frequently disappointed in his efforts (not least because of the internal crises besetting the Spanish monarchy after 1640 and the French from 1648) and the revelation of his European (and Irish) schemes presented a propaganda gift to his enemies, they nevertheless attest to his continuing conception of himself as a European, as well as a British monarch.

A sense of Britain was important to him, however. He was conscious that he had inherited 'three flourishing kingdoms', and he had endeavoured to bring them into greater uniformity with each other. This had led him to the Act of Revocation and the imposition of new canons and a new prayer book in Scotland, as well as Strafford's stern rule in Ireland, both of which, as seen, to some extent mirrored policies being pursued by continental monarchs. He nevertheless saw the value of his British kingship, in terms of resources as well as status, and in the 1640s he sought to use this to his advantage by the deals he made sought with the Irish Confederates and with the Scottish Engagers. His decision to surrender to the Scots in 1646 rather than to his English parliamentarian opponents also showed an awareness of how the competing interests and agendas visible within the British Isles might play to his advantage. Though his strategy ultimately failed, and, ironically the Commonwealth regime achieved (if brutally, in Ireland) a greater level of unity and control than he had, the differing religious and political arrangements in the other kingdoms would continue to vex many future regimes in England.

Another important continuity was his fervent belief in the interdependence of Church and State. Like Laud, he saw monarchy and an episcopal Church as inextricably linked, as well as mutually reinforcing. Hence Puritan critics of Arminianism in the 1620s were denounced for subverting monarchical authority by questioning the direction of the Church, while Prynne, Burton and Bastwick were punished in 1637 for attacking the bishops

Epilogue 255

and thereby the king's episcopal appointments and for suggesting that *iure divino* episcopacy and monarchical authority were in tension. Charles continued to regard his opponents as using religious language to cloak straightforward political rebellion with a spurious legitimacy, whether the Scottish Covenanter rebels or his English parliamentarian opponents. Nevertheless, while contested in his lifetime, the Church of England that was restored after 1660, and which survives to this day, was, in many ways, the Church of Charles I and Laud.

Though often thought to be aloof and inflexible, in many ways Charles was less than his critics claimed of him. He did issue public justifications of big decisions he took, notably his declarations following the dissolution of Parliament in 1629, and his *Large Declaration* during the Scottish crisis a decade later, while in the period 1641–42 as he sought to present himself as a moderate defender of constitutional and religious norms he issued, or had issued in his name, strong statements of his public position on a variety of issues and events, including the refusal of his entry into Hull and Parliament's *Nineteen Propositions* for a settlement. Charles's willingness to explain himself may militate against the image of an entirely inaccessible monarch who believed himself entirely unaccountable, as he himself said on the scaffold, 'A subject and a sovereign are clear different things', though the fact of his having to state and assert his authority in such terms might rather be suggestive of an insecurity surrounding its exercise.

Insecurity appears to have produced indecision: one of Charles's most persistent traits, and one that frustrated his wife, his advisers, and his opponents alike, was his vacillation and inconsistency. He lurched between concession and coercion, between gestures of compromise with his opponents (whether Scottish Covenanters or English parliamentarians) and acts of deceit and deception. He could offer olive branches in public while renouncing them in private correspondence, as with the Scots, or appear to be co-operating with Parliament while hatching or approving Army plots or attempts to seize his opponents by force. And yet, when steely-eyed and ruthless dishonesty was pragmatically expedient, for instance when Henrietta Maria and the foreign-alliance faction among his advisers suggested giving in to Scottish demands for a Presbyterian Church and then reneging on it later, he invoked

256 *Epilogue*

his conscience as an insuperable obstacle. In captivity and while awaiting death, he consistently stated his determination to act according to his conscience and the image he sought to construct of himself and have constructed for him posthumously by his supporters emphasised his martyr-like commitment to principle and scruple. The tragedy is that he showed enough irresolution and indecision, enough lurching between ideas of authority built on 'force' or on 'love' to convince his enemies that he was disingenuous at best and dishonest at worse, while if he had indeed lived up to the ruthless and calculated disregard for principle (episcopacy in particular) that his enemies alleged but which he could never quite muster, he might, just might, have recovered his throne and eventually the plenitude of his royal power.

In the last analysis, Charles was of course a failure as a British monarch. He ultimately forfeited his throne, his life, and, for time, his dynasty. Yet it is important to appreciate the mitigating effect of the context in which he operated. His inheritance was challenging, in many ways invidious, both religiously and politically, and his initial attempts to live up to the expectations of his subjects were genuine, if ultimately unsuccessful though this was due at least as much to parliamentary obstructionism as to his own mistakes. When he then charted a different path, one based on an imperial vision of his rule of three kingdoms brought into greater conformity with his rule of England, he was pursuing something for which there were clear continental parallels, and which represented a political and cultural conception of monarchy with an internal consistency. His kingship during his personal rule possessed a sense of history, underpinned and reinforced by a cultural and aesthetic vision based on a revived chivalric ideal (notably in the attention given to the Order of the Garter) and with financial policies rooted in medieval precedents; yet it was also contemporary, rich in the appreciation of the visual arts and the political ideas of the Renaissance state, both the projection of power and its exercise based on coercive as well as affective bonds. When his kingdoms dissolved into civil war he proved a divisive figure, able to inspire great loyalty as well as hostility, capable of great personal courage as well as political cowardice and as a negotiator possessed of unshakeable conviction in some things and irresolution in others. Unable to settle definitively

Epilogue 257

either on coercion or concession, he failed nevertheless to instigate the forceful reclamation of his throne that he in the end yearned for, and, as his most candid private reflections demonstrated, he constructed a Manichean world-view in which his enemies were irredeemable rebels and his supporters devoted adherents. In life this was an obstacle to any kind of settlement, but in death it gave his followers the basis of a martyrology around which they could coalesce and through which his son could recover the throne for the Stuart dynasty.

Notes

1 Gardiner, *History of the Great Civil War*, III, pp. 604–05. As Gardiner explains, while no first hand testimony of this survives, it is recounted in Spence's *Anecdotes* via Pope, and has a semblance of plausibility about it.
2 *The Trial of Charles I*, ed. Roger Lockyer (London, 1959), p. 146.
3 Gardiner, *History of the Great Civil War*, III, pp. 598–9.
4 Petrie, *Letters of Charles I*, pp. 261–72.
5 Michael Braddick, *God's Fury, England's Fire: A New History of the English Civil Wars* (London, 2008), p. 580.
6 'Gauden, John', *ODNB*.
7 *Eikon Basilike* (1649), p. 3.
8 Ibid., pp. 12–3.
9 Ibid., pp. 19–21, 25–6, 32, 36.

Guide to further reading

Given the voluminous writing on seventeenth-century British history, this is necessarily selective.

The printed primary sources on the period are themselves many and varied, but for an examination of the king's own thoughts and motivations, the selection of Charles's correspondence edited by Sir Charles Petrie, *The Letters of King Charles I* (London, 1935) is a good starting point. Also useful is the selection of his letters to and from Henrietta Maria edited by Mary Anne Everett Green, *Letters of Queen Henrietta Maria, including her Private Correspondence with Charles the First* (London, 1857). The views of those around Charles, advising him and often commenting to each other on his actions, can be gleaned from a range of edited collections. For the earlier part of the reign, including the Personal Rule, the edition of Strafford's correspondence by William Knowler, *The Earl of Strafforde's Letters and Dispatches* (2 vols, London, 1729) and the diary of William Laud, found in volume three of *The Works of the Most Reverend Father in God, William Laud, D.D. Sometime Lord Archbishop of Canterbury*, eds. William Scott and James Bliss (7 vols, Oxford, 1847–60) are particularly useful. For the period after 1641 the views of two of Charles's closest advisers, Edward Hyde and Sir Edward Nicholas are essential, found most accessibly in the *State Papers Collected by Edward, Earl of Clarendon* (3 vols, Oxford, 1767) and the first volume of, *The Nicholas Papers, 1641–1652* respectively, while Clarendon's later *History of the Rebellion*, edited by W.D. Macray (6 vols, Oxford, 1888), provides a very good, if not always entirely reliable, retrospective

Guide to further reading 259

on the vicissitudes of the reign. Sir Philip Warwick's *Memoirs of the Reign of Charles I* (London, 1701), while distinctly partisan, supplies the nuanced perspective of a nevertheless dedicated royalist. For official papers, particularly relating to the Privy Council, the *Calendar of State Papers Domestic* is invaluable while the collection of constitutional documents in J.P Kenyon, *The Stuart Constitution, 1603–1688* (Cambridge, 1988) has some helpful commentary on parliamentary and conciliar pronouncements. The most recent and fullest collection of such documents is, however, *English Historical Documents, 1603–1660* (London, 2010), edited by Barry Coward and Peter Gaunt.

The secondary literature is extraordinarily extensive, and some of it has been discussed at length in the Introduction, but in many ways the standard narrative of the period remains Samuel Rawson Gardiner's *History of England from the Accession of James I to the Outbreak of the Civil War, 1603–1642* (10 vols, London, 1883–4) along with his *History of the Great Civil War* (3 vols, London, 1886–91), both of which are thorough, rigorous, and pay due attention to the British and religious contexts, even if they are infused with a latent bias towards the parliamentarian cause. For more recent work on the early Stuarts, Tim Harris's *Rebellion: Britain's First Stuart Kings, 1567–1642* (Oxford, 2014) is among the best surveys. For the European and global context the breadth and scope of Geoffrey Parker's *Global Crisis: War, Climate Change & Catastrophe in the Seventeenth Century* (New Haven and London, 2013) is matchless. For Charles's role as Prince of Wales and his first five years as king, Glyn Redworth's account of his mission to Madrid, *The Prince and The Infanta: The Cultural Politics of the Spanish Match* (New Haven and London, 2003) is excellent, while Tom Cogswell's *Blessed Revolution English Politics and the Coming of War, 1621–1624* (Cambridge, 1989) is particularly good on the detail of the politics of the Parliament of 1624. As a guide to the politics of the 1620s, Conrad Russell's *Parliaments and Politics, 1621–1629* (Oxford, 1979) remains unrivalled even if some of its conclusions no longer stand.

On Charles himself, the best (and most balanced) biographical study is Richard Cust's *Charles I: A Political Life* (Harlow, 2005) though Mark Kishlansky's *Charles I: An Abbreviated Life* (London, 2014) is the most trenchant defence of the king. On the

260   *Guide to further reading*

Personal Rule, Kevin Sharpe's magisterial *The Personal Rule of Charles I* (New Haven, 1992) is the fullest study, even if some of his conclusions have been revised since it was written. On Charles as an art-collector, see Jerry Brotton, *The Sale of the Late King's Goods: Charles I and His Art Collection* (Basingstoke, 2006). The politics and political thought of the Personal Rule are impressively analysed in the essays edited by Julia Merritt, *The Political World of Thomas Wentworth, Earl of Strafford, 1621–1641* (Cambridge, 1996) while Richard Cust's monograph on *Charles I and the Aristocracy* (Cambridge, 2011) highlights the importance of Charles's relationship to his elite subjects. The recent collection of essays edited by Ian Atherton and Julie Sanders, *The 1630s: Interdisciplinary Essays on Culture and Politics in the Caroline Era* (Manchester, 2006) provides a much-needed and impressively wide-ranging set of new approaches and perspectives. On Scotland, Laura Stewart's *Rethinking the Scottish Revolution: Covenanted Scotland, 1637–1651* (Oxford, 2016) is the best recent examination of the complex religious and political dynamics. On the centrality of hysteria surrounding Catholicism to the collapse of the Personal Rule, Caroline Hibbard's *Charles I and the Popish Plot* (Chapel Hill, 1983) is a thorough account.

With regard to the Civil Wars and their causes, Austin Woolrych's *Britain in Revolution, 1625–1660* (Oxford, 2004) is a wonderfully mellow integrated history of the causes, course, and consequences of the Civil Wars across the British Isles while Mike Braddick's *God's Fury, England's Fire: A New History of the English Civil Wars* (London, 2008) is particularly good on the role of popular politics and print culture. The collection of essays edited by John Adamson, *The English Civil War: Conflicts and Contexts* (Basingstoke, 2009) presents a nuanced consideration of the key themes and some new approaches. Adamson's own *Noble Revolt* (2007) is the key work on the role of the aristocracy in the political crisis of 1640–42. The collection of essays edited by Jason McElligott and David L. Smith (eds.), *Royalists and Royalism during the English Civil Wars* (Cambridge, 2007) is a much-needed and thorough examination of the previously neglected subject of Royalism. The contributions by David Scott to both of those collections are particularly important re-evaluations of the nature of royalist politics during the Civil Wars. On the military campaigns,

Guide to further reading 261

Peter Gaunt's *The English Civil War: A Military History* (London, 2014) is the best recent synthesis of the key arguments while John Kenyon's *The Civil Wars of England* (London, 1996) remains a strong analysis of both the political and military dimensions.

On the search for settlement between 1646 and 1648, Robert Ashton's *Counter Revolution: The Second Civil War and its Origins, 1646–1648* (New Haven and London, 1994) is the best guide, and for the politics surrounding the trial and execution of the king, the collection of essays edited by Jason Peacey, *The Regicides and the Trial and Execution of Charles I* (2001). For the king's trial itself, C.V. Wedgwood's *The Trial of Charles I* (London, 1964) is still a readable narrative account.

Index

Abbot, George, Archbishop 20, 50, 57, 66
absolutist rule: Charles I and 79–80; of Wentworth in Ireland 103
Act of Revocation 104
Addled Parliament 19
Anglo-French War 58–60, 67, 76
Anglo-Spanish War 23–24, 23–25, 27, 32, 34, 37–38, 47, 49, 76
Anne of Austria (Queen of France) 169, 186
Anne of Denmark 20, 21
armed forces: British 'Union of Arms' conception 58–59; Charles I reform of 85; commissions of array 150–151; *see also* militia
Arminianism 48, 54–55, 66, 68, 254
Army *see* New Model Army
army oath 110
Army Plots 134–135
arts, the: Inigo Jones designs 29, 99, 100; neo-Roman motifs and Charles I monarchy 99–101; patronage by Charles I and Henrietta Maria 113, 253; Renaissance aesthetic favoured by Charles I 31, 253; Rubens

paintings 1, 88–89, 101, 240; Van Dyck portraits of Charles I 88, 99, 100, 161
Arundel, Thomas Howard, 21st Earl of 65, 66, 88, 93, 108, 110, 111
Ashburnham, John ('Jack') 166–167, 185, 188, 197, 204–205, 212, 213–214

Bacon, Sir Francis 25
Balcanquhall, Walter 108, 109
Banqueting House 1, 99, 101, 240
Bastwick, John 97
Berkeley, John, 1st Baron Berkeley of Stratton 209–210, 212, 213, 216
Berwick, Pacification of 110–111
Bishops' Exclusion Bill 146–147
Bishops' Wars, the 108–112, 127–129
Book of Common Prayer 163, 203, 219; burial of Charles I without use of 247; Directory of Public Worship to replace 177
Book of Orders 84–85
Book of Sports 96
Bradshaw, John (Chief Justice) 232, 235, 236, 237

Index 263

Bristol: capture by royalists 164–165; defeat of royalists at 183–184

Bristol, John Digby, 1st Earl of 29, 33, 52, 54, 131

Buckingham, George Villiers, 1st Duke of: accusations and hostility against 7, 34, 37–38, 48–49, 52–54, 60, 63, 96; Cadiz naval expedition 49; death of 65–66, 85, 253; Hugh Despenser and Sejanus, likened to 25, 54; influence and royal favourite 20–21, 31, 43–44, 48–49, 50, 87–88, 251; interred in Westminster Abbey 247; La Rochelle naval expedition 59–60; and religious controversy 54–55; Spain, agitates for war against 31, 33; Spain journey of 28–30, 33

Burton, Henry 97

Cadiz naval campaign 49

Carey, Lady Elizabeth 15–16

Carey, Robert, 1st Earl of Monmouth 15–16, 21

Carisbrooke Castle 214, 218, 226

Carleton, Sir Dudley, later Viscount Dorchester 15, 56, 77

Carlton, Charles 4

Carr, Robert 19, 20

Catholicism/Catholics: Charles I accused of being soft on 181; Charles I marriage negotiations and 29, 36, 44, 45; Charles I proclamations against 142, 145, 147; conversions at royal court to 98; foreign alliances with 168; hostility to, in Parliament 44, 47–48; in Ireland 102–103; parliamentary proposals concerning 177; popery, accusations of 98–99, 108, 129, 135, 140, 141, 143, 147, 241; in Scotland 107–108; service towards royalist army 159, 160; suspension of laws against 36, 45, 176, 180, 182

Charles I, King of Britain: accession 43–44; aloofness of 89, 255; appraisal of reign 2–4, 251–257; art and 31, 88, 99–101, 113, 161, 253; burial at Windsor 246–247; Canterbury Quadrangle statue of 98; chivalry in battle, display of 165–166; coronation 50–51; early life and education 13–19; Emperor Tiberius, likened to 25, 54; European Renaissance, admiration for 31, 253, 256; execution 239–241; family honour, sense of obligation to 25, 53, 56; Henry VIII, compared to 13; imperial motifs and 99–101; insecurity and inconsistency of 255–257; marriage to Henrietta Maria 44–45; 'medievalism' of 4, 87–89, 130, 133, 151, 256; military competence of 161–162, 165, 190; Nero, likened to 97; personality of 4–5, 10, 114; and posterity 247–251; religious beliefs 239, 241; royal court of 85–89; Royalist defeat, responsibility for 189–191; stammer 16, 46, 234; surrender to Covenanter forces 188, 196, 254; trial 227–239; *see also specific topics*

Charles II, Prince of Wales 187, 200, 219, 228, 250; Charles I

264 *Index*

correspondence with 225–226, 247–249

chivalry, revival of 5–6, 87, 113, 130, 256; Order of the Garter 88–89, 147

Church of England: Charles I advice to the Prince of Wales on 248; Charles I as defender of 95–99, 139–140, 142, 147, 159; Charles I view of monarchy as inseparable from 199–200, 251, 254–255; 'Laudian' direction of 89–90, 95–96; Protestant ceremonialsm in 113; Protestant divisions over 47–48, 54–55, 68, 132, 253, 254–255; Scottish and Irish uniformity with 91, 95, 105–106

Civil War, English: Battle of Edgehill and 161–162, 189, 190; Battle of Lostwithiel in 156, 174, 175, 190; Battle of Marston Moor in 171–175; Battle of Naseby in 180, 189; Battle of Newbury in 165–166; Bristol in 164–165, 183–184; Charles I, petitions for return of 218–219; Charles I responsibility for starting 225, 231, 240; Charles I surrender to Covenanters 188, 196, 254; council of war in 8, 166–167, 189; fiscal expedients implemented in 170–171; foreign assistance sought by Royalists 168–169, 184–186, 201–202; Heads of Proposals issued by Army 209–212; proximate cause of 139; recruitment of troops for 150–151, 158; Royalist defeat, causes of 156–157, 189–191;

Treaty of Oxford 163–164; Treaty of Uxbridge 177–178

Civil War, English, second 219–221; Treaty of Newport in 221–224

coat and conduct money 109, 121, 123, 127–128

Cogswell, Thomas 7, 31, 35

Coke, Sir John 58–59

commissions of array 150–151, 158

Con, George 107–108, 110, 138

coronation, of Charles I 50–51; oath 50–51, 191, 198, 203

Cottington, Francis, 1st Baron Cottington 29, 30, 90, 91, 92, 108, 112, 123–124, 179

council of war, Charles I and 166–167, 179, 189

court culture and politics 85–91, 113, 253

Court of High Commission 137, 141

Covenant *see* National Covenant

Covenanters, the: alliance and Engagement with Charles I 184–186, 188, 197, 216–217, 221; Battle of Marston Moor 171–175; Bishops' Wars 108–112, 127–129; Catholics, hostility to 107–108; Charles I rallying cry against 128–129; Charles I royal authority threatened by 106–107, 108–109, 114, 129; Charles I surrenders to 188, 196; context of conflict with 105–106; French reluctance to intervene against 169, 188; Irish assistance against, Charles I hopes of 109, 120, 175–176; Louis XIII correspondence with 120, 121; National Covenant of

Index 265

105–106, 107, 108–109, 177, 199, 206, 207, 216, 222; Parliament members accused of supporting 122, 124, 125–126; Scottish Affairs committee advises force against 123–124; Treaty of Ripon 130–131

Cressy, David 7, 75, 89

Cromwell, Oliver: in Battle of Naseby 180; Charles I, appeal for the life of 228–229; Charles I attitude to 210; Charles I, attitude to 209–210, 225; Charles I negotiating with Scots, suspicions about 215–216; Charles I seizure at Holdenby, suspected of 208; Charles I vigil, apocryphal story about 246; Pembrokeshire uprising and 219; Pride's Purge, suspected of involvement in 227; in second Civil War 220, 221, 224

Culpeper, Thomas, 1st Baron Culpeper 144, 150, 175, 183, 185, 187, 200, 202, 204–205

Cust, Richard 5, 8, 27, 56, 75, 249

Denbigh, Basil Lord Fielding 217, 228–229, 231

D'Ewes, Sir Simonds 36–37, 82–83; on Buckingham 60; on Laud 94–95

Digby, George, Lord: foreign alliances, pushes for 179, 182, 184–185, 204–205; and Glamorgan's Irish expedition 187; impeachment of 145; rise and influential role of 144–145, 167, 182, 189; Rupert, clash with 167, 173, 174, 175, 179, 184

Directory for Public Worship 177, 216, 247

divine-right kingship 2, 191, 236, 251

Dorset, Edward Sackville, 4th Earl of 60, 67, 157, 229

Edgehill, Battle of 161–162, 189, 190

Edinburgh: Castle, Charles I recovers 110; Charles I visits 137–138; christening of Charles I in 14; coronation of Charles I in 95; religious riots in 105–106

Eikon Basilike 237–238, 239, 249

Elector Palatine *see* Frederick V, Elector of the Palatinate

Eliot, Sir John 54, 74, 252

Elizabeth of Bohemia 16, 18, 22, 32, 38, 86, 92

Engagement, the 197, 216–217, 221, 227

episcopacy: Army proposals concerning 210–212; Charles I consents to suspend 111–112, 202–204, 216–217, 222–223; Charles I followers advise concessions on 198–199, 202–205; Charles I principled attachment to 133, 183, 186, 191, 199, 202, 203, 251, 254–255; 'Engagement' with Scots concerning 216–217; monarchy as inseparable from 199–200, 202, 251, 254–255; parliamentary proposals to abolish 163, 177, 222–223; popular hostility towards 143

Essex, Robert, 3rd Earl of 19, 122, 147, 151, 161, 165, 172, 174

executions: of Charles I 239–241; of Hamilton 241; of Laud 176–177; of Strafford 136

266   *Index*

Fairfax, Thomas, 3rd Baron
    Fairfax 169, 209, 220, 221, 239
Falkland, Lucius Carey, 2nd
    Viscount 101, 102, 144,
    150, 165
Felton, John 65
finances, royal 19, 24–25,
    47, 56–58, 67, 69, 79–84,
    119–120, 127–128, 130–131,
    133, 137, 158, 168, 253;
    Charles I wartime fiscal
    expedients 170–171; corporate
    monopolies 81–82; 'fiscal
    feudalism' 79–81, 114; Ship
    Money 82–84, 113, 120–121,
    123, 124, 129, 132, 137;
    Tonnage and Poundage 47, 54,
    56, 67, 137, 253
Finch, Sir John, Lord 120–121,
    124, 132
Five Members, the 143–146
Forced Loan 56–58, 60, 61, 67, 253
foreign policy 92–94
Forest Fines 81, 121, 137
Four Bills, The 215–217
France: Anglo-French War 58–60,
    67, 76; Charles I hopes for
    assistance from 169, 186,
    201–202, 224; Charles II sent
    to Maria Henrietta in 187, 197;
    Charles I marriage negotiations
    with 35–37, 44–45; Fronde
    rebellion in 103, 224; Henrietta
    Maria departs to 146; La
    Rochelle expedition 59–60;
    suspected of aiding Scottish
    rebels 108
Frederick V, Elector of the
    Palatinate 18, 22, 38, 92, 93

Gardiner, S.R. 2, 165, 224–225, 259
Grand Remonstrance 140–143
Great Council of Peers 129–131

Greenwich, Palace of 20, 86
Gunpowder Plot 16

Hamilton, James, 1st Duke of
    94, 106–107, 108, 109–110,
    111, 112, 134, 212; Battle of
    Preston defeat 220–221; and
    The Incident 138–139; trial and
    execution of 241
Hammond, Robert 213, 214, 224
Hampden, John 82, 83, 126, 144
Hampton Court: Charles I escape
    from 1, 212–214; Charles I
    paintings at 100
Heads of the Proposals 209–212
Heath, Robert 62, 66
Henrietta Maria, Queen: accused
    of popery and Irish rebellion
    support 144; Berkeley sent
    back to England by 209;
    Canterbury Quadrangle statue
    of 98; Catholic interests and
    36, 45, 98, 144, 180, 187;
    Charles I marriage negotiations
    and 35–37; court culture
    and politics, role in 86, 167;
    dissidents condemn 96, 97;
    dowry used to fund Cadiz
    campaign 49; foreign assistance,
    attempts to secure 160, 172,
    224; hard-line advice to Charles
    I 147, 148–149, 156, 160, 164,
    167, 189; marriage to Charles
    I 44–45; Oxford court arrival
    167; Oxford court departure
    172; Prince of Wales entrusted
    to 187; quarrel at Charles I
    coronation 51; relationship
    with Charles I 45, 85–86,
    87; religious concessions,
    pushes for 185, 202, 217;
    royal prerogative, attempts to
    preserve 139

Index 267

Henry, Duke of Gloucester 209, 228, 239

Henry, Prince of Wales 14, 17

Henry VIII, Charles I compared to 13

Herbert, Sir Thomas 230, 239–240, 246–247

High Commission, Court of 137, 141

High Court of Justice: Charles I attacks legitimacy of 238–239; Charles I trial in 230–239; establishment of 229, 231

Holdenby House 206, 208

Holland, Henry Rich, 1st Earl of 36, 81, 86, 123, 151, 206; campaign against Scots at Kelso 110; Charles I takes away office from 147; Charles I treatment after defection of 168; Prince of Wales appoints commander 219; trial and execution of 241

Holmes, Clive 8–9, 229–230

Hopton, Sir Ralph 165, 170, 171

House of Commons: Arminianism and 66, 68; Buckingham, hostility to 47, 48–49, 52–54, 63; Charles I attacks during trial 236, 238–239; Charles I funding for war, withholding of 35, 47–49, 52, 61, 62, 69, 121–123; Charles I orders arrest of opponents in 125–126; Charles I response to grievances of 124–126; *Declaration* against Charles I 217–218; freedom of speech protestation 26–27; grievances against Charles I 48–49, 52, 121–123, 217–218; Militia Ordinance issued by 147, 148, 150, 151, 201; Ordinance for Charles I trial 230–233; Protestation of

1641 135–136; Remonstrance of 63–64; supremacy claimed by 231–232; Ten Propositions of 137

House of Lords: Charles I denied access to his clergy by 206; Charles I support among 122–123; Commons asserts supremacy over 229, 231–232, 236; Ordinance for Charles I trial challenged by 231; oversteps Commons and grants Charles I supply 231

Howard, Thomas, 1st Earl of Suffolk 19, 20, 85, 108, 128

Huguenots, the 59–60, 65, 169

Hume, David 9–10

Hurst Castle 224, 226

Hyde, Sir Edward, 1st Earl of Clarendon 168, 169, 175, 177, 181, 185, 187, 196, 213, 223, 258; alliance with Scots and Irish, opposition to 204, 205, 227; on Ashburnham 166–167; on Charles I surrender to Scots 196; in royalist party 142–143

impeachment: of bishops 143; of Buckingham 37–38, 52–54, 63–64; of Charles I, contested 238; of Digby 144; of Henrietta Maria, Charles I pre-empts 144; of Laud 132; of Strafford 144

Incident, The 138–139

Independent party 183, 188, 190, 203, 205, 206, 210, 215

Ireland: Ormond joins Catholic Confederates in 224, 225, 234; Royalist requests for assistance from 168–169, 176, 180–182, 184; Scottish war assistance requested from 109, 112, 120; Strafford rule in 90, 91, 101–103

268   *Index*

Ireton, Henry 180, 213, 215, 225
Irish Rebellion 103, 140–141,
  144, 233
Isle of Wight: Charles I escapes
  from 218–219; Charles I flees
  to 213–214

James VI and I, King of Britain
  7, 21–23; belief in divine-right
  kingship 251; Buckingham,
  relationship with 20–21;
  Charles I and Buckingham
  accused by Spanish of
  conspiring against 34; Charles
  I and Buckingham alleged
  murder of 37–38, 52, 233;
  Charles I early life and 13–16,
  17; Charles I Madrid journey
  and 28, 30–31; Charles I
  represents the interests of
  23–24, 26, 33; Commons
  Declaration on freedom of
  speech, disputes 26–27; court
  and household of 16–17; court
  politics under 19; death and
  funeral of 37–38, 44; Palatine,
  attempts to assist Frederick V
  recovery of 22, 38; Parliament
  of 1621 summoned by 22–25;
  qualities of, compared to
  Charles I 46; reappraisal of
  3–4; religious policies of 105,
  106; Scottish identity of 104;
  Spanish Match negotiations
  and 21–22, 30; Spanish war,
  secures parliamentary funding
  for 22–25, 33
Jones, Inigo 29, 99, 100
Juxon, William, Bishop 91, 98,
  198, 239, 240, 241, 246

Kelsey, Sean 8, 227–230, 233,
  234, 237

King's Cabinet Opened, The 180
kingship: divine-right 2, 191, 236,
  251; 'two bodies' theory of 149
Kishlansky, Mark 6–7, 51, 54, 58,
  97, 106, 196–197, 230
Knighthood Fines 80, 121, 137

La Rochelle expedition 59–60
Laud, William, Archbishop
  89–91, 94, 123; Arminianism
  and 55, 66, 68; Buckingham
  death, grief over 65; Charles I
  coronation, presides at 50–51;
  Charles I raises to bishopric
  of London 64; Charles I
  shows favour to 98; Church
  policy, influence over 89–90,
  94–96, 106, 113; crypto-
  Catholic charges, refutes 98;
  dissidents, condemnation
  of 96–98; execution of
  176–177; impeachment and
  imprisonment of 132; popular
  protests against 126–127;
  prerogative taxation, supports
  57; Privy Council appointment
  57; Remonstrance, drafts reply
  to 64; Scottish affairs and 106,
  112; Strafford and 90–91, 101,
  137; 'Thorough' approach to
  government 90–91; Weston
  and Cottington, dislike for 89,
  90, 91
Leicester, sacking of 179
Leighton, Alexander 96
Le Sueur, Hubert 100
local government, Charles I
  reforms 84–85
London, City of: Charles I and
  Henrietta Maria arrive in,
  after marriage 45; Charles I
  flight from 146, 250; Charles
  I requests loan from 127, 131;

Index 269

Charles I returns to, from Scotland 140; Crown taxes and fines in 81, 83; plague in 46, 48; 'popish plot' rumours and unrest in 140, 143; Royalist forces attempt to reclaim 161–162
Long Parliament 131–137, 249, 250
Lostwithiel, Battle of 156, 174, 175, 190
Louis XIII (King of France), Covenanter correspondence with 120, 121

Madrid journey 28–31
Mansfield, Count 37
Maria, Infanta of Spain 28, 29, 30
Marston Moor, Battle of 171–175
Mary, Princess 134
Mazarin, Cardinal 103, 169, 186, 188, 201–202
militia: Charles I reforms of 85; commissions of array 150–151; dispute over control of 143–144, 147, 148, 149, 150, 163, 198, 199, 201, 204, 205, 206, 207, 211, 212, 215–217, 222, 224–225
Militia Ordinance 147, 148, 150, 151, 201
Mompesson, Sir Giles 25
monarchy: Church as inseparable from, Charles I views 199–200, 251, 254–255; divine-right and 2, 191, 236, 251; imperial motifs in Charles I reign 99–101, 151–152; 'two bodies' theory and 149
monopolies, corporate 81–82
Montagu, Richard, Bishop 48, 55, 57, 64, 66, 67–68
Montagu, Wat 93, 167
Montrose, James Graham, 1st Marquess of 138, 179, 182

Murray, Thomas 17, 21
Murray, William 138–139, 203–204

Naseby, Battle of 180, 189
National Covenant 105–106, 107, 108–109, 177, 199, 206, 207, 216, 222
Newbury, Battle of 165–166
Newcastle Propositions 197–201, 206, 211
New Model Army: Charles I taken into custody of 208; guards against Charles I escape 224; Heads of Proposals issued by 209–212; makes final offer to Charles I 224–225; Parliament, conflict with 206–209, 212, 227; *Remonstrance of the Army* 225, 227–228, 230; republican sympathies within 213
Newport, Treaty of 221–224
Nicholas, Sir Edward 138, 139, 152, 177–178, 181, 182, 183–184, 204, 223, 227
nobility, Charles I and the 5–6, 87–88, 113, 148, 151, 169–170; *see also* Great Council of Peers
Northumberland, Algernon Percy, 10th Earl of 112, 119, 121, 126, 206; Charles I children in custody of 209, 212; complaints about Strafford, Laud and Hamilton 94; complaints about the army 128; Short Parliament dissolution, disapproves 123, 126; on Strafford and Laud impeachments 131–132; on treason charges against Charles I 231
Nottingham 151, 158
Noy, William 74, 81, 97

270 *Index*

Olivares, Gaspar de Guzman, Count-Duke of 102, 103, 253
Order of the Garter 88–89, 113, 147; burial of Charles I in chapel of 247
Ormond, James Butler, 12th Earl and Marquis of: Catholic Confederates, alliance with 224, 234–235; Charles I correspondence with from Isle of Wight 224; Charles I inadvertently alienates 186–187; Charles I pushes for Irish assistance 168–169, 176, 181–182
Oxford: Charles I wartime court at 164, 166–171, 175, 178–180; Parliament (1925) adjourned to 48; royal progress to 89, 98
Oxford, Treaty of 163–164

Palatinate, the 31, 36, 38, 92, 93–94
Parliament: of 1614 19; of 1621 22–28; of 1624 31–35; of 1625 45–50; of 1626 51–54; of 1628 60–65; of 1629 66–70; Army, conflict with 227; Buckingham, hostility to 47, 48–49, 52–54; Catholicism, hostility to 47–48; declaration of war and raising of army 151; distrust between Charles I and 61, 70, 122, 253; fiscal and administrative wartime changes 170; Long Parliament 131–137, 249, 250; Nineteen Propositions of 149–150; Oxford Parliament (during Civil War) 164, 166–171, 175, 178–180; petition for Charles I to summon 129–130; Short Parliament 120–127; Vote of No Addresses to Charles I 217, 221; *see also* House of Commons; House of Lords
parliaments: Charles I advises the Prince of Wales on 249; Charles I claims to love 61, 68; Charles I defends prerogative to summon 133–134; Charles I mistrust of 124–125, 249; petition demanding summons of 129–130; Wentworth's attitude to 102–103
Pembroke and Montgomery, Philip Herbert, 4th Earl of 127
Pembroke, William Herbert, 3rd Earl of 20, 32, 33, 55, 60, 65–66
Personal Rule 74–76, 256; Charles I defence of 124–125; Commons grievances concerning 121, 122; court culture and nobility under 86–89; end of 112–114; Privy Council's increased powers under 78–79, 84
Petition of Right 61–65
Philip IV, King of Spain 30, 31, 80, 100, 102, 127
popery: allegations of 98–99, 108, 129, 135, 140, 141, 143, 147, 241; Charles I promises to destroy 145
'popularity,' disdain and fear of 3, 5, 66, 96, 249
Porter, Endymion 138, 166
Poyning's Law 176
Presbyterianism/Presbyterians: Charles I advisers urge compromise with 185–186, 198, 202; Charles I condemnation of, to the Prince of Wales 200; Charles I denies rumours of his intention to import 139–140; Charles I

Index 271

equates with 'Papists' 183; Charles I makes concessions to 216–217, 222–223; Charles I makes counter-propositions to 202–203; Charles I refusal to make concessions to 183, 185–186, 198–200; Directory of Public Worship 177, 216; Independents and 188; National Covenant 105–106, 107, 108–109, 177, 199, 206, 207, 216, 222; purge of, in Commons 227

Pride's Purge 227

Privy Council: Charles I begins attending 21; Charles I offers remodelling of, to spare Strafford 134; Charles I reconfigures 49; factional divisions in 60; Laud and Neile appointed to 150; official papers relating to 259; Parliament seeks to vet appointments to 150; Personal Rule and increasing powers of 78–79, 84; Poyning's Law and 176

Privy Seal loans 56–58

Prynne, William 96–97

Puritanism 79, 96, 97, 183, 199

Pym, John: arrest of, Charles I issues 126; chancellorship of the Exchequer, Charles I offers 144; Charles I and royal prerogatives criticised by 121, 122; Grand Remonstrance presented by 140–141; impeachment of, Charles I issues 144; 'Popish Plot' fears of 135; Scottish truce, plans to petition for 123; Strafford and Laud impeachment sought by 132; Ten Propositions of 137

religious toleration: of Catholicism, as condition for French marriage treaty 36; of Catholicism, as condition for Irish assistance 168, 182; Charles I promise to Army of 217; of episcopalianism, sought by Charles I 103; of Wentworth in Ireland 103

Revocation, Act of 104, 254

Richelieu, Cardinal 103, 136, 169

Richmond, James Stuart, 3rd Duke of and 4th Duke of Lennox 176, 185, 187, 189, 205, 212, 226, 247

Richmond, Palace of 18, 21

Ripon, Treaty of 130–131

royal court *see* court culture and politics

Royalists 142–143, 146–152; aristocratic commanders *vs.* merit 169–170; Battle of Edgehill failure of 161–162, 189; Battle of Lostwithiel victory of 174, 175, 190; Battle of Marston Moor defeat of 171–175; Battle of Naseby defeat of 180; Battle of Newbury defeat of 165–166; Bristol and 164–165, 183, 189, 190; Catholics in the ranks of 159; conscription, Charles I authorises 171; defeat, causes of 157, 188–191; defeat in the second Civil War 221–222; factional divisions in 8, 167–169, 175, 179, 204–205; fiscal expedients to fund, Charles I issues 170–171; foreign assistance sought by 168–169, 184–186, 201–202; indisciplined army of 128, 161, 174; Oxford government of

166–167; party, construction of 142–143, 146–152; popular support for 218–219; Powick Bridge victory of 159–160; recruitment of 148, 151–152, 158–159; Scots in the ranks of 171

royal prerogative: Charles I defence of, to Parliament 61–63, 125, 133, 150; Charles I makes concessions on 134, 137; Commons erosion of, James I and Charles I fear 27–28; Henrietta Maria acts to preserve 139; James I and Charles I divine-right belief in 251; Laud seen as attempting to enhance 50–51; Petition of Right challenging 61–63, 69; prerogative taxation 19, 79, 80–84, 113, 114, 121, 130, 151; Pym fears Charles I extension of 121, 122; Triennial Bill and 134

Rubens, Peter Paul 1, 88–89, 240

Rupert, Prince 158, 159–160, 161, 162, 170, 182; appointed to command naval forces 224; in Battle of Marston Moor 171, 172–174, 189; in Battle of Naseby 180; Bristol governorship, Charles I decides to offer 165; Bristol, loss of 183, 189, 190; Digby, clash with 167, 174, 175, 179; dismissal of 183–184, 189; Henrietta Maria suspicions of 167; influential role of 166, 179; Powick Bridge victory of 159–160

Russell, Conrad 22–23, 27, 35, 119

Scotland 104–108; Battle of Marston Moor 171–175;

Bishops' Wars 108–112, 127–129; Charles I surrenders to 188, 196; Charles I visit to 137–140; "confessionalisation" policy in 105–106; National Covenant of 105–106, 107, 108–109, 177, 199, 206, 207, 216, 222; Parliament convenes in Edinburgh 111–112; Strafford trial and execution demanded by 134; Treaty of Ripon 130–131; Wentworth strategy for 112, 123–124; see also Covenanters, the

Scott, David 8

Scottish prayer book, revolt against 105–106

Sharpe, Kevin 7, 75, 90, 95

Ship Money 82–84, 113, 120–121, 123, 124, 129, 132; abolition of 137

Short Parliament 120–127

Southampton, Thomas Wriothesley, 4th Earl of 26, 33, 176, 188, 189, 212, 229, 246, 247

Spain: Castile and Irish rule, parallels between 102, 103; Charles I and Buckingham in 28–31; marriage negotiations with 28–31; as model for British policy 58–59, 102; Strafford requests loan from 127; see also Anglo-Spanish War

Star Chamber, Court of 78, 137

Stewart, Lady Margaret 14

Strafford, Earl of see Wentworth, Thomas, later Viscount Wentworth and 1st Earl of Strafford

Suffolk, Earl of see Howard, Thomas, 1st Earl of Suffolk

Index 273

taxes: Civil War, fiscal expedients to fund 170–171; coat and conduct money 109, 121, 123, 127–128; corporate monopoly sales 82; Forced Loan 56–58, 60, 61, 67, 253; Forest Fines 81, 121, 137; Knighthood Fines 80, 121, 137; prerogative taxation 19, 79, 80–84, 113, 114, 121, 130, 151; Ship Money 82–84, 113, 120–121, 123, 124, 129, 132, 137

Ten Propositions 137

Thirty Years War 76, 86, 224

Tonnage and Poundage 47, 54, 56, 67, 137, 253

torture, Charles I authorising 126–127

Traquair, John Stewart, 1st Earl of 111–112

treason: Charles charged with 231–232; king's "two bodies" theory against charges of 149; redefinition of 231, 233; royalist commanders executed for 221, 241; Strafford and Laud charged with 132

treaties *see specific treaties*

Triennial Act 133–134, 250

Uxbridge, Treaty of 177–178

Van Dyck, Sir Anthony 88, 99, 100

Vane, Sir Henry 123, 129, 138

Villiers, George *see* Buckingham, George Villiers, 1st Duke of

Wales, Prince of *see* Charles II, Prince of Wales; Henry, Prince of Wales

Waller, Sir William 162, 172

wars *see specific wars*

Warwick, Robert Rich, 2nd Earl of: Armianism controversy and 55; arrest of 125–126; Charles I bars from taking control of the army 148; Covenanters assisted by 122

Warwick, Sir Philip: on the cause of Royalist defeat 157; on Charles I fleeing to Isle of Wight 214; on Charles I in Army custody 209, 222; *Memoirs of the Reign of Charles I* 259; Nicholas warns Charles I through 227

Wentworth, Thomas, later Viscount Wentworth and 1st Earl of Strafford: Charles I contrition over the death of 240, 250; Charles I grant of earldom to 112; Charles I refusal of earldom to 88; funding and troops, makes requests to Irish and Spanish for 112, 120, 127; hard-line view of dissidents 87, 106; Irish rule of 90, 91, 101–103; Laud and 90–91, 101, 137; Scottish Affairs and 112, 123–124; treason charges and execution of 132, 134–136, 177, 203

Weston, Sir Richard, later 1st Earl of Portland 80, 81, 83, 89, 90, 91, 100

Whitehall, Palace of 1, 99, 100–101

Whorwood, Jane 220

William of Orange, Prince 134

Williams, John, Dean and Bishop 46, 49–50, 98, 136, 143, 167, 173

Windebank, Sir Francis 108, 110, 112, 120, 124, 132

Wren, Matthew 95, 120, 198

York 129–130, 147–148, 172–173

Young, Michael B. 4–5

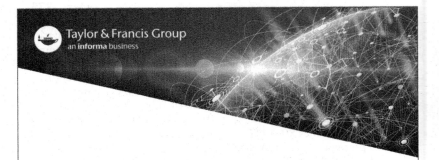

Taylor & Francis eBooks

www.taylorfrancis.com

A single destination for eBooks from Taylor & Francis with increased functionality and an improved user experience to meet the needs of our customers.

90,000+ eBooks of award-winning academic content in Humanities, Social Science, Science, Technology, Engineering, and Medical written by a global network of editors and authors.

TAYLOR & FRANCIS EBOOKS OFFERS:

- A streamlined experience for our library customers
- A single point of discovery for all of our eBook content
- Improved search and discovery of content at both book and chapter level

REQUEST A FREE TRIAL
support@taylorfrancis.com